Dante's 'Comedy'
Introductory Readings of Selected Cantos

Dante's *Comedy*
Introductory Readings of
Selected Cantos

UBERTO LIMENTANI

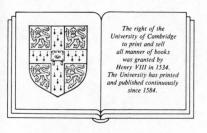

The right of the
University of Cambridge
to print and sell
all manner of books
was granted by
Henry VIII in 1534.
The University has printed
and published continuously
since 1584.

CAMBRIDGE UNIVERSITY PRESS

Cambridge
London   New York   New Rochelle
Melbourne   Sydney

Published by the Press Syndicate of the University of Cambridge
The Pitt Building, Trumpington Street, Cambridge CB2 1RP
32 East 57th Street, New York, NY 10022, USA
10 Stamford Road, Oakleigh, Melbourne 3166, Australia

First published 1985

Printed in Great Britain at
the University Press, Cambridge

Library of Congress catalogue card number: 85–4168

British Library cataloguing in publication data
Limentani, Uberto
Dante's *Comedy*: introductory readings of
selected cantos.
1. Dante Alighieri. *Divina commedia*
I. Title II. Dante Alighieri. *Divina commedia*
851'.1   PQ4390
ISBN 0 521 30031 2

GG

Contents

Preface

The ten readings in this volume were originally written as *Lecturae Dantis* in the ten series given in the University of Cambridge between 1969 and 1984 — the first, as far as I know, to be organized in Britain. Their purpose was twofold: to offer a well-informed commentary on single Cantos of the *Comedy*; and to prove to those who wished to read Dante's poem but did not have a close familiarity with the language — or, indeed, had little or no knowledge of it — that it could be done with the help of a prose translation line-for-line, facing the original text; difficulties of a linguistic nature confronting English readers of Dante are not, in fact, as formidable as one might imagine, particularly if they have some acquaintance with French and/or Latin. The continued response of Cambridge audiences over the years was taken as an indication that the experiment was not too ambitious. In their printed form these essays will now reach a wider public. If they encourage some to read further into Dante's poem, their original intention will be entirely fulfilled.

I have deliberately referred to a prose translation as being the most useful aid to a full appreciation of Dante's poetry; it will obviously be more literal than a verse translation, and it will thus prove a more trustworthy guide to the understanding of the original — for which there can be no adequate substitute. Dante explained it all, in a nutshell, long ago with his usual clarity and forthrightness (*Convivio*, I, vii, 14): 'nulla cosa per legame musaico armonizzata si può de la sua loquela in altra transmutare, sanza rompere tutta sua dolcezza e armonia' ('no work of poetry can be translated from its own into another language without destroying all its sweetness and harmony'). At least two prose translations of the *Comedy* are known to be in print, one by John D. Sinclair (the Bodley Head Ltd); the other by C. S. Singleton (London: Routledge and Kegan Paul). The former has been used in this volume, with two exceptions: the translation of the text of *Inferno*, I is by Patrick Boyde, and of *Paradiso*, XVII by Kenelm Foster. (In a few places I have altered the wording slightly, mainly in order to make the translations more literal.)

The fact that these commentaries are all by the same author may be found to impart to this volume some greater measure of continuity and cohesion than can be expected in collections of *Lecturae Dantis*.

Preface

I am more indebted than I can say here to the two distinguished scholars I have already referred to, Father Kenelm Foster and Professor Patrick Boyde, for the assistance they generously gave me. They read each commentary at different times and offered detailed advice that was highly valued. I am deeply grateful to these two colleagues, with whom I had the good fortune to work for many years. My thanks are also due to Mr Terence Moore and Miss Jane Hodgart of the Cambridge University Press for their help and assistance with the typescript.

The first nine readings have never been published before; the tenth was included in *Cambridge Readings in Dante's 'Comedy'*, ed. K. Foster and P. Boyde (Cambridge, 1981).   U. L.

Inferno I

All the hundred Cantos of the *Comedy* have a distinctive character of
their own, and this first one is no exception. To begin with, it is very
much the prologue, not just to the *Inferno*, but to the whole work. The
very fact that in the meticulously symmetrical architecture of the *Comedy* the *Inferno* has been assigned one Canto more than the *Purgatorio*
and the *Paradiso* already points to the introductory nature of this ex-
tra Canto; Dante knew from classical authors and medieval rhetoric
that a statement of the contents and a justification of the story were called for at the beginning of a work; and this is precisely what he does
here. He explains the circumstances in which the journey had its origin
and, as we shall see later, briefly declares the theme of the poem. But
there is more to differentiate it from the rest of the *Comedy*. Canto I
being a prologue, the story, the real story, has not yet begun. It begins
not so much in Canto II, which is a continuation and a clarification of
the first Canto, but in Canto III, when Dante and Virgil cross the gate
of Hell. From that moment onwards the journey, the literal journey,
is described with almost historical precision, concretely, to the minutest
detail: detail of space, detail of time; you can draw maps, you can write
accurate timetables. In Canto I it is otherwise. Twilight prevails in this
prologue of a work that begins in darkness and ends in dazzling splendour; a kind of mist envelops some, at any rate, of the concrete details;
things are seen as seeming to be, rather than being what they are: for
example, the words 'parea' and 'sembiava' appear three times between
lines 46 and 50, and there are a number of half-veiled statements and
ambiguous allusions. Dante finds himself in a dark wood (we don't
know where it is); he is not yet in the nether world and therefore,
somehow, he is still on earth (yet he has crossed 'lo passo Che non lasciò
già mai persona viva', the straits from which no one had ever emerged alive: 27); he tries to climb a hill (possibly a foreshadowing of the
mountain of Purgatory, but we can't be sure), is impeded in his way
by three beasts that appear from nowhere, is given assistance by Virgil,
is advised by him to take an 'altro viaggio', a longer route rather than
this short cut; but the particulars of what the shorter route is, its
topographical outline as well as its underlying meaning, are given in
the vaguest possible terms: perhaps, deliberately (there is little or

1

nothing that is not carefully thought out in detail in the *Comedy*), perhaps because Dante was still in the process — in the final stages of the process — of achieving that ultimate mastery of poetic expression that very soon becomes apparent and is sustained, almost miraculously, throughout, to achieve unthought-of heights as the poem progresses. This vagueness as to details adds to the Canto the air of a dream-like scene that I myself find very appealing or, more precisely, poetical; but its elusiveness may well have deterred some readers from proceeding further with the *Comedy*.

And now I come to another reason why the first Canto, the prologue, is different from the rest. It is a reason concerning the obstacles that face a modern reader. Let me put it this way: we feel that the *Comedy*, for all that it vibrates with the ideas and passions of one individual and with the echoes of long-past events, is timeless, dealing, as it does, with humanity, with the human predicament; but it is a medieval work, and it often demands of the modern reader the effort of adapting himself to Dante's way of thinking, to the way of thinking of 650 years ago. This effort is, perhaps, nowhere more necessary than in Canto I, at least in its first half. In Dante's time things were seen not only for what they were, or appeared to be, but also for what they stood for. Although his contemporary readers did not have to be warned about the polivalence of what they read, Dante took the trouble to explain in a letter to his patron of later years, Cangrande della Scala (which we assume to be genuine), that one should see several different layers of meaning in the *Comedy*; not all the time, not always all of them at once; but allegory looms as large as the literal story in the work as a whole. Now, in the prologue the story has not yet begun, and its first half, at least, seems to me to be pure, unalloyed allegory. Incidentally, there appears to be little doubt that a close relation exists between, on the one hand, the allegory of the prologue, with its wood, its hill, which Dante attempts to climb, its sun glimpsed from the lowest slopes of the hill, and, on the other hand, the broad allegory that unfolds through the *Comedy*, interwoven with the literal story. Dante himself hints at this, or even vaguely and indirectly states it, here and there in the course of the poem.

And now let us look at the text in some detail. The Canto falls, one might say, naturally, into two halves, with Virgil appearing on the scene almost exactly half-way through. Whether this is a coincidence or part of that symmetry I have already referred to, there is no way to tell. Each of these two halves can again be divided more or less precisely into two sections.

Inferno I

Nel mezzo del cammin di nostra vita
mi ritrovai per una selva oscura,
ché la diritta via era smarrita.   3
    Ahi quanto a dir qual era è cosa dura
esta selva selvaggia e aspra e forte
che nel pensier rinova la paura!   6
    Tant' è amara che poco è più morte;
ma per trattar del ben ch'i' vi trovai,
dirò de l'altre cose ch'i' v'ho scorte.   9
    Io non so ben ridir com' i' v'intrai,
tant' era pien di sonno a quel punto
che la verace via abbandonai.   12

(In the middle of our life's journey I came to myself in a dark wood, for the straight road was lost. Ah, how hard it is to say what the wood was like — so wild, hostile and harsh that it terrifies me again even to think about it, and death itself can scarcely be more bitter. But if I am to give an account of the good I found, I must talk about the other things I noted there. I cannot rightly say how I got into the wood, I was so full of sleep at the point where I wandered off the true path.)

The first division, then, deals with Dante's predicament in the wood; and right from the first line (notice the word 'nostra') points to the scope of the whole work, which is the account of a personal and at the same time universal experience, so that throughout the allegory of this section of the first Canto one has to bear in mind that Dante is talking about himself and about all of us, in the sense that we are all liable to stray into the wood of sin. Like so many passages of the *Comedy* and of Canto I in particular, the initial statement resonates with echoes from the Bible. The year is 1300, the year of the first Jubilee (the Holy year proclaimed by Pope Boniface VIII), and therefore a year of expiation and forgiveness; it was also Dante's thirty-fifth year, the middle of three score years and ten, that is, of the point described elsewhere by him as the highest of the arc that is human life. In line 7 the poet declares beyond doubt that the dark wood (entered because the straight way has been lost) is allegorical; the wood is scarcely less bitter than death itself, in so far as it stands for a deviation from virtue, from the 'diritta via', whether this be a moral deviation, a falling into vice to which Dante had succumbed (and any man not pursuing virtue succumbs), or an intellectual deviation, the pursuit of philosophy rather than of theology. The second terzina begins with a cry from the heart, and is itself a cry from the heart, with the inversion of the normal order of the words in the first line meant to make one's voice dwell on the rhyming word 'dura', and with the final word of the terzina, 'paura', receiving most of the emphasis. The fact that the word 'paura' is repeated three times in the first nineteen lines has led some commentators to single out fear as the key-note to the Canto. I myself prefer to see in 'paura' only a manifestation of that weakness, that fallibility, he confesses to; a weakness to overcome which he undertook the journey and which is very much in evidence particularly in the early part of the *Comedy*. It is this human fallibility, sinfulness, or pursuit of the wrong objects, as the case may be, that is referred to in the 'sonno' of line 11, and it is what happens to all of us so that 'we cannot rightly tell how we entered there'. However Dante, in his desire to overcome this weakness, finds a 'bene', a good (8) in it, an assistance sent from Heaven, that he is about to give us an account of.

> Ma poi ch'i' fui al piè d'un colle giunto,
> là dove terminava quella valle
> che m'avea di paura il cor compunto, 15
> guardai in alto e vidi le sue spalle
> vestite già de' raggi del pianeta
> che mena dritto altrui per ogne calle. 18
> Allor fu la paura un poco queta,
> che nel lago del cor m'era durata
> la notte ch'i' passai con tanta pieta. 21

(But when I got to the foot of a hill that closed off the valley which had struck such fear into my heart, I looked up and saw that the shoulders of the hill were already clothed in the rays of the planet that leads men straight on every path. Then the fear subsided a little, that had tossed in the lake of my heart all through the night I had passed in such horror.)

I have said enough of the vagueness and uncertainty of interpretation surrounding the hill and the planet (that is, the sun, turning round the earth according to the notions of cosmology current in those times) to attempt now a more precise explanation of the next six lines; the hill is in contrast with the wood, it is high while the wood is low, and leads on higher, clothed as it is in the beams of divine light. Its sight soothes the fear in the lake of Dante's heart, a reference to the anatomical view of the heart that he accepted.

> E come quei che con lena affannata,
> uscito fuor del pelago a la riva,
> si volge a l'acqua perigliosa e guata, 24
> così l'animo mio, ch'ancor fuggiva,
> si volse a retro a rimirar lo passo
> che non lasciò già mai persona viva. 27
> Poi ch'èi posato un poco il corpo lasso,

4

ripresi via per la piaggia diserta,
sì che 'l piè fermo sempre era 'l più basso.   30

(I was like a survivor — his lungs still bursting, having made it from the sea
to dry land — who turns to the menacing waves, and stares; my mind was still
in full flight, but it swung round to look back on the straits, from which no one
had ever emerged alive. When I had rested my tired body a while, I set out again
across the deserted slope, and every step forward was a step higher.)

And now we come suddenly upon the first of the many similes that
enrich the *Comedy* with their telling economy of words and uncanny
realism that make a symbolical situation become concrete, almost visible; even though we are still within the compass of allegory, the feeling of one who has escaped from drowning is conveyed with physical
('lungs still bursting') and psychological directness, and I should like
to underline the daring, the immediacy of the image of line 25: 'l'animo
mio, ch' ancor fuggiva', the mind being still in flight from peril, while
the body is resting.

A short parenthesis on metre may not be out of place at this point:
line 22 will supply the pretext, and show what a pliable instrument the
hendecasyllabic line (or verse of eleven syllables) had become in
Dante's hands. It is enough to read it ('E come quei che con lena affannata') to notice how effectively it conveys the feeling of panting, of
fright and anguish. This may be due, partly, to the position of its verse
accents (or rhythmic stresses) — the accents falling on the fourth,
seventh and tenth syllables, a pattern that we have not yet encountered
in the previous twenty-one lines — and partly to the concurrence of two
'a's (at the end of 'lena' and at the beginning of 'affannata') which are
elided for the purpose of scanning, but voiced for the purpose of
recitation.

I am not going to try to solve the minor puzzle of line 30, which concludes the first division of the Canto, when Dante begins his effort to
ascend the hill. That the still (or is it firm?) foot was always the lower
can be understood in many, more or less satisfactory, ways, but can
only mean that he was moving, and that he was moving upwards.

Ed ecco, quasi al cominciar de l'erta,
una lonza leggiera e presta molto,
che di pel macolato era coverta;   33
    e non mi si partia dinanzi al volto,
anzi 'mpediva tanto il mio cammino,
ch'i' fui per ritornar più volte vòlto.   36
    Temp' era dal principio del mattino,
e 'l sol montava 'n sù con quelle stelle

ch'eran con lui quando l'amor divino   39
  mosse di prima quelle cose belle;
sì ch'a bene sperar m'era cagione
di quella fiera a la gaetta pelle   42
  l'ora del tempo e la dolce stagione;
ma non sì che paura non mi desse
la vista che m'apparve d'un leone.   45
  Questi parea che contra me venisse
con la test' alta e con rabbiosa fame,
sì che parea che l'aere ne tremesse.   48

(Suddenly, more or less where the real ascent began, a leopard appeared, lightly built, a very fast runner, and covered all over in dappled fur; it simply would not shift from in front of me; indeed, it was blocking my path so effectively, that several times I turned round to turn back. The time was early morning, and the sun was rising with those stars with which it had been conjoined when God in his love first set their loveliness in motion: so there were good grounds for hope — concerning the beast with its alluring fur — in the hour of the day and the mild season; but not enough to save me from the fear occasioned by the appearance of a lion. He seemed to be coming straight for me, his head held high, and furious with hunger, so that a tremor seemed to shake the air.)

The next thirty lines tell us of the beasts that impede Dante's way up the hill. They are a 'lonza' (usually described as some kind of leopard), a lion and a she-wolf; they appear one after the other, each more formidable than the previous one. Indeed Dante, harassed repeatedly by the first one, the leopard, did not lose hope of overcoming it (41), encouraged as he was by the hour of day (the beginning of the morning) and the sweet season (spring). I cannot go on to the next beast without first drawing attention to a lyrical passage of great beauty (37–43) and pointing to the skill with which Dante has managed to insert it in the middle of the allegory; these lines have considerable lyrical impact, in spite of the astronomical and astrological detail of the sun mounting within the same sign of the zodiac in which it was believed to be at the time of the creation of the world.

The second beast, the lion, although vividly described, occupies only four lines; the word 'tremesse', at the end of line 48, replaces the formerly accepted 'temesse' in Petrocchi's recent edition, which we are following, and seems to be a more natural sequel to the impressive line that precedes it.

Ed una lupa, che di tutte brame
sembiava carca ne la sua magrezza,
e molte genti fé già viver grame,   51
  questa mi porse tanto di gravezza
con la paura ch'uscia di sua vista,

ch'io perdei la speranza de l'altezza.   54
    E qual è quei che volontieri acquista,
e giugne 'l tempo che perder lo face,
che 'n tutti suoi pensier piange e s'attrista;   57
    tal mi fece la bestia sanza pace,
che, venendomi 'ncontro, a poco a poco
mi ripigneva là dove 'l sol tace.   60

(And with him a she-wolf — no more than skin and bone, but apparently filled with a craving for everything (in her time she had brought hardship to many)
— and she crushed my spirits so completely, through the fear inspired by her
appearance, that I lost hope of gaining the summit. Imagine a man who is
devoted to making money; the day comes when he loses it all, and in every cor-
ner of his mind he broods and groans; that is how the insatiable wolf made me
feel, running at me, and little by little driving me back to where the sun's voice
cannot be heard.)

But it is the third beast, the she-wolf, that makes Dante despair
altogether, relentlessly driving him back towards the wood, 'là dove
'l sol tace' (60), an audio-visual image, or, more precisely, a
synaesthetic image of great effect. It is the she-wolf that Virgil, on his
appearance, has to protect Dante from, and it is the she-wolf that will
be seen later on as the target of the Greyhound's hunt. The spotlight,
then, seems to be on the last of the three beasts. We must consider what
they mean, and more than one interpretation has to be considered. This
is not because one cannot pick on one of these interpretations as being
obviously preferable. Rather, these allegories are complex by their
nature, in the same way as Dante's predicament in real life at that time
was complex: he was in political, moral and intellectual trouble, in the
same way as man's predicament as he saw it (and as we see it today) is
complex in the moral, in the intellectual, and in the political spheres.
(Dante was in political trouble because he was living in a town torn by
strife at the time in which he placed the fiction of the *Comedy* (1300)
and was compelled by events to take sides with one of the conflicting
factions. He was in moral trouble because, it seems, at one time he had
gone astray (there are obscure hints only; e.g. *Purgatorio*, XXIII,
115–20). He was in intellectual trouble because, he felt, he had
neglected theology to pursue philosophy in the preceding years.) It is
reasonable to suggest that, while he wanted to convey a specific and
well defined meaning that the beasts symbolized, there may have been
other less obvious meanings, resonating in his mind.

Briefly, three main sets of explanations have been proposed, none
of which can be ruled out, although they do not seem to me to carry
equal weight. The least weighty one, to my mind, identifies the leopard

covered with a spotted hide with Florence, divided by strife among parties and factions; the lion with the House of France, which had interfered with Florentine affairs, so disastrously for Dante and so many of his fellow-citizens; and the wolf with the Church, whose temporal power Dante never tired of condemning. I am loath to discard this interpretation, since political considerations often arise in Dante's work, and since the three Powers I mentioned could be regarded by Dante as the three main obstacles to the attainment of that world order he envisaged as ordained by God; but I find it difficult to square it with the prophecy of the Greyhound, whose task, as we shall see, is to send the wolf back to Hell (110), after bringing her to a miserable death (102). Could Dante then have meant the Church? Surely not. Nevertheless it is possible that he may have wished to interweave a reference to political disorder with the main significance of the allegory of the beasts, which must surely be that of man's three dispositions to sin, impeding the path towards virtue. The suggestion of the three beasts comes from Jeremiah 5: 6: 'Wherefore a lion out of the forest shall slay them, and a wolf of the evenings shall spoil them, a leopard shall watch over their cities'.

This brings us to the other two interpretations. One, more general, equates the three beasts with 'Le tre disposizion che il ciel non vuole' (the three dispositions of the mind that are against the will of Heaven) of Canto XI, namely the three classes of sins punished in Hell: the leopard — incontinence; the lion — violence; the wolf — fraud. The other interpretation sees in each beast a particular sin: lust in the leopard, pride in the lion and avarice (or covetousness) in the wolf. While the second of the three interpretations (the general one) has some attractions, the obviousness of the fact that sin as such is an obstacle to virtue seems to suggest that an allegory so conceived has less point than an allegory based on three specific sins; and, if Dante had it in mind, it probably counted for less than the lust—pride—avarice interpretation. The latter, moreover, has stronger arguments in its favour. That the she-wolf meant avarice for Dante is clear from another passage in *Purgatorio* where, in cursing covetousness, he calls it 'antica lupa' in terms strongly reminiscent of Canto I; the identification of the lion with pride is almost self-evident; the equation leopard—lust is disputed, and would involve a lengthy discussion, bound up as it is with other passages from the *Inferno*, but is supported by the earliest commentators. I mentioned stronger arguments above; and these must surely rest on the appositeness of the choice of these three sins as

Inferno I

obstacles on the path towards expiation and salvation. Sensuality and pride seem to have loomed large in Dante's eyes as vices by which he was beset; there are several places in the *Comedy* where this is acknowledged. Covetousness was seen by him as the prime cause of the corruption and disorder in the world (the avarice of the Church aroused Dante's particular indignation, which goes to show the ways in which the different interpretations can co-exist). To conclude these remarks on the beasts, I think that, by putting them at the beginning of his poem, Dante was not only pinpointing the three sinful attitudes that seemed to him most reprehensible in man, but was himself making an almost penitential act of humility, by confessing two of his own chief vices: a repentance and a confession that justify the extraordinary journey he is about to embark on.

> Mentre ch'i' rovinava in basso loco,
> dinanzi a li occhi mi si fu offerto
> chi per lungo silenzio parea fioco. 63
>   Quando vidi costui nel gran diserto,
> '*Miserere* di me', gridai a lui,
> 'qual che tu sii, od ombra od omo certo!'. 66
>   Rispuosemi: 'Non omo, omo già fui,
> e li parenti miei furon lombardi,
> mantoani per patrïa ambedui. 69
>   Nacqui *sub Iulio*, ancor che fosse tardi,
> e vissi a Roma sotto 'l buono Augusto
> nel tempo de li dèi falsi e bugiardi. 72

(As I was plunging to the bottom again, there manifested before my very eyes one whose voice seemed faint through long silence. When I saw him in the deserted plain, I called out: 'Help me, take pity, whatever you may be, ghost or living man.' 'Not a man', he replied, 'although once I used to be. My parents were from Lombardy, both citizens of Mantua. I was born under Julius Caesar, although late in his time, and I lived in Rome under the good Augustus, in the age when there were many gods, all false and lying.)

At the beginning of the second half of the Canto, a human figure (or is it a shade?) becomes visible, at first indistinctly, and then drawing from Dante a cry of assistance: '*Miserere* di me!' The silence that reigned in the first half is broken; Virgil has appeared and from now on the Canto takes on the form of a dialogue. As has been noted by others, classical reminiscences replace the Biblical ones of the first half, so that the Canto can be seen moving between two poles — the two great texts that had most influenced Dante's intellectual formation: the Scriptures and the poetry of ancient Rome at its highest. Line 63 marks the border between the vision of the first half and the dialogue of the second. The adjective 'fioco', indicating dimness to the eye, and referring at the same

9

Dante's 'Comedy'

time to the weakness of a voice that had remained unheeded for a long time, characterizes accurately a figure half seen at first, as if during sleep, and Dante had in fact already used it in the *Vita Nuova* (XXIII, 24) to describe a person seen in the context of a dream. It is at this point that we enter the world of the marvellous, of the supernatural, with the introduction of the soul of one who had died many centuries before, and yet the transition takes place so smoothly (with the words: 'Not man, though once I used to be': 67) that we hardly notice it. The fact is that the transition is really from the abstract world of allegory, in which we have found ourselves until now, to the verisimilitude of history: a transition that no writer, as far as I know, had managed so credibly before.

The second most important character of the *Comedy* (the most important after Dante) has come upon the stage that he will occupy uninterruptedly for nearly two thirds of the work. Right from the beginning, Virgil appears in all his capacities, fully-fledged as we will find him throughout his role as a guide. He is at once the historical Virgil, the character in the fiction of the *Comedy*, and the allegorical Virgil. Indeed, when he is described as 'one whose voice seemed faint from long silence' (63), Dante probably had in mind in the first place the symbol or symbols for which Virgil stood: he represents human reason, the highest, sanest wisdom of antiquity, unaided by Revelation, and, therefore, also the Empire decreed by God to guide mankind to happiness. The meaning of line 63 must be that the voice of reason had been silent for long to the sinner, and was only beginning to make itself heard; and, at the same time, on a different plane, that Virgil's message had failed to be understood for a long period of time.

Virgil, however, is first and foremost the historical Virgil, and he introduces himself, slowly and precisely, in lines 68 to 72; the mention of the place of his birth (Lombardy — indeed, Mantua) is indicative of the strong feeling of belonging to a city and its territory that permeated the medieval Italy of communes and city-states; a feeling that will find a warmer expression in *Purgatorio*, VI, where the mere mention by Virgil of his native town will elicit from Sordello the cry: 'O Mantovano, io son Sordello Della tua terra' ('O Mantuan, I am Sordello of thy city'). The details of his life, '*sub Iulio*' (notice the solemnity of the Latin formula: 70), though late in his time, and 'under the good Augustus', emphasize the connection between Virgil and the Roman Empire.

Inferno I

> Poeta fui, e cantai di quel giusto
> figliuol d'Anchise che venne di Troia,
> poi che 'l superbo Ilïón fu combusto.   75
> Ma tu perché ritorni a tanta noia?
> perché non sali il dilettoso monte
> ch'è principio e cagion di tutta gioia?'.   78

(I was a poet, and I wrote about a man of justice, Anchises' son, who came from Troy after proud Ilium had been burnt to the ground. But you — why are you going back to all that torment? Why don't you climb the pleasant mountain, the foundation and cause of every happiness?')

If we were to inquire: why was Virgil chosen to guide Dante as far as human reason, but human reason unaided by Revelation, can go, through Hell and Purgatory to the Terrestrial Paradise? why was he preferred to, say, Aristotle (to name the most obvious other choice), that is, to a philosopher for whom Dante had shown the highest esteem? The answer would be supplied, in a nutshell, by the passage that follows (73–87); it opens with the proud statement 'Poeta fui'. Virgil was chosen as a guide because he was a poet, Dante's favourite poet, the greatest he knew, the one whom he had been reading in the previous years with 'lungo studio' and 'grande amore' (83), and whom he acknowledges as his master, his author: teacher of wisdom ('famoso saggio': 89) and master of style. The 'bello stile' of line 87 is, of course, the 'tragic' style, as Dante calls it in the *De Vulgari Eloquentia*, which he had employed in his lyrical poems, and which, he states, he had derived from Virgil. But he found in the *Aeneid* not only real poetry, but an idea of empire with which he was in complete harmony: that Roman Empire which he saw as the instrument of the will of God intended to ensure order and justice on earth. The journey of Aeneas to Italy (73–5) was for Dante a crucial link in the chain of providential events that led to the establishment of the Empire of Rome, and Virgil supplied the evidence, considered by Dante to be historically true, and went on to provide an epic of Rome, a celebration of the destiny of the city that was the capital of the world and of the new era inaugurated by Julius Caesar and Augustus.

These are the most powerful motives that suggested the choice of Virgil as a guide; there were others that are not evident in this Canto, but appear elsewhere: the sixth book of the *Aeneid* contains an account of a descent into the invisible world, and was, therefore, an inspiration for the *Comedy*; the supposed Messianic prophecy of the Fourth Eclogue, which caused Virgil to be regarded in the Middle Ages as a herald of Christianity, was accepted by Dante, although he does not

11

Dante's 'Comedy'

employ it until Canto XXII of *Purgatorio*; finally, he found in the *Aeneid* the allegorical expression, whether it be there or not, of man's journey towards contemplation and perfection, which is the subject of the *Comedy*.

> 'Or se' tu quel Virgilio e quella fonte
> che spandi di parlar sì largo fiume?',
> rispuos' io lui con vergognosa fronte. 81
> 'O de li altri poeti onore e lume,
> vagliami 'l lungo studio e 'l grande amore
> che m'ha fatto cercar lo tuo volume. 84
> Tu se' lo mio maestro e 'l mio autore,
> tu se' solo colui da cu' io tolsi
> lo bello stilo che m'ha fatto onore. 87
> Vedi la bestia per cu' io mi volsi;
> aiutami da lei, famoso saggio,
> ch'ella mi fa tremar le vene e i polsi'. 90

('Can you be Virgil? Are you the spring from which there flows such a majestic river of words?', I answered, with my head bowed in reverence. 'You who have shed light and glory on other poets, help me, for the sake of the long study and great love that have made me search your volume through. You are my master, my author; it's from you alone that I've taken the beauty of style that has brought me honour. You can see the wolf who has made me turn back; protect me from her, in your fame and wisdom, for she makes me shudder in my pulse and veins.')

But no enumeration of motives can convey Dante's attitude towards Virgil: his admiration, his gratitude, indeed, his love, as much as the thrill of joy, of wonder that runs through the words spoken by Dante with brow covered with shame, that is to say with his head bowed in reverence (79–81). One senses here that Virgil's role in the *Comedy*, as deliverer from sin and guide through purgation, may have had its counterpart in Dante's real, personal experience, and that Virgil's works may have had as much of an impact on Dante's spiritual life as his intervention has in the fiction of the *Comedy*. The third section of the Canto closes with a renewed appeal for Virgil's assistance.

> 'A te convien tenere altro vïaggio',
> rispuose, poi che lagrimar mi vide,
> 'se vuo' campar d'esto loco selvaggio; 93
> ché questa bestia, per la qual tu gride,
> non lascia altrui passar per la sua via,
> ma tanto lo 'mpedisce che l'uccide; 96
> e ha natura sì malvagia e ria,
> che mai non empie la bramosa voglia,
> e dopo 'l pasto ha più fame che pria. 99

12

Inferno I

('You will have to go by a very different road', he replied, when he saw my tears, 'if you want to escape from this wild place; for the beast you complain of will not let anyone pass her way; she blocks his path until she kills him. Her nature is so vicious and bad that she can never satisfy her longings, and after a meal, she is hungrier than before.)

The final division deals with Virgil's advice and with his prophecy of the coming of the Greyhound; after the moving encounter of the two poets, it takes us straight back into allegory. The advice is that another road should be followed in order to escape from the she-wolf. An early commentator takes this to mean that the time has not yet come for ascending the mountain, for a man cannot suddenly turn from a sinner into a saint, but must first descend into Hell, that is to the confession of his sins; such confession is the beginning of penitence and purgation and, if evil is not recognized, it cannot be avoided. Line 100 probably indicates that many people become infected with avarice, which in Dante's time was a far stronger word than it is today, and conveyed excessive attachment to material goods, in contrast with love for God, the Creator of all things.

> Molti son li animali a cui s'ammoglia,
> e più saranno ancora, infin che 'l veltro
> verrà, che la farà morir con doglia.   102
>   Questi non ciberà terra né peltro,
> ma sapïenza, amore e virtute,
> e sua nazion sarà tra feltro e feltro.   105
>   Di quella umile Italia fia salute
> per cui morì la vergine Cammilla,
> Eurialo e Turno e Niso di ferute.   108
>   Questi la caccerà per ogne villa,
> fin che l'avrà rimessa ne lo 'nferno,
> là onde 'nvidia prima dipartilla.   111

(She couples with many animals, and will do so with many more, until the Hound comes who will make her die in torment. He will not feed on land or coin, but on wisdom, love and power; and he will be born among felts. He will be the deliverance of the plains of Italy, for the sake of which Camilla the Maid, Euryalus, Turnus and Nisus endured their mortal wounds. He will hunt the wolf through every town, until he has driven her back to Hell, from where Envy first set her loose.)

And now we come to the prophecy of the Greyhound, which has taxed the ingenuity of interpreters for six and a half centuries. On the one hand, it is deliberately couched in such obscure terms as not to permit of a straightforward explanation; on the other hand, it cannot be lightly dismissed; it is a very important pronouncement, because Dante ex-

13

pected the Greyhound to kill the she-wolf (102) and send her back to Hell (110), that is, to restore order and justice in the world by eliminating the chief cause of corruption. This would make it possible for the Spiritual and the Temporal Powers to fulfil the functions assigned to them by God and thus to secure happiness for men. One must try, therefore, to understand it as far as it can be understood. The word 'Veltro' (101) is the first puzzle. Why a greyhound? Boccaccio says: 'È il veltro una spezie di cani maravigliosamente nimica de' lupi' ('the greyhound is a species of dog with a peculiar hatred for wolves'), and this simple comment may suffice; all the more so, as the *motif* of the greyhound appearing in dreams to defend men from ferocious beasts had occurred twice in the *Chanson de Roland*. Next, its attributes, the only clues to an identification: he shall not feed on land or coin (103), that is, he shall not covet land or wealth, as befits one who is to hunt avarice, but on wisdom and love and valour — a reference possibly to the three attributes of the Holy Trinity, possibly to the highest virtues man can attain. Line 105 is the real riddle, and Boccacio prefaces his explanation with an apology, which many interpreters ought to bear in mind: 'la qual parte io manifestamente confesso ch'io non intendo' ('I candidly confess that I don't know what region is referred to'). 'Nazion' is now mostly taken to signify 'birth', rather than 'nation'. 'Felto' should, emphatically, be spelt with a small 'f' both times: the geographical explanations (Feltre, Montefeltro) are too far-fetched to hold water. The most plausible explanation follows from the fact that, felt being a cheap sort of cloth, one who was clothed in felt when he was born will be of humble birth, and perhaps will even follow the rule of poverty of a Franciscan order. However evidently Dante uses mysterious language here in order to be as non-specific as possible.

There is no uncertainty, however, as to the results of the coming of the Greyhound: he shall be the salvation of 'humilis Italia' (the word 'umile' is a Virgilian echo, meant in this context to stress the absence of the exalted state particularly appropriate to Italy as the seat from which the two highest authorities should exercise their functions), that Italy for which Trojan and non-Trojan heroes alike died: the Trojans, Euryalus and Nisus, and their Latin foes, Turnus and Camilla, are listed without distinction of nationality. Since they all shed their blood to further the design of God, which is the creation of the Roman Empire, they all fought for a good cause, and neither the victors nor the vanquished were dishonoured. We see, then, in the prophecy of the coming of the 'Veltro' an intimation of Dante's view of the ideal world that had already taken shape in his mind: herein lies the seed of the *Monarchia* and of much else in the *Comedy*.

One further question should be answered: who is to be this 'Veltro'? It has been said that every interpreter of Dante tries to slip his own collar on to the Greyhound. I feel that we ought to resist the temptation, and indeed reject the innumerable identifications with this or that historical character of Dante's time, on the grounds that if he had wanted to refer to a particular person, he would have given clearer clues. Obviously, the prophecy is the expression of a profound faith in a future event. Dante could not believe that what was manifestly God's will was not, in the end, to triumph, and that covetousness, the main cause of the confusion of the two powers and of the ensuing disorder, was not to be removed. He did not know who was to be the instrument of Providence, but he was sure that one would come. Some unspecified pope, or some emperor of the future, has been suggested. If we consider that the whole system expounded in the *Monarchia* and in the *Comedy* is based on the collaboration of the two highest powers for the earthly and eternal welfare of man, we must conclude that Dante is unlikely to have singled out *one* of these powers as destined to bring order to the world. An attractive theory has recently been revived which sees in the 'Veltro' Dante himself; it is grounded on the explanation of the words 'tra feltro e feltro' as referring to the sign of the Zodiac under which Dante was born: the Heavenly Twins, the *pilleati fratres* with their felt caps. While one recognizes that Dante was sustained in his work by a sense of mission, that he was fully aware of revealing truths of which the discovery had never been attempted before and of writing a poem 'to which both Heaven and Earth have set their hand' (*Paradiso*, XXV, 2) one has, nevertheless, to discard this theory, reluctantly, for a number of reasons, and particularly because Dante explicitly indicated in *Purgatorio*, XX, 15 that the coming of the Greyhound was still in the future. Clearly, Dante envisaged the *Comedy* as preparing a pattern of life and purpose for the Greyhound, whom I think he conceived as some exceptional man, to be sent by God, not on account of his birth or office, but on account of his being 'chosen' to redeem humanity.

> Ond' io per lo tuo me' penso e discerno
> che tu mi segui, e io sarò tua guida,
> e trarrotti di qui per loco etterno,   114
>   ove udirai le disperate strida,
> vedrai li antichi spiriti dolenti,
> ch'a la seconda morte ciascun grida;   117
>   e vederai color che son contenti

nel foco, perché speran di venire
quando che sia a le beate genti.   120
    A le quai poi se tu vorrai salire,
anima fia a ciò più di me degna:
con lei ti lascerò nel mio partire;   123

(And so I consider and judge it best for you to follow me; and I shall be your guide. I shall lead you from here through a world without end, where you shall hear the screams of despair, and see tormented spirits from times long past, each of them lamenting the second death. And you shall see those who are content in the fire because sooner or later they hope to join the ranks of the blessed. Should you then wish to ascend among the blessed, another soul will come, more worthy for that task than me; I shall leave you with her on my departure.)

These four terzine succinctly declare the subject of the work — a journey through Hell, Purgatory and Paradise. The 'second death' (117) of the 'spirits from times long past' (that is, of souls from the earliest beginnings of mankind) is probably to be understood as the final death on the Day of Judgement; 'anima . . . più di me degna' (122) is, of course, Beatrice, who will guide Dante through Paradise, from which Virgil was banned, because he was a rebel against God's law (125). That is to say, having lived before Christianity, Virgil had incurred the guilt of 'not worshipping God aright' (*Inferno*, IV, 38).

ché quello imperador che là sù regna,
perch' i' fu' ribellante a la sua legge,
non vuol che 'n sua città per me si vegna.   126
    In tutte parti impera e quivi regge;
quivi è la sua città e l'alto seggio:
oh felice colui cu' ivi elegge!'.   129
    E io a lui: 'Poeta, io ti richeggio
per quello Dio che tu non conoscesti,
a ciò ch'io fugga questo male e peggio,   132
    che tu mi meni là dov' or dicesti,
sì ch'io veggia la porta di san Pietro
e color cui tu fai cotanto mesti'.
Allor si mosse, e io li tenni dietro.   136

(For the Emperor who reigns on high has decreed that I may not enter his city, because I was a rebel to his law. His authority is universal, but there he rules in person. There lies his capital city and his high judgement-seat. Happy indeed are those whom he chooses to go there!' And I said to him: 'Poet, I entreat you in the name of the God you did not recognise, in order that I may escape this present danger, and worse, that you should lead me where you said just now, so that I may see Saint Peter's gate, and those whom you describe as so full of woe.' Then he set out, and I kept close behind.)

We should pause for a moment here to consider lines 124–9, where another aspect of Dante's Virgil is revealed for the first time in all its pathos. We have already seen him as a paternal figure, solicitous for the welfare of his charge, trustworthy, wonderfully knowledgeable, as steady as a rock. It is a joy, for the reader of the *Comedy*, to follow the development of the relationship between the two main characters, with the stern taskmaster of the earlier Cantos mellowing to become almost an elder brother, and with his pupil clinging more and more affectionately to his guide. But through all the strength and steadfastness of Virgil's character there runs a vein of infinite sadness, which here comes to the surface — its cause is a longing never to be fulfilled, to enter the city of God: 'Happy indeed are those whom he chooses to go there!' (129). It is with an almost audible sigh of 'desio', of yearning (*Inferno*, IV, 42) that Virgil pronounces these words; salvation will be denied to this soul that, in the story of the *Comedy*, is represented as having saved others; hopeless nostalgia will be eternal for him.

Then Dante formally and solemnly accepts Virgil's advice, and asks to be led to Saint Peter's gate (134), which he places at the entrance to Purgatory. Virgil sets out: 'Allor si mosse, ed io li tenni dietro' (136). With this line begins the most venturesome journey ever undertaken by the human mind.

Inferno VI

Dante and Virgil began their journey by crossing the gate of Hell into the Vestibule where the Slothful are punished (Canto III), and had then proceeded to the first Circle, or Limbo, the abode of the Virtuous Heathen and unbaptized infants (Canto IV), and to the second Circle (The Lustful, Canto V). They have now reached the third Circle (line 7); here they find the souls of those who sinned by gluttony.

We all know that, as George Herbert put it, 'gluttony kills more than the sword'; but at first the terrible inevitability of eternal retribution in Hell may strike us as a harsh punishment indeed. Dante, of course, was on firm ground, theologically, when he placed the Gluttonous in Hell, immediately below the Lustful. The gluttonous, no less than the lustful, have been unable to control their appetite; they are guilty of what Dante will later describe as 'incontinenza' (Canto XI), inability to exercise self-restraint. Let us be quite clear: Dante is not thinking of the occasional and excusable indulgence in the pleasures of the palate, but of a habitual excess, a habitual lack of measure or order, in this indulgence. So conceived, gluttony (*gula*) was traditionally counted among the Seven Capital Vices, or Deadly Sins: excessive preoccupation with food and drink in the sense not only of overeating, but of love for rare dishes and expensive wines could so contaminate the spiritual life of man as to divert his mind from its supreme purpose — from the thought of God and of salvation. Medieval attitudes to gluttony are well illustrated by the commonplaces put into the mouth of Chaucer's Pardoner (*Pardoner's Tale*, I, 170): 'O glotonye, ful of cursednesse, O cause first of our confusion, O original of our dampnacioun!' Dante leaves us in no doubt about his abhorrence for this offence, which is described as 'dannosa' (53), a word of which the context shows that it has a stronger meaning than usual; its force is adequately rendered by the translation 'ruinous'. The lesson imparted in the *Inferno* is further driven home in Cantos XXII–XXIV of *Purgatorio*, where, as here, the solitary indulgence of the gluttonous in their craving is seen as more degrading, and therefore, to some extent, as a more serious offence, than the mutual indulgence of the lustful. Through a series of examples of temperance and abstinence, Dante portrays an ideal life of austerity, frugality and renunciation, which we know was fully congenial to

18

him. Boccaccio reports in his *Trattatello in laude di Dante* that he had been extremely frugal both in eating and in drinking. That ideal way of life was totally opposed to the pursuit of worldly pleasures and materialistic gratification of the senses, of which gluttony was a manifestation. There is an indication later on that for Dante gluttony was spiritual blindness.

The Canto can be roughly divided into three sections; the first one, down to line 33, describes the third Circle and its guardian, the monster Cerberus; the second one, up to line 93, presents Dante's encounter with Ciacco and recent political events in Florence; in the third and final section Virgil informs Dante about the state of the damned souls and their fate at the Last Judgement and after. The three sections may seem heterogeneous and unrelated, but I hope to show that this apparent diversity conceals a substantial unity within the Canto as a whole, and that the various themes are linked to one another in a logical sequence. For the time being, it is enough to remark that Canto VI derives its special appeal from its variety and from its first introduction of some of the issues that the poet has not yet had a chance of broaching, issues that will loom larger and larger as the poem progresses. Thus, even though it comes immediately after the lyrical climax at the end of Canto V, this Canto is no anticlimax. Indeed, the sharp contrast with Canto V heightens its impact on the reader.

> Al tornar de la mente, che si chiuse
> dinanzi a la pietà d'i due cognati,
> che di trestizia tutto mi confuse,   3
>   novi tormenti e novi tormentati
> mi veggio intorno, come ch'io mi mova
> e ch'io mi volga, e come che io guati.   6

(With the return of my mind that was shut off before the piteous state of the two kinsfolk, which quite confounded me with grief, new torments and new souls in torment I see about me, wherever I move and turn and look.)

The opening lines still reverberate with the emotions kindled by Dante's encounter with Paolo and Francesca, and recall, by way of transition, the grief and anguish that assailed him on hearing the story of the two lovers, and that still affected him on recovering from his swoon; while the second terzina is meant to strike the imagination of the reader and to convey, just as several other passages in the *Inferno* do, the almost visual effect of the multitudes of souls that since the beginning of time have come to people the nether regions.

> Io sono al terzo cerchio, de la piova

etterna, maladetta, fredda e greve;
regola e qualità mai non l'è nova.   9
    Grandine grossa, acqua tinta e neve
per l'aere tenebroso si riversa;
pute la terra che questo riceve.   12

(I am in the third circle, of eternal, accursed rain, cold and heavy, never changing its measure or its kind; huge hail, black water and snow pour down through
the gloomy air, and the ground that receives it stinks.)

How Dante has been transported from the second to the third Circle,
he does not tell us. Line 7 starkly registers this fact and implies that, having left behind him the sin of lust, he can now turn to another deadly
sin. The punishment of the Gluttonous is described with typical directness and economy in lines 7–12: as in the case of the ceaseless storm that
buffets the Lustful, here too the elements are the agents of God's wrath;
but sinners receive the full force of the pelting rain, hail and snow,
crouched on the ground and motionless, in the stinking mud (12). Note
the rare accumulation of adjectives in line 8. Dante is habitually very
sparing in his use of epithets, and so it is all the more striking that a
whole line should consist of nothing else. His purpose is to emphasize
that the deluge is no ordinary rainstorm, but an implacable torment,
in fact, a fitting 'contrappasso' (retribution); the Gluttonous have been
attached to earthly things, so they are condemned to lie in mud. It has
been argued repeatedly that the substances that poured down onto the
stinking ground were malodorous and nauseous. There is little
justification for this in the text, bearing in mind that had Dante meant
to say what some interpreters think they can perceive, he would have
left us in no doubt. I prefer to see the 'acqua tinta' of line 10 as taking
its colour from the surrounding atmosphere, described as 'aere
tenebroso' in the next line.

    Cerbero, fiera crudele e diversa,
con tre gole caninamente latra
sovra la gente che quivi è sommersa.   15
    Li occhi ha vermigli, la barba unta e atra,
e 'l ventre largo, e unghiate le mani;
graffia li spirti ed iscoia ed isquatra.   18
    Urlar li fa la pioggia come cani;
de l' un de' lati fanno a l'altro schermo;
volgonsi spesso i miseri profani.   21
    Quando ci scorse Cerbero, il gran vermo,
le bocche aperse e mostrocci le sanne;
non avea membro che tenesse fermo.   24
    E 'l duca mio distese le sue spanne,
prese la terra, e con piene le pugna

20

Inferno VI

la gittò dentro a le bramose canne. 27
    Qual è quel cane ch'abbaiando agogna,
e si racqueta poi che 'l pasto morde,
ché solo a divorarlo intende e pugna, 30
    cotai si fecer quelle facce lorde
de lo demonio Cerbero, che 'ntrona
l'anime sì, ch'esser vorrebber sorde. 33

(Cerberus, a beast fierce and monstrous, with three throats barks like a dog over the people that are immersed there; he has red eyes, a beard greasy and black, a great belly, and clawed hands, and he scars and flays and rends the spirits. The rain makes them howl like dogs, and the profane wretches often turn themselves, of one side making a shelter for the other. When Cerberus, the great monster, perceived us, he opened his mouths and showed us the fangs, not one of his limbs keeping still, and my Leader spread his hands, took up earth, and with full fists threw it into the ravenous gullets. As the dog that yelps for greed and becomes quiet when it bites its food, being all absorbed in struggling to devour it; such became these foul visages of the demon Cerberus, who so thunders at the souls that they would fain be deaf.)

The appalling condition of the damned (a penalty of which, we are later told (48) that, if some are greater, none is so loathsome) is further exasperated by the presence of Cerberus. Once again Virgil, the guide in the journey, is also the literary model. In the *Aeneid* (VI, 417–23) Cerberus barks with three throats, as he does here; and there too the Sybil throws him a morsel as a sop. But Dante, vying with his master and summoning all the resources of his imagination, recreates the monster; the differences between the model and this passage are more important than the similarities. First of all, we notice that the traditional Cerberus, as depicted by Virgil, guarded the entrance to Hades; here he is the guardian only of the Circle of the Gluttonous. It was appropriate to give him this role, as dogs were usually associated with voracity, and Cerberus's very name was believed (wrongly, as is often the case with medieval and classical etymologies) to mean 'the flesh-devouring one'. Secondly, we find that in the *Comedy* Virgil (25–7) does not throw flesh or a honey-cake to the dog, but the mud lying on the ground, to denote not only the foulness and degradation, but also the futility, of gluttony. Finally, and above all, 'Cerberus is here to indicate the sin of gluttony', as Boccaccio stated in his commentary 600 years ago; Dante's Cerberus seems the quintessence of gluttony, the concrete personification of an abstract concept, to the point that after the passage devoted to him — in fact, after line 33 — Dante does not expatiate further on gluttony as a sin. He identifies Cerberus with gluttony itself, and this by two principal means: by the many realistic

21

touches in the grotesquely medieval description of the monster, in contrast with the conventional portrayals by classical authors (it is enough to point to lines 16–17, and particularly to the greasy beard and turgid belly); and, secondly, by making him a repulsive mixture of man and beast, the symbol of a failing through which men descend to the level of animals. The deliberate ambiguity of such a depiction is suggested throughout the passage by the indiscriminate mingling of human and canine attributes and actions: Cerberus barks like a dog (line 14 — a remarkable line, stretched out, as it were, by the two stresses that fall on 'caninamente', which give the impression of the unendurable protractedness of his barking) and shows his fangs (23); but, at the same time, he has a beard and hands, as well as the glutton's paunch (16–17), and three faces, rather than three snouts, on his three heads (31); conversely, the sinners have acquired some canine features and howl like dogs under the rain (19). Thus, Dante's Cerberus is a striking, as well as highly original, embodiment of gluttony; his presence adds colour and interest to the discussion of a sin that is, in itself, somewhat prosaic. While he is still the fierce and very strange beast of classical tradition (line 13: the adjective 'diverso' has the meaning of 'out of the ordinary' more than once in the *Comedy*), he is also the medieval monster ('il gran vermo': 22) conjured up by Dante's imagination; and he is a demon (32), like the other Pagan deities that inhabit this Christian Hell.

> Noi passavam su per l'ombre che adona
> la greve pioggia, e ponavam le piante
> sovra lor vanità che par persona.   36
> Elle giacean per terra tutte quante,
> fuor d'una ch'a seder si levò, ratto
> ch'ella ci vide passarsi davante.   39

(We passed over the shades that were beaten down by the heavy rain, setting our feet on their emptiness, which seemed real bodies. They were all lying on the ground, except one who sat up as soon as he saw us passing before him.)

The central part of Canto VI is taken up by the dialogue with Ciacco. We know little, or nothing, about this character, although several early commentators, including Boccaccio, volunteer a good deal of picturesque information about his name and habits. But the details, for the most part, have all the air of being embroiderings on what Dante says or implies. The same can be said of one of the short stories in Boccaccio's *Decameron* (IX, 8), where Ciacco figures prominently; it tells us no more about him than we can learn from Canto VI. The very name Ciacco has caused some controversy; it has been taken by some to be a nickname, referring perhaps to some physical peculiarity; by others to be a shorter form of a first name such as Giacomo; or even to mean simply 'pig' or 'swine'. Now, it is true that the word *ciacco* has been frequently used, mainly in Tuscany, to mean *porco*, but no example has been found before Dante's time, and it seems likely that the powerful suggestion of the episode in the *Comedy* was itself responsible for this usage. Dante certainly addresses Ciacco in terms that rule out any derogatory overtones in his name. As for its being a nickname or an abbreviation, we just do not know; there are other people with the same name on record in Florentine annals.

> 'O tu che se' per questo 'nferno tratto',
> mi disse, 'riconoscimi, se sai:
> tu fosti, prima ch'io disfatto, fatto'.   42
> E io a lui: 'L'angoscia che tu hai
> forse ti tira fuor de la mia mente,
> sì che non par ch'i' ti vedessi mai.   45
> Ma dimmi chi tu se' che 'n sì dolente
> loco se' messo, e hai sì fatta pena,
> che, s'altra è maggio, nulla è sì spiacente'.   48
> Ed elli a me: 'La tua città, ch'è piena
> d'invidia sì che già trabocca il sacco,
> seco mi tenne in la vita serena.   51
> Voi cittadini mi chiamaste Ciacco:
> per la dannosa colpa de la gola,
> come tu vedi, a la pioggia mi fiacco.   54
> E io anima trista non son sola,
> ché tutte queste a simil pena stanno
> per simil colpa'. E più non fé parola.   57

('O thou who art led through this Hell,' he said to me, 'recall me, if thou canst; thou wast made before I was unmade.' And I said to him: 'The anguish thou hast perhaps takes thee from my memory, so that I do not seem ever to have seen thee; but tell me who thou art, put in a place of such misery and under such a penalty that, if any is greater, none is so loathsome.' And he said to me: 'Thy city, which is so full of envy that already the sack runs over, held me within it in the bright life, when you citizens called me Ciacco. For the ruinous fault of gluttony, as thou seest, I lie helpless in the rain; and in my misery I am not alone, for all these are under the same penalty for the same fault.' And he said no more.)

That Dante was acquainted with Ciacco there can be no doubt; line 41 (where a trace of jocularity may be detected, or of ever so slight irony in the implicit reference to the results of his punishment) indicates that, if he had not been disfigured by suffering, Dante would have recognised him, just as he recognised Dante; no precise clue emerges from line 42 as to the time at which he lived. He died after Dante's birth, when the latter was old enough to have known him. No other facts concerning him can be culled from the text, but some traits of his personality can be discerned. One surmises that he thought and expressed himself with some precision, that he was educated and spoke well (line 42, to which I have just drawn attention, is not to be taken as a pun [*fatto — disfatto*], but as an example of ornate style, such as Dante sometimes used); it seems that he was not given to circumlocutions, but stuck to fact; one can even perceive a certain brusqueness in his speeches, or perhaps only a clipped way of finishing his sentences (line 57 and, even more, line 90). Apart from this, we can accept the almost universal testimony of the early commentators, that he was a courtier or a kind of courtier. There was, of course, no court in the modern sense in the Florentine republic; 'courtier' must have meant a gentleman, a diner-out, a *causeur*, a person whose company was welcomed in the houses of prominent families and, possibly, whose opinion was sought.

> Io li rispuosi: 'Ciacco, il tuo affanno
> mi pesa sì, ch'a lagrimar mi 'nvita;
> ma dimmi, se tu sai, a che verranno   60
>   li cittadin de la città partita;
> s'alcun v'è giusto; e dimmi la cagione
> per che l'ha tanta discordia assalita'.   63

(I answered him: 'Ciacco, thy distress so weighs on me that it bids me weep. But tell me, if thou canst, what the citizens of the divided city shall come to and whether any there is just, and tell me the cause of such discord assailing it.')

Finally, we must assume that Dante thought well of him; once Ciacco has introduced himself, Dante addresses him with some affection and expresses sorrow at his predicament (58–9); even more remarkable is the fact that he makes this fellow-citizen, the first of many Florentines he is to meet in Hell, utter an important prophecy of events in Florence in the crucial first few years of the fourteenth century: those events in which Dante had been so intimately involved, and about which he felt so passionately. The first five Cantos of *Inferno* deal with problems that do not necessarily relate to Dante's experiences after he had left Florence; the only reference to politics in the broadest sense of the word is the prophecy of the coming of the Greyhound in Canto I. Now the time has arrived to raise a theme that must have been ever-present in his mind during the long years of exile: the conditions in his native city that had caused his banishment. This theme comes gradually to the fore, and is further explored and expanded as the poem progresses:

here, the events leading up to the revolution of 1301–2 in Florence, and their aftermath; in Canto VI of *Purgatorio*, the condition of the whole of Italy; and in Canto VI of *Paradiso* the providential designs for the happiness and welfare of mankind. Canto VI of each Cantica, then, is constantly reserved for political considerations, so minutely thought out is the architectural plan of the poem.

Several commentators have wondered whether it was seemly to entrust such a weighty pronouncement to a glutton. Would it not have been better, asked the sixteenth-century critic Castelvetro, to talk to him 'd'alcuna ghiottornia', of some delicacy? And where, at any rate, is the connection between gluttony and Florentine politics? That Dante saw a link, and chose the third Circle advisedly to introduce the topic, is clear from the fact that in Cantos XXIII and XXIV of *Purgatorio* too, when he discourses with his old friend and boon companion Forese Donati in the Circle of the Gluttonous, the conversation soon turns to conditions in Florence and to political events (the corruption of Florentine women, and the death of Corso Donati). Now, during his exile Dante must have been reflecting upon the causes of recent upheavals in Florence, and he must have gradually come to the conclusion that the growing mercantile prosperity of his town was responsible for the pre-conditions that led to strife and violence — i.e., for the prevalent corruption and luxury, the 'orgoglio e dismisura' (arrogance, or pride, and excess), as he will say a few Cantos further on (XVI, 73–4), brought about by 'la gente nuova e i subiti guadagni' (the new people, the influx of strangers from the surrounding countryside, and the sudden large profits). A conspicuous facet of the luxury and corruption he deplored was a more refined way of life with its possible corollary, gluttony. In other words, he saw the political problem as just an aspect of a wider moral problem, and related politics to a particular sin, or to several sins. The obverse was the mythical Florence of a previous age, such as he imagines it and cherishes in his dreams, 'sobria e pudica' (*Paradiso*, XV, 99), sober and chaste, without moral laxity, and also austere and frugal, i.e., without gluttony.

Right from the speech where he introduces himself, Ciacco reveals a deep and enduring interest in Florence, and a sense of resentment for the injustice that reigned in it, obliquely conveyed by such expressions as 'thy city' and 'you citizens' (49, 52), instead of 'our city' and 'our fellow-citizens', as we would expect. He also supplies the pretext for Dante's three precise questions as to the future course of events, by his allusion to the envy with which Florence is filled (50). Dante quickly follows up his cue and elicits from him his prophecy — the first of many prophecies after the event, the fictional date of his journey being 1300, whereas the Canto we are reading was written at least a few years later.

> E quelli a me: 'Dopo lunga tencione
> verranno al sangue, e la parte selvaggia
> caccerà l'altra con molta offensione. 66
> Poi appresso convien che questa caggia
> infra tre soli, e che l'altra sormonti
> con la forza di tal che testé piaggia. 69
> Alte terrà lungo tempo le fronti,
> tenendo l'altra sotto gravi pesi,
> come che di ciò pianga o che n'aonti. 72
> Giusti son due, e non vi sono intesi;
> superbia, invidia e avarizia sono
> le tre faville c'hanno i cuori accesi'. 75

(And he said to me: 'After long strife they shall come to blood and the party of the rustics shall drive out the other with much offence; then that party is destined to fall within three years, and the other to prevail, by the force of one who is now manoeuvring. Long will it hold its head high, keeping the first under grievous burdens, for all their tears and anger. Two men are just and are not heeded there. Pride, envy and avarice are the three sparks that have set these hearts on fire.')

With the authority of a direct witness of these vicissitudes, Dante through Ciacco gives us his interpretation of them and recounts how the 'divided city' of line 61 came to bloodshed. The split within the Florentine Guelphs had been caused by a number of factors: a conflict of personalities between the two leading citizens, Vieri de' Cerchi and Corso Donati; the crystallizing round each of them of two groups of interests, one that came to be known as the Whites, firmly in the saddle and holding the reins of power, the other, the Blacks, seeking to oust them; the rancour and desire for revenge engendered by the laws passed in previous years against the older noble families (Grandi, or Magnati), and especially by the *Ordinamenti di Giustizia* of 1293. But contemporaries, including Dante and the Florentine chroniclers Dino Compagni and Giovanni Villani, saw the long strife ('lunga tencione': 64) as having entered its acute phase following a brawl on 1 May 1300, when one of the Cerchi family was wounded (this is the bloodshed in the next line); subsequently, in the summer of 1301, several prominent Black Guelphs were banished 'with much offence' (66) by the republic, which, as I have just observed, was controlled by the Whites, here called 'parte selvaggia' (65), a reference to the recent rustic origin of the Cerchi family. In Dante's aristocratic eyes, they were upstarts. Then, the

26

Whites themselves fell from power (67) and were banished, in their turn, by the triumphant Blacks, between November 1301 and April 1302 ('within three years', that is, from the fictional date of 1300). This was brought about by the intervention of Charles de Valois, brother of Philippe le Bel, King of France, who had been sent to Florence for this purpose by that powerful supporter of Corso Donati and the Blacks, Pope Boniface VIII (here described as 'one who is now manoeuvring': 69). By sending Charles to drive out the White Guelphs the Pope was trying to exert his own control over Florence; but in 1300 he was still giving the impression of sitting on the fence, of 'manoeuvring' with both parties. Line 70 has been eagerly analysed and carefully weighed by interpreters to see if it can yield a clue for determining the precise year in which this Canto was written, and thus provide a point of reference for the dating of the *Inferno*; the victorious party, the Black Guelphs, will hold their heads high for a long time. In fact, this is exactly what happened; the Whites never regained power. But how soon could Dante write this statement, with the certainty of not being proved wrong by events? In other words, how long is a long time? Obviously, individual judgements will differ as to the exact meaning of such a vague expression; but I think one would be justified in assuming that Dante would hardly have used it if only a few months had elapsed from that fateful early November 1301; at least six or seven years seems a safer guess. As for the grievous burdens, the tears and the disdain (71–2), these had been part and parcel of Dante's everyday life since 1302, and we can well imagine how heavy his heart was while writing such words.

The reply to Dante's second question (73) takes us back to 1300. He asked: are there any just men in Florence (62)? Ciacco says that there are two, but they are not heeded. The identification of these two men has exercised the ingenuity of commentators and critics through the centuries; and recently, although no new theories have been proposed, some of the old ones have been forcefully restated. That Dante included himself among this very small number of just men left in Florence, has been believed by several, and one cannot rule out the possibility that this thought was at the back of the poet's mind; it seems, however, difficult to believe that, if he had wished to make so boastful an allusion to himself, he would have put it so baldly. The arguments in favour of other candidates (Guido Cavalcanti, Dino Compagni, etc.) are so slender as to allow us to disregard them out of hand. An interpretation given by no lesser authority than Dante's own son, Pietro,

Dante's 'Comedy'

has been recently refurbished. It consists in reading 'giusti' as a noun, rather than as an adjective, and an abstract noun at that, and giving it the same meaning as the Latin *jus*, a meaning that can be found elsewhere in Dante's works; thus the two 'giusti' would be natural justice, and legal justice. It is hard to reconcile this interpretation with Dante's original question, which was clearly intended to ask whether there are still any in Florence who pursue justice; and I follow the majority of recent commentators, and interpret Ciacco's answer as being decidedly in the negative: there are so few (the number two is possibly an echo of Ezekiel's, 14: 14–16, three righteous men in a corrupt city), that it is as though there are none. What no interpreter, as far as I know, has noticed is that the mention of the word 'giusti' is, in all likelihood, also intended to introduce at this point the concept of justice, as the direct counterpart of the three scourges of Florence (and of mankind), pride, envy and avarice, mentioned in the next line as the three sparks that have caused all evil.

Justice is a key word and a key concept for Dante; he was one of those who (in his own words) 'esuriunt et sitiunt iustitiam' (*Epistola* V, i, 3), hunger and thirst after righteousness; his mission in life was to preach justice (he described himself as 'vir predicans iustitiam' (*Epistola* XII, iii, 7)); his intense need for justice (justice for himself, but above all for all men) permeates the *Comedy*, as well as his other works and particularly the *Monarchia*, and is solemnly restated both in *Purgatorio*, VI, and in *Paradiso*, VI. Now, the main obstacle to justice is greed (*cupiditas*), or avarice ('iustitie maxime contrariatur cupiditas' ('the thing most contrary to justice is greed'), he remarks: *Monarchia*, I, xi, 11). Thus, avarice takes the first place, in Dante's eyes, among the evil dispositions of man; in this he followed St Augustine and several medieval thinkers, such as Giacomo da Viterbo, for whom, as for St Paul, it was 'radix omnium malorum' (the root of all evils: *De regimine christ.*) But, while these thinkers considered avarice in terms of individual psychology as the foremost sin (for it hinders the exercise of charity), Dante's reasoning was different: he saw avarice as the main cause of the corruption of contemporary society; it affected whole communities, like Florence, which became tainted with greed; it affected popes in particular, and thus prevented the establishment of justice, harmony and happiness in the world, with a universal emperor exercising temporal power over the whole of mankind. 'Maladetta sie tu, antica lupa' ('accursed be thou, ancient wolf [the symbol of avarice]'), he will exclaim in *Purgatorio* (XX, 10). Envy and pride, or

28

arrogance (*superbia*) were concurrent causes of the disorder prevailing in Florence and outside, for they generated hatred and strife; envy, in particular, is closely connected with avarice, in Dante's thought, for it is easily kindled by greed; and it was envy that had first loosed the she-wolf out of Hell, as we are told in Canto I of *Inferno*. As for pride, the sin that induced Lucifer to rebel against God, it came first in the list of the Seven Deadly Sins, being considered the most serious. Dante acknowledges this, in spite of the special emphasis he set on avarice, by placing the Proud in the first Cornice of *Purgatorio*. This trio of sins — 'superbia, invidia e avarizia' — almost the epitome of injustice, sets the seal on Ciacco's prophecy; his judgement of the plight of Florence will be echoed by others in similar vein later in the *Comedy*.

> Qui puose fine al lagrimabil suono.
> E io a lui: 'Ancor vo' che mi 'nsegni
> e che di più parlar mi facci dono.   78
>   Farinata e 'l Tegghiaio, che fuor sì degni,
> Iacopo Rusticucci, Arrigo e 'l Mosca
> e li altri ch'a ben far puoser li 'ngegni,   81
>   dimmi ove sono e fa ch'io li conosca;
> ché gran disio mi stringe di savere
> se 'l ciel li addolcia o lo 'nferno li attosca'. 84

(Here he made an end of his grievous words. And I said to him: 'I would still learn from thee, and I beg thee to grant me further speech. Farinata and Tegghiaio, men of such worth, Jacopo Rusticucci, Arrigo and Mosca and the rest whose minds were set on well-doing, tell me where they are and give me knowledge of them; for I am pressed with a great desire to know whether they share Heaven's sweetness or the bitterness of Hell.')

Dante's thirst for knowledge is not yet satisfied, and he asks his fellow-citizen one more question. At first sight it seems unconnected, but in fact it arises quite logically from what has gone before. His inquiry is about the fate of the souls of five Florentines, all of them clearly entitled to a share in the praise that is specifically given first to two of them (79), and then to others who are not named (81); they were men who were normally regarded, in the popular view, as having deserved well of their city. Opinions differ regarding the identity of Arrigo (80), whose name does not occur again in the *Comedy*; but it is pointless to review them, as there is no real evidence on which to reach a decision. The other four had all lived in the first half of the previous century, three of them, in fact, up to the 1260s. Farinata degli Uberti and Mosca dei Lamberti had been Ghibellines; Tegghiaio Aldobrandi and Jacopo Rusticucci, Guelphs. The nature of their services to Florence can be judged from the fact that Farinata had protected his native city from

Dante's 'Comedy'

destruction by his fellow-Ghibellines after the battle of Montaperti in 1260, as Villani reported and Dante will openly acknowledge in Canto X of *Inferno*; and Tegghiaio Aldobrandi and Jacopo Rusticucci were said to have tried in vain to persuade their Guelph fellow-citizens to give up their plan to engage the overwhelming Ghibelline forces in the same disastrous battle; they seem to have also played a leading part in the successful conclusion of a peace negotiation between Volterra and San Gimignano. Whether Guelph or Ghibelline, they had cared, first and foremost, for their country, rather than for themselves; yet, Ciacco informs Dante that they have all been damned (85–7); and, indeed, they are all to be met lower down in Hell, Farinata among the Heretics, in a celebrated episode, Tegghiaio Aldobrandi and Jacopo Rusticucci among the homosexuals (Canto XVI), Mosca dei Lamberti among the Sowers of Discord (Canto XXVIII). The lesson to be learnt by the reader seems to be that, however great the praise one has earned as a citizen, it will be of no avail if one has not resisted individual passions. But this would not be sufficient reason for mentioning the five men; nor is it enough to say, as some commentators have recently suggested, that Dante names these Florentines here simply because he wants to whet his readers' appetite, and spur them to read on and find out about their fate. His main motive is clearly to stress the lack of merit and virtue in his own times, and to compare it with the higher civic standards of a supposedly uncorrupted previous age, when righteous men were more plentiful. Nor is he just harking back to a mythical past in a sterile attempt to escape from an unbearable present; he is seeking there above all a blueprint for a better world and for a purer spiritual life; as far as Florence is concerned, this means the hope that the town might become once more 'un popol giusto e sano' ('a people just and sane') (*Paradiso*, XXXI, 39), without pride, envy and avarice. The myth of the former purity of Florence, which is given a first airing here, will be further developed in Cantos XV–XVII, as we shall see, and even more fully in *Paradiso*, in the Cacciaguida Cantos.

> E quelli: 'Ei son tra l'anime più nere;
> diverse colpe giù li grava al fondo:
> se tanto scendi, là i potrai vedere.   87
>   Ma quando tu sarai nel dolce mondo,
> priegoti ch'a la mente altrui mi rechi:
> più non ti dico e più non ti rispondo'.   90
>   Li diritti occhi torse allora in biechi;
> guardommi un poco e poi chinò la testa:
> cadde con essa a par de li altri ciechi.   93

Inferno VI

(And he: 'They are among the blackest souls and different faults weigh them down to the depth; if thou descend so far thou canst see them. But when thou shalt be in the sweet world I pray thee bring me to men's memory. I tell thee no more nor answer thee again.' With that he turned his direct look askance, gazed at me for a moment, then bent his head and so dropped to the level of the other blind.)

Before Ciacco has to sink down again under his eternal punishment, his request to be remembered among the living (a request that Dante often hears from the souls) adds another human touch to a sympathetically drawn portrait. 'Sweet world' (88) means life on earth for the damned, and there are several examples in the *Comedy* of similar expressions, one of them to be found in this same Canto ('bright life': 51). The suggestion that it might refer to a particular period of revelling and merry-making in Florence seems untenable, in view of the context.

> E 'l duca disse a me: 'Più non si desta
> di qua dal suon de l'angelica tromba,
> quando verrà la nimica podesta: 96
>   ciascun rivederà la trista tomba,
> ripiglierà sua carne e sua figura,
> udirà quel ch'in etterno rimbomba'.   99
>   Sì trapassammo per sozza mistura
> de l'ombre e de la pioggia, a passi lenti,
> toccando un poco la vita futura;   102
>   per ch'io dissi: 'Maestro, esti tormenti
> cresceran' ei dopo la gran sentenza,
> o fier minori, o saran sì cocenti?'.   105

(And my Leader said to me: 'He wakes no more till sounding of the angel's trumpet, when the adverse Judge shall come; each shall find again the sad tomb and take again his flesh and form, and hear that which echoes in eternity.' So we passed on through the foul mixture of the shades and the rain with slow steps, touching a little on the life to come. I said therefore: 'Master, will these torments increase after the great judgement, or become less, or continue as fierce as now?')

After the finality of line 90 comes the even more terrible finality of the angel's trumpet at the Last Judgement, when the 'adverse Judge', that is, Christ, will come; he is strikingly called 'inimical', that is, no longer a friend to the damned. Line 96 has a Biblical, or even apocalyptic, ring, which is echoed in the next three lines down to line 99. This is achieved partly by the choice of rhyming words, partly by the four strongly stressed verbs in the future tense ('verrà', 'rivederà', 'ripiglierà', 'udirà'). Virgil's solemn, yet dramatic words introduce a short doctrinal excur-

31

Dante's 'Comedy'

sus, one of the few in the *Inferno*. The transition is effortless, and follows quite naturally: first, a slow, pensive terzina (100–2), whereupon Dante, pursuing the train of thought begun by Virgil, expresses his doubt as to the intensity of the sufferings of the damned after the Last Judgement: will it be greater, slighter, or the same (103–5)?

> Ed elli a me: 'Ritorna a tua scïenza,
> che vuol, quanto la cosa è più perfetta,
> più senta il bene, e così la doglienza.   108
> Tutto che questa gente maladetta
> in vera perfezion già mai non vada,
> di là più che di qua essere aspetta'.   111
> Noi aggirammo a tondo quella strada,
> parlando più assai ch'i' non ridico;
> venimmo al punto dove si digrada:
> quivi trovammo Pluto, il gran nemico.   115

(And he answered me: 'Go back to thy science, which requires that in the measure of a creature's perfection it feels more both of pleasure and of pain. Although these people who are accursed never come to true perfection, they look to be completer then than now.' We went round that curving road, with much more talk than I repeat, and reached the point where the descent begins. Here we found Plutus, the great enemy.)

Virgil's answer refers Dante expressly to 'tua scïenza' ('thy science': 106); this indicates unequivocally the doctrines of Aristotle, constantly described by Dante as *the* master, philosopher, teacher (*preceptor*) *par excellence*, while Virgil often places the pronoun 'thy' before the titles of Aristotle's individual works when he mentions them to Dante. The Italian poet, of course, read Aristotle in a Latin translation together with the commentaries of St Thomas Aquinas. As for line 111, one has only to read *Paradiso*, XIV, 43–59 to have the full sense. When the human body is restored, the human being is then perfected, and capable of experiencing more joy in Paradise or, conversely, more torment in Hell; in other words, as Dante puts it here, the damned expect to possess a more complete human form after the Last Judgement than before ('di là più che di qua': 111), and therefore will feel their punishments more intensely.

The Canto closes with the poets' descent from the third to the fourth Circle, that of the Hoarders and Spendthrifts; in order to leave the third Circle, they must follow its circumference ('that curving road': 112) until the point where the passage is to be found. Line 115, as pithy as an epigram, is typical of this fast-moving Canto and brings it to an abrupt close, leaving the reader in a state of suspense and curiosity: it is an invitation not to stop here. 'Pluto' is, of course, the guardian of the fourth Circle, and is described as 'the great enemy'; but this does not suffice to tell us whether Dante wishes to refer to Pluto, the god of the nether world (in which case 'gran nemico' means the Devil), or to Plutus, the god of wealth and an appropriate choice for a place of punishment of the Avaricious and Prodigals (in which case the attribute 'gran nemico' would imply that acquisitiveness, and therefore avarice, is the greatest enemy of mankind). It is likely that Dante did not really distinguish between Pluto and Plutus and, in some way, means us to understand both here.

In conclusion, it is worth considering some general aspects of the style and manner of this, the shortest Canto in the *Comedy*, apart from *Inferno* XI which is of exactly the same length. I have already hinted that its brevity and conciseness were deliberate. This mode of treatment of the subject-matter of Canto VI seems to have been adopted for the sake of variety. In Canto V the poet, limiting himself to a single theme, can allow himself, with a more leisurely development, a more complex sentence structure. In Canto VI he seeks, by contrast, directness as well as diversity, both in substance and in style, and manages to pack all he has to say into these 115 taut lines, with a rapid succession of realistic description, interpretation and discussion of political events, and disquisition on moral and philosophical issues. Such an undertaking requires a considerable variety of language and style; after the apprenticeship of his lyrical poems and experimentation in the previous Cantos, he is quite ready for this (note for example several of the rhyming words, some harsh in sound, some solemn and resounding: not only obvious examples such as 'latra', 'atra', 'isquatra': 14, 16, 18; but also 'pugna', 'agogna', ' 'introna', 'attosca': 26, 28, 32, 84, etc.). One can find a remarkable range of style even in the last few lines, from the solemnity of the references to the Last Judgement, to the technical, prosaic, scholastic language of Virgil's second speech, to the startling abruptness of the very last line.

Inferno VIII

In the first seven Cantos of the *Inferno* we have already made considerable progress together with our two pilgrims, Dante and his guide, Virgil; or, rather, we have been plunged ever deeper into the huge funnel-like-chasm that is Hell as Dante represented it. There are ten divisions in the *Inferno* — as many as in the other two Cantiche, *Purgatorio* and *Paradiso* — and by the time we get to Canto VIII, we have left five of them behind — in fact, most of Upper Hell; after the Gluttons (Canto VI) come the Avaricious and Prodigals, who are punished in the fourth Circle (Canto VII). We are still in the region reserved for the sins of incontinence, that is, for sins that are relatively less heinous than those of violence and fraud, since they are due to impulse and want of self-control; they harm only the sinner and do not affect others.

Before we reach the beginning of Canto VIII, we have already entered another Circle, the fifth, as the word 'seguitando' in line 1 tells us. Dante meant it to indicate that, unlike its predecessors, Canto VIII is not self-contained, in the sense that it does not start afresh with a new Circle of damned souls, but continues the narrative of the incidents marking Dante's and Virgil's visit to the fifth Circle of the Incontinents and of their entrance into the City of Dis — a vast narrative that had begun half-way through Canto VII and will stretch across to occupy the first section of Canto IX as well; so that Canto VIII represents, in a way, the central panel of a triptych.

We learnt in Canto VII that the two poets, having already descended through four Circles of Upper Hell, entered the last of these Circles where the most serious among the sins of incontinence is punished — wrath together with another sin, described as 'accidia', possibly a variety of wrath, i.e., sullen wrath that, instead of exploding into violent actions, makes one sulk and harbour a grudge; or, possibly, the opposite of wrath, i.e., slothfulness where righteous indignation would be called for. The former (the Wrathful) are immersed in a marsh, identified with a river of the classical underworld, the Styx, where they squabble ferociously, inflicting grievous bodily harm on one another; the second group are totally under water in the murky pond. At the end of Canto VII the two poets arrived at the foot of a tower; and this is

where the narrative is now resumed, 'seguitando', or rather, as stated
in lines 1 and 2, going back to some time before they found themselves
at the foot of that high tower.

The Canto could be divided into two parts of almost exactly equal
length; the events in the Circle of the Wrathful, and the drama enacted
before the entrance into the City of Dis. But drama and tension run
through it all, from the very beginning.

> Io dico, seguitando, ch'assai prima
> che noi fossimo al piè de l'alta torre,
> li occhi nostri n'andar suso a la cima   3
>   per due fiammette che i vedemmo porre,
> e un'altra da lungi render cenno,
> tanto ch'a pena il potea l'occhio tòrre.   6
>   E io mi volsi al mar di tutto 'l senno;
> dissi: 'Questo che dice? e che risponde
> quell' altro foco? e chi son quei che 'l fenno?'.   9
>   Ed elli a me: 'Su per le sucide onde
> già scorgere puoi quello che s'aspetta,
> se 'l fummo del pantan nol ti nasconde'.   12

(Continuing, I have to tell that long before we were at the foot of the high tower
our eyes rose to its top on account of two lights which we saw put there and
to which another, so far off that we could hardly make it out, sent back a signal.
And I turned to the sea of all wisdom and said: 'What does this mean? And that
other fire, what does it answer? And who are they that have have made it?' And
he said to me: 'Over the foul waves thou mayst discern already that which we
wait for, if the marsh's fumes do not hide it from thee.')

The immense dark space in which Dante finds himself is made still
darker by the fumes rising from the marsh. This darkness is suddenly
punctuated by bewildering flashes of light from the top of a tower (4)
and by another fainter light answering them from a great distance
(5–6), signals that appear and disappear in an almost hallucinatory
fashion. Dante's disquiet is apparent from his short, breathless questions — three of them in two lines (8–9) — addressed to his omniscient
guide, 'the sea of all wisdom'. No sooner is Virgil's reply uttered than
it is followed by the event it has announced; indeed, everything in this
Canto happens with extraordinary rapidity and alarming overtones.

> Corda non pinse mai da sé saetta
> che sì corresse via per l'aere snella,
> com' io vidi una nave piccioletta   15
>   venir per l'acqua verso noi in quella,
> sotto 'l governo d'un sol galeoto,
> che gridava: 'Or se' giunta, anima fella!'.   18
>   'Flegïàs, Flegïàs, tu gridi a vòto',
> disse lo mio segnore, 'a questa volta:

Dante's 'Comedy'

più non ci avrai che sol passando il loto'.   21
    Qual è colui che grande inganno ascolta
che li sia fatto, e poi se ne rammarca,
fecesi Flegïàs ne l'ira accolta.   24
    Lo duca mio discese ne la barca,
e poi mi fece intrare appresso lui;
e sol quand' io fui dentro parve carca.   27
    Tosto che 'l duca e io nel legno fui,
segando se ne va l'antica prora
de l'acqua più che non suol con altrui.   30

(Never string drove arrow from the bow that ran so swiftly through the air as at that moment I saw a little boat approaching us over the water in the charge of a single oarsman, who cried: 'Now thou art caught, guilty soul!' 'Phlegyas, Phlegyas, this time thou criest in vain,' said my Lord; 'thou shalt have us no longer than the passing of the slough.' Like one that hears of a great fraud practised on him and then resents it, such Phlegyas became in his pent-up rage. My Leader went down into the boat, then made me enter after him, and not until I was in did it seem laden, and as soon as he and I had embarked the ancient prow moved off, cutting deeper into the water than it was wont with others.)

The event which Virgil anticipates, and which is already upon them with the speed of an arrow in flight (13–14), is the arrival of a little boat in the charge of Phlegyas; at one moment the boat has only just been discerned through fumes and mist from the marsh, and then, in the twinkling of an eye, it is already beside them, with its oarsman shouting at Dante — the first of the characters encountered in this Canto, all of whom will be hostile and threatening both in what they do and what they say. Phlegyas, the mythological son of Mars and King of the Lapithae, was said to have revenged himself on Apollo, who had seduced his daughter Caronis, and to have set fire to his temple. Although Phlegyas is clearly the personification, or one of the personifications, of wrath in this episode, it would be wrong to conclude that he is nothing but a symbol. It is true that he is sketched in rather than described in the round (in any case, little about him could have been gleaned from classical sources); but he is shown in action, so to speak, and this is enough to bring him to life. Dante's art is so mature by now that he does not have to supply details of a character or of what he stood for; he is able to convey these things dramatically and, as a result, poetically. A freely recreated figure, then, having its origin in fragments from mythology, filtered down to Dante through several classical writers, and in particular through Virgil's *Aeneid* (VI, 618), where Phlegyas is made to cry out loudly, as he does in this passage. He is at once a demon, displaying in his anger the attributes of the place

Inferno VIII

where Dante has put him, a guardian of the fifth Circle; and a ferryman, although there is disagreement as to whether the latter was his usual function. Dante is reticent on this point, and we can assume that he is deliberately vague; all we need to note is that Phlegyas's name not only suggests anger etymologically (*Phleg-*, to burn) but is also especially appropriate to one who conveys souls to the city of fire.

Phlegyas utters only five words here (18), and about as many, still shouting, later on; no more are needed to leave the ring of his angry voice in our ears. As for Virgil, who is usually composed and self-possessed, this time one detects, I think, more than a trace of irritation and impatience in his speech; he too seems affected by the general atmosphere of tenseness and apprehension.

The scene that follows in the next 33 lines is one of violence and passion; at the centre of the storm is a Florentine character named Filippo Argenti. The encounter with him unfolding in these eleven compact terzine can be divided into three sections (almost the three acts of a drama), the first and the last consisting of twelve lines each, and the second of nine.

> Mentre noi corravam la morta gora,
> dinanzi mi si fece un pien di fango,
> e disse: 'Chi se' tu che vieni anzi ora?'.   33
> E io a lui: 'S'i' vegno, non rimango;
> ma tu chi se', che sì se' fatto brutto?'.
> Rispuose: 'Vedi che son un che piango'.   36
> E io a lui: 'Con piangere e con lutto,
> spirito maladetto, ti rimani;
> ch'i' ti conosco, ancor sie lordo tutto'.   39
> Allor distese al legno ambo le mani;
> per che 'l maestro accorto lo sospinse,
> dicendo: 'Via costà con li altri cani!'.   42

(While we were running through the stagnant channel there rose up in front of me one covered with mud and said: 'Who art thou that comest before thy time?' And I said to him: 'If I come I do not stay. But thou, who art thou that art become so foul?' He answered: 'Thou seest I am one that weeps.' And I to him: 'In weeping and in misery, accursed spirit, remain; for I know thee, for all thy filth.' Then he reached out to the boat with both hands; on which the wary Master thrust him off, saying: 'Away there with the other dogs!')

A distinguished Italian critic, Momigliano, has called it one of the most finished achievements of Dante's mature dramatic style. The hand of a master is evident from the start, in the taut, rapid exchange: 'Chi se' tu ...' — 'ma tu chi se' ... '; 'vieni ...' — 'vegno ...'; 'rimango ...' — 'rimani ... '; 'piango ...' — 'piangere ... ' (33–8). It is a *tour de force* of concision and rhetorical skill. The meaning of line 36 is slightly controversial, and several modern commentators choose to give to the statement 'I am one that weeps' the force of 'I am one who expiates his sin'; Boccaccio, whose ear must have been trained to distinguish inflections in the speech of his fellow-townsmen, remarks in his commentary that this is truly the reply of one who is irascible and wrathful, and who is in the habit of answering in a grumbling and offensive tone. But we are not allowed to dwell on these sullen words for long, for almost immediately after they have been uttered comes Dante's disdainful retort, which contains the unkindest cut of all. Despite his effort to conceal his identity, the soul has been recognized (39), and as a result his degraded condition will be revealed to the living. The implied threat rouses Filippo Argenti to violent anger and to a rapid menacing gesture with both hands (40), which is foiled by Virgil with equal swiftness.

> Lo collo poi con le braccia mi cinse;
> basciommi 'l volto e disse: 'Alma sdegnosa,
> benedetta colei che 'n te s'incinse! 45
>   Quei fu al mondo persona orgogliosa;
> bontà non è che sua memoria fregi:
> così s' è l'ombra sua qui furïosa. 48
>   Quanti si tegnon or là sù gran regi
> che qui staranno come porci in brago,
> di sé lasciando orribili dispregi!'. 51

(Then he clasped me with his arms about my neck, kissed my cheek and said: 'Indignant soul, blessed is the womb that bore thee! In the world this man was full of arrogance; no good there is to adorn his memory, therefore is his shade here furious. How many above there now account themselves great kings who shall lie here like swine in the mire, leaving of themselves horrible dispraises!')

In contrast, the rhythm of the second section of the episode is slower and the tone is solemn. It offers a commentary on the scene that has passed, without any further action. Virgil pointedly approves of Dante's spiteful behaviour towards Filippo Argenti. His language is quite extraordinary, to the extent that he paraphrases a passage of the Gospels: 'Blessed is the womb that bare thee' (Luke XI: 27). The Scriptural formula applied to Dante establishes an analogy between him and Christ; and it is worth observing the contrast between the two adjectives 'sdegnosa' and 'orgogliosa', which are in a rhyming position in lines 44 and 46, and thus receive greater stress, for we will shortly see that this contrast is significant. Finally, before we move on, we must pay attention to the vocabulary, for plebeian language is introduced to good effect in order to stress the undignified condition in which the

wrathful in general and Filippo Argenti, their prototype, in particular,
find themselves: I mean words like 'porci' and 'brago' (50), soon to be
reinforced by expressions such as 'attuffare in questa broda' (53), which
are made even more striking by being placed side by side with a choice
latinism like 'regi' (49) and similar terms.

> E io: 'Maestro, molto sarei vago
> di vederlo attuffare in questa broda
> prima che noi uscissimo del lago'.   54
>   Ed elli a me: 'Avante che la proda
> ti si lasci veder, tu sarai sazio:
> di tal disïo convien che tu goda.'.   57
>   Dopo ciò poco vid' io quello strazio
> far di costui a le fangose genti,
> che Dio ancor ne lodo e ne ringrazio.   60
>   Tutti gridavano: 'A Filippo Argenti!';
> e 'l fiorentino spirito bizzarro
> in sé medesmo si volvea co' denti.   63

(And I said: 'Master, I should like well to see him plunge in this broth before
we leave the lake.' And he to me: 'Before the shore comes in sight thou shalt
have satisfaction; in such a wish thou art sure to be gratified.' Soon after I saw
such a rending of him by the muddy crowd that I still give praise and thanks
to God for it; all cried: 'At Filippo Argenti!' and the frenzied Florentine spirit
turned on himself with his teeth.)

The figure of the villain in this episode has aroused much curiosity.
Who was Filippo Argenti? There is no lack of information about him
in the early commentaries to the poem, not all of it reliable or consistent; writers of short stories, too, seized upon him as a protagonist for
some of their tales, but they are less useful as sources of information
than one might have hoped, since they often based Argenti's character
on details borrowed from Dante's episode rather than on independent
accounts. It is not even clear from them whether Argenti was his surname or a nickname he had acquired because of his habitual ostenta-
tion of luxury (he was said to have had his horse shod with silver). At
any rate, he is likely to have been a member of the rich and powerful
Adimari family, and it is certain that Dante branded the Adimari, one
and all, in *Paradiso* (XVI, 116–20) as insolent and overbearing,
'dragons' to the timid, but to men with teeth or purses, 'lambs'. They
were Dante's neighbours and are said to have been hostile to him.
Moreover, they were bitter political rivals, for they belonged to the faction of the Black Guelphs, whereas Dante was exiled in 1301 as a White
Guelph; and it seems that one of them seized Dante's possessions on this
occasion.

Dante's 'Comedy'

These facts go some of the way towards explaining Dante's hostility to this spirit, but surely they do not fully account for the venomously spiteful tone of the whole episode. As though it was not enough to present Filippo Argenti in the most humiliating situation, covered with mud, to stress his abject state repeatedly with degrading epithets, such as 'brutto' ('foul': 35) and 'lordo' ('filthy': 39), and to liken the sinner to a dog (42) and a swine (50) — even Virgil is pressed into service to abuse the wretched soul. In the end, one is struck by the disproportion between Virgil's exaggerated praise of Dante and what the latter has just done (uttered wounding words against one who, for all his sulky tone, has given him no immediate occasion for taking offence). But there was more to come: the poet expresses the perverse wish of seeing Filippo 'plunge' in the mud of the marsh (53) and Virgil promises not just satisfaction (56), but even gratification (57). Soon after, the climax of the scene and the cruel fate of the sinner bring forth a solemn expression of thanksgiving to God (60). His fellow-penitents (the 'muddy crowd': 59) turn on him, rending his limbs and shouting his name loud and clear at the same time, while in his fury the unfortunate Florentine, far from trying to evade his assailers, turns on himself with his teeth. In the *Comedy* the act of biting oneself expresses an extreme degree of frenzy, brought on either by great rage — as is the case with the Minotaur (*Inferno*, XII, 14–15) and with Minos (XXVII, 126) — or great grief, as with the damned Ugolino in Canto XXXIII, 58. Now, a strong element of personal dislike or even hatred between Dante and Filippo can be taken for granted. There are accounts of the latter having slapped the poet in the face. But, even making allowances for this rooted antipathy, one is still left with the feeling that there must be a better reason for this aspect of the episode; indeed, commentators and readers have striven over the centuries to find it and to see if the sin of anger in Filippo could have been an adequate — or less inadequate — target for such an onslaught. Of the several explanations that have been put forward, I will select three, all of which seem to me to have a good deal of weight, though they are not equally cogent.

Filippo Argenti, it has been argued, should not be seen just as a private enemy of Dante, but as a representative of that upstart class which the poet blamed for all the social and political misfortunes that had befallen Florence. Virgil's scathing remarks (49–51) on the pride and arrogance that accompany anger do lend support to the view that Dante had principally in mind those *parvenus* of rich upper-class families whom he also attacked elsewhere. A rather more laboured variant of this theory maintains that Argenti symbolizes the resistance of the Florentines against the Emperor Henry VII, whereas Dante is alleged to represent those Florentines who were true to the idea of the Roman Empire — an allegory that will culminate later in this Canto and in the next one with the arrival of the Envoy from Heaven.

The identification of Filippo with a Florentine class or faction may be well grounded, but perhaps one might attach greater significance to the second interpretation. This goes beyond historical considerations and, taking its cue from the extraordinary language of line 45 and also of line 60 (Dante's thanksgiving to God), interprets this episode as a first threat by the forces of evil, represented by Argenti, against Dante's journey willed by Providence. A second and more serious onslaught by the devils and the Furies in the latter half of this Canto and in the first section of the next one will require the intervention of grace to repel it, but this time human resources (Virgil) are enough to remove the threat. According to this interpretation, these assaults also represent a renewal of the fears and uncertainties that confronted Dante at the beginning of his journey; now, as he is about to embark on the most perilous stage, it is natural that they should recur with increased strength.

Finally, those who are struck by the different shades and degrees of anger exhibited by the three characters who hold the stage, by the violence repeatedly displayed and by the fact that the episode is specifically situated in the Circle of the Wrathful, prefer to give prominence to a distinction that had been clearly indicated by Boccaccio, and to see in it a violent clash between two kinds of anger, 'ira mala' and 'ira buona', well-directed and misdirected anger. Dante, then, the 'Alma sdegnosa' ('indignant soul') of line 44, is contrasted with the proud arrogance (46) of wrathful Filippo. The nature itself of the sin punished in this Circle would explain, according to this theory, the violence and ruthlessness that typify the episode; in addition, Dante (I mean Dante the poet, rather than Dante the character) may well have consciously or unconsciously overreacted in the presence of anger, aware as he was that he was not altogether fully armed against this sin. This is possibly hinted at the beginning of Canto XVI of *Purgatorio*.

> Quivi il lasciammo, che più non ne narro;
> ma ne l'orecchie mi percosse un duolo,
> per ch'io avante l'occhio intento sbarro. 66
>   Lo buon maestro disse: 'Omai, figliuolo,
> s'appressa la città c'ha nome Dite,
> coi gravi cittadin, col grande stuolo'. 69

41

Dante's 'Comedy'

E io: 'Maestro, già le sue meschite
là entro certe ne la valle cerno,
vermiglie come se di foco uscite   72
   fossero'. Ed ei mi disse: 'Il foco etterno
ch'entro l'affoca le dimostra rosse,
come tu vedi in questo basso inferno'.   75
   Noi pur giugnemmo dentro a l'alte fosse
che vallan quella terra sconsolata:
le mura mi parean che ferro fosse.   78
   Non sanza prima far grande aggirata,
venimmo in parte dove il nocchier forte
'Usciteci', gridò: 'qui è l'intrata'.   81

(Here we left him, so of him I have no more to tell; but on my ears smote a sound of grief, at which with eyes wide open I looked intently forward. The good Master said: 'Now, my son, the city draws near which bears the name of Dis, with its grave citizens and great garrison.' And I said: 'Master, already I make out distinctly its mosques there within the valley, red as if they had come out of the fire.' And he said to me: 'The eternal fire which burns within them makes them show red, as thou seest, in this nether Hell.' We got right into the deep moats entrenching that unhappy city, whose walls seemed to me to be of iron, and when we had first made a wide circuit we came to a place where the boatman cried loudly: 'Go out, that is the entrance.')

Line 64, abruptly dismissing Filippo Argenti as unworthy of further discourse, marks the transition from the first to the second part of the Canto. The two pilgrims are approaching a walled city that Virgil calls Dis (68), one of the classical names of the god of the underworld. They have left behind them (or, rather, above them) the five Circles of Upper Hell and the sins of incontinence and are about to enter Lower Hell (75) with its four Circles where the more serious sins of violence and fraud are expiated.

The mood and tonality of the Canto are affected to some extent by this transition. Movement and action are accentuated and the atmosphere of tension is heightened, if anything, in the second half, to become at times dismay, if not panic. Dante's journey takes on the character of an adventure: you will remember that the Dante-character was shown in physical danger only at the very beginning of the poem, and that the intermediate Cantos have been devoted to exploration and dialogue. Now once again, as in the dark wood of Canto I, the protagonist is in fear of his life. There are, however, links between the two halves of Canto VIII. Even after the two poets have left the Circle of the Wrathful, anger is still in the air. It shows itself not only in the speeches of the devils (see line 83, and the fierce resentment, 'gran disdegno', of line 88), but even, it seems, in Virgil's reaction to the devils' hostility which, as we shall see towards the end of the Canto, is described with a word — 'adirarsi' (121) — expressing anguish in its context, but having in itself more than a suggestion of wrath. The element that does most to guarantee the unity of the Canto, however, is the meaning of the story at the moral level. We can be sure that this meaning is an essential part of the narrative, because we are explicitly warned by Dante that we must take notice of it in three lines in the middle of the next Canto:

> O voi ch'avete li 'ntelletti sani,
> mirate la dottrina che s'asconde
> sotto 'l velame de li versi strani.

(Ye that are of good understanding, note the teaching that is hidden under the veil of the strange lines.)

Like the encounter with Filippo Argenti, the confrontation with the devils guarding the City of Dis can be divided into three sections of almost equal length, preceded by five terzine describing the two poets' approach to the walled town. Its towers and fortifications are called 'mosques' (70) — the churches of the enemies of Christ — a word that must have had a special ring in the ears of Dante's contemporaries, many of whom undoubtedly had heard vivid accounts of the eighth and last crusade, which had taken place during the poet's childhood in 1270. The landscape that comes into sight as Dante looks intently forward (66) is awe-inspiring indeed, glowing with the redness of the eternal fire that burns within (73–4); fire is the dominant factor, as stressed by the word 'foco' repeated twice (72–3), and closely followed by 'affoca' in the next line.

In the rest of this episode and, in fact, throughout Canto VIII Virgil as a character is more prominent than usual. His role is not just to explain, to teach, to guide and defend; here he is involved in the action as the protagonist. We notice that he has not lost his self-assurance; he describes almost objectively what lies before him. His affectionate vocative 'figliuolo' (67), however, indicates that he is drawing nearer his pupil and is ready to protect him as they are about to face what he expects will be an ordeal, while Dante's speech already betrays a feeling of disquiet; this is conveyed by word-order, syntax and rhythm, and by a very bold enjambment ('come se di foco uscite Fossero': 72–3), where the word 'fossero', stressed on the first syllable, is followed by a most unusual pause. The feeling of profound unease is heightened by alliterations ('foco' — 'fossero' — 'foco').

Lines 76–81 tell us that from the marsh the boat of Phlegyas entered the deep moats surrounding the walled city, and that it had to make a wide circuit before it reached the point where the boatman bade his two passengers land.

> Io vidi più di mille in su le porte
> da ciel piovuti, che stizzosamente
> dicean: 'Chi è costui che sanza morte   84
> va per lo regno de la morta gente?'.
> E 'l savio mio maestro fece segno
> di voler lor parlar segretamente.   87
> Allor chiusero un poco il gran disdegno
> e disser: 'Vien tu solo, e quei sen vada
> che sì ardito intrò per questo regno.   90
> Sol si ritorni per la folle strada:
> pruovi, se sa; ché tu qui rimarrai,
> che li ha' iscorta sì buia contrada'.   93
> Pensa, lettor, se io mi sconfortai
> nel suon de le parole maladette,
> ché non credetti ritornarci mai.   96

(I saw above the gates more than a thousand of those rained down from Heaven, who cried angrily: 'Who is this that without death goes through the kingdom of the dead?' And the Sage my Master made a sign that he would speak with them apart. Then they restrained a little their fierce resentment and said: 'Come thou alone, and let him go off who has dared thus to enter on this kingdom. Let him return alone on his mad way and see if he knows it, for thou shalt stay here who hast been his guide on that dark road.' Judge, reader, if I did not lose heart at the sound of the accursed words; for I did not think I should ever return here.)

The first section of the final episode begins here, with the appearance of a multitude of devils who have 'rained down from Heaven' (83), when they rebelled with Lucifer against God. Now for the first time the two poets are face to face with the devils of popular belief. In due course, Dante will see many more of them, but the first meeting presents the most formidable challenge, since they declare that they are determined to oppose his entrance — the entrance of a living person (84) — into the City of Dis, and order him to return alone 'on his mad way' (91). The adjective 'folle' here means 'foolhardy', 'presumptuous', 'doomed to disaster'; it is the same as that which the Dante-character used to describe the journey when it was first proposed to him by Virgil at the beginning of the *Comedy* in Canto II (35), and it is meant to link his present plight with his fears and hesitations in the dark wood, in the presence of seemingly insurmountable obstacles.

> 'O caro duca mio, che più di sette
> volte m'hai sicurtà renduta e tratto
> d'alto periglio che 'ncontra mi stette,   99

44

> non mi lasciar', diss' io, 'così disfatto;
> e se 'l passar più oltre ci è negato,
> ritroviam l'orme nostre insieme ratto'.   102
>   E quel segnor che lì m'avea menato,
> mi disse: 'Non temer; ché 'l nostro passo
> non ci può tòrre alcun: da tal n'è dato.   105
>   Ma qui m'attendi, e lo spirito lasso
> conforta e ciba di speranza buona,
> ch'i' non ti lascerò nel mondo basso'.   108
>   Così sen va, e quivi m'abbandona
> lo dolce padre, e io rimango in forse,
> che sì e no nel capo mi tenciona.   111

('O my dear Leader, who seven times and more hast restored my confidence and drawn me from great peril confronting me, leave me not', I said, 'so undone; and if going farther is denied us, let us quickly retrace our steps together.' And my Liege who had brought me there said to me: 'Do not fear, for none can hinder our passage, by such an One is it granted us; but wait for me here and comfort thy weary spirit and feed it with good hope, for I will not forsake thee in the nether world.' He goes away and leaves me there, the gentle Father, and I remain in doubt, ay and no contending in my head.)

In the next section Dante manifests his anguish and turns to his 'dear leader' for assistance. Virgil, 'the gentle Father' (110), tries to comfort him by assuring him that the divine will guarantees the continuation of their journey (104–5). Note the effectiveness of the sudden change to the present tense in lines 109–11, as the poet relives the terror of the moment. Virgil does not quite succeed in reassuring Dante, particularly since he has to leave him for a while in order to parley with the devils. Line 111 has become almost proverbial, and was singled out by Ugo Foscolo in his essay entitled 'Parallel between Dante and Petrarch' as a typical example of Dante's style. 'Instead of selecting, as Petrarch does, the most elegant and melodious words and phrases,' he wrote, 'Dante often creates a new language. The conflict of opposite purposes *battles in the brain* of Dante.'

> Udir non potti quello ch'a lor porse;
> ma ei non stette là con essi guari,
> che ciascun dentro a pruova si ricorse.   114
>   Chiuser le porte que' nostri avversari
> nel petto al mio segnor, che fuor rimase
> e rivolsesi a me con passi rari.   117
>   Li occhi a la terra e le ciglia avea rase
> d'ogne baldanza, e dicea ne' sospiri:
> 'Chi m'ha negate le dolenti case!'.   120
>   E a me disse: 'Tu, perch' io m'adiri,
> non sbigottir, ch'io vincerò la prova,

qual ch'a la difension dentro s'aggiri.   123
    Questa lor tracotanza non è nova;
ché già l'usaro a men segreta porta,
la qual sanza serrame ancor si trova.   126
    Sovr' essa vedestù la scritta morta:
e già di qua da lei discende l'erta,
passando per li cerchi sanza scorta,
    tal che per lui ne fia la terra aperta'.   130

(I could not hear what he put before them; but he was not long there with them
when they all ran in headlong, and these our adversaries shut the gates in the
face of my Lord, who was left outside and turned back to me with slow steps.
His eyes were on the ground and his brow shorn of all boldness and he said between his sighs: 'See who has denied me the abodes of pain!' And to me he said:
'Do not thou be dismayed for my distress, for I shall prevail in the contest, no
matter who is plotting within to hinder us. This insolence of theirs is not new,
for once they showed it at a less hidden gate, which still stands without a bolt.
Over it thou sawest the deadly writing, and already within it one descends the
steep and passes without escort through the Circles, by whom the city shall be
opened to us.')

In the last section Virgil is again the protagonist; the momentary check
he suffers when the devils shut the gates in his face (115–16) causes him
to take on a dejected appearance and to lose that quiet confidence that
comes from feeling sure of oneself: this is the force of the word
'boldness' (119). His remark in the next line (120) is uttered in sorrow
and bewilderment, rather than in doubt and uncertainty, and should
be read as an interjection, not as a question. But when he speaks to
Dante again he has recovered his confidence as well as his dignity. He
reminds him that on a previous occasion the devils' defiance was shown
at a 'less hidden gate' (125), that is, at the first and outer gate of Hell,
in order to prevent Christ from entering into Limbo: Dante had already
seen it, as recounted in Canto III; the door had been left without a bolt
(126), for Christ had forced it open. The 'deadly writing' to be read on
it (127) refers to the inscription 'in dull characters' ('di colore oscuro':
Inferno, III, 10) announcing the 'second death' (*Inferno*, I, 117) of all
who enter. And now, surprisingly, the last three lines bring in a note
of optimism; such is the variety and alternation of moods in this stormy
Canto. A ray of sunshine breaks through the clouds for an instant, with
the promise of a happy ending; an Envoy of God is already on his way
to open the gate for them, as indeed he will do in the next Canto,
although this will not happen before a renewal of terrors and uncertainty. Dante never precisely identifies the Messenger of Heaven, either
here or in Canto IX, where he is seen passing on foot over the Styx dry-

shod, and effortlessly opening the gate of the City of Dis with a little wand. I think it is safe to interpret this Envoy of God as an angel; this interpretation suggests itself almost naturally on reading the text, and it is that of the majority of the early commentators, including Boccaccio, who appropriately linked Dante's description in Canto IX ('one sent from Heaven', 'da ciel messo') with the etymological meaning of the word 'angel' (from the Greek *angelos*, 'messenger', 'envoy').

The change of harmony and key between the sombre tone of the bulk of this Canto and this finale is artistically satisfying, and keeps the reader's curiosity continuously alive. Artistic motives certainly played a part in suggesting to Dante the tense atmosphere of the Circle of the Wrathful and this climax of the disputed entrance into the City of Dis, to all of which the sudden calm in the next Canto, following the arrival of the heavenly creature, will stand in sharp contrast; that calm itself being foreshadowed in the last three lines of Canto VIII. In the *Comedy* artistic and moral, religious and political themes are constantly intertwined; some being more stressed or more important than others; but each playing its part. Likewise, several layers of meaning — literal, allegorical and moral — are frequently, if not always, intermingled. To recapitulate, the general theme of the Canto is the portrayal of that stage of the journey of Dante's soul in its progress towards moral enlightenment and liberation from evil and sin, where it is confronted by the most serious of the sins of incontinence and is about to face the even more serious sins of violence and fraud. In this light the devils' opposition takes on a greater significance and becomes logically connected with the earlier part of the narrative.

One of the fourteenth-century commentators of the *Comedy*, Benvenuto da Imola, wrote: 'This Canto which looks easy and ordinary as to its subject-matter (*facile et de materia communi*) is very difficult and beautiful, and its author introduces into it original and ingenious inventions (*auctor facit novas et artificiosas fictiones*).' Even after almost 600 years it would be hard to improve on this summary.

Inferno XVII

The journey of the two poets through the sixth Circle (the Heretics) is related in Cantos IX and X, and through the seventh Circle (the Violent) in Cantos XII–XVII. The latter are punished in three separate Rings: the Violent against others (murderers, plunderers, tyrants); the Violent against themselves (suicides, squanderers); and the Violent against God (blasphemers), nature (sodomites) and art, or handiwork (usurers). Having left the Ring of the sinners against nature (Cantos XV–XVI) behind them, Dante and Virgil are now approaching the precipice that separates the Circle of the Violent from those of the Fraudulent.

All readers of Canto XVII will, I am sure, feel its especial fascination. It is provided by the monster Geryon, who occupies the first part of the Canto (1–32) as well as the last (79–136), Dante's encounter with the usurers being deftly sandwiched in between to add variety to the narrative. Everything about Geryon is a constant source of wonder and delight — particularly the detailed description of his movements and of their effect on Dante.

The approach of the monster is described in the last seven lines of Canto XVI. Its visual impact on Dante is rendered with one of those marvellous, uncannily effective comparisons that came so naturally to the poet by now, his art having reached its full maturity. Geryon is represented as rising up through the abyss separating the Violent in the seventh Circle of Hell, from the Faudulent in the Circles below; and the as-yet-unidentified something is said to look like a diver who, having gone down to free an anchor, returns to the surface, thrusting his arms above him and drawing up his feet. In other words, he seems to be swimming, but swimming up through the gross and murky air. In this way the simile serves to establish from the outset the parallelism between the movements of a swimmer (the only ones that Dante could personally have observed) and the imagined experience of flying:

> i' vidi per quell'aere grosso e scuro
> venir notando una figura in suso,
> maravigliosa ad ogne cor sicuro,
> sì come torna colui che va giuso
> talora a solver l'àncora ch'aggrappa
> o scoglio o altro che nel mare è chiuso,
> che 'n sù si stende e da piè si rattrappa.

Inferno XVII

(I saw swimming up through that gross and murky air a figure amazing to the
stoutest heart, even as he returns who goes down perchance to loose the anchor
that is caught on a reef or something else hid in the sea, stretching upward and
drawing in his feet.)

Two general points about the Canto should be noted. The position of
each Canto is usually significant within the meticulously thought-out
architecture of the poem. This one is placed exactly at the end of the first
half of the Inferno; indeed it marks a full-stop. It rounds off the description of those whose sin is violence, and leaves the whole of the second
part of the *Inferno* for the Fraudulent and the Traitors. The Fraudulent
(Cantos XVII–XXX) practise fraud on those who do not confide in them
and thus destroy the natural bond of love that should unite all men, as
explained in Canto XI, 52–66. The Traitors (Cantos XXXII–XXXIV) are
those whose guilt consists of a betrayal of trust.

The other point I should like to mention is that Canto XVII abounds in
similes. There are more of them than in any other Canto of the *Comedy*
— fifteen altogether. This constant and exceptionally frequent use of
comparisons serves to make Geryon and the circumstances of his extraordinary appearance more credible, and to infuse life and realism into
allegory.

> 'Ecco la fiera con la coda aguzza,
> che passa i monti e rompe i muri e l'armi!
> Ecco colei che tutto 'l mondo appuzza!'.   3
>   Sì cominciò lo mio duca a parlarmi;
> e accennolle che venisse a proda,
> vicino al fin d'i passeggiati marmi.   6
>   E quella sozza imagine di froda
> sen venne, e arrivò la testa e 'l busto,
> ma 'n su la riva non trasse la coda.   9

('Behold, the beast with the pointed tail, that passes mountains and breaks
through walls and arms! Behold, he that infects all the world!' Thus my Leader
began to speak to me, and he beckoned him to come ashore near the end of the
rocky path; and that foul image of fraud came on and landed his head and chest,
but did not draw his tail onto the bank.)

What sources did Dante draw upon for his conception of Geryon? The
pedigree of this creature is far from straightforward or, rather, its nature is composite. Commentators have pointed out that the name of the
mythological king who was killed by Hercules — Geryon — was mentioned by Virgil, Ovid and Horace; and they have also listed the many
suggestions from Biblical sources and medieval legends that may have
had some influence on Dante; they have even recalled the fantastic

49

stone monsters with which contemporary sculptors used to adorn cathedrals and churches. But in all these models, whether literary or in the figurative arts, Geryon himself had remained a nebulous figure. Dante, on the contrary, described him with his usual clarity and allowed his powerful imagination to recreate freely a being capable of holding our attention on the literal level of the narrative, while at the same time concentrating our minds on the image and concept of fraud. And it is precisely in this combination of realism and symbolism that Dante stands apart from all his alleged models.

> La faccia sua era faccia d'uom giusto,
> tanto benigna avea di fuor la pelle,
> e d'un serpente tutto l'altro fusto;　　　　　　　　　　12
> 　　due branche avea pilose insin l'ascelle;
> lo dosso e 'l petto e ambedue le coste
> dipinti avea di nodi e di rotelle.　　　　　　　　　　15
> 　　Con più color, sommesse e sovraposte
> non fer mai drappi Tartari né Turchi,
> né fuor tai tele per Aragne imposte.　　　　　　　　18
> 　　Come talvolta stanno a riva i burchi,
> che parte sono in acqua e parte in terra,
> e come là tra li Tedeschi lurchi　　　　　　　　　　21
> 　　lo bivero s'assetta a far sua guerra,
> così la fiera pessima si stava
> su l'orlo ch'è di pietra e 'l sabbion serra.　　　　　　24
> 　　Nel vano tutta sua coda guizzava,
> torcendo in sù la venenosa forca
> ch'a guisa di scorpion la punta armava.　　　　　　27

(His face was the face of a just man, so gracious was its outward aspect, and all the rest was a serpent's trunk; he had two paws, hairy to the armpits, and the back and breast and both the flanks were painted with knots and circlets — Tartars or Turks never made stuffs with more colours in ground and embroidery, nor were such webs laid by Arachne on the loom. As boats sometimes lie at the shore, part in the water and part on land, and as there among the German gluttons the beaver settles itself to wage its war, so the vile brute lay on the rim that bounds the great sand with stone. All his tail was quivering in the void, twisting upwards the poisonous fork that armed the point like a scorpion's.)

A constant and distinctive feature in the myth of Geryon is that the monster had three heads and three bodies. Dante gives him a single body blending together three different natures; thus, we learn that he has a human face (10–11) — the face of a just man, suggesting the deceptive appearance of fraud; while all the rest is a serpent's trunk, with a poisoned forked tail (25–7) representing the deadly reality of fraud. To complete the triple nature of the monster his forelegs are hairy, like those of a lion (13). It has been suggested that if duplicity is the equivalent of fraud, triplicity is almost its superlative; this may be stretching the point a bit too far, but there is little doubt that all sorts of variations on number three could be detected in connection with Geryon, whether deliberate or accidental there is no way to tell. I will mention just one: the creature is at the same time a vehicle, a beast, and a demon.

One thing about him is, however, unquestionably deliberate: the air of mystery and ambiguity surrounding him. This incarnation of fraud gives nothing away about himself; in fact, he never utters a word throughout the whole episode; moreover, we are told nothing about his habitual function in Hell or about his precise place of abode. The ambiguity that attaches to all his attributes and actions is intended to mark duplicity; the seemingly dignified face of a good man is tantamount to a mask and reminds us that seeming is not the same as being and, perhaps more banally, that one who is about to commit fraud usually contrives to take on the appearance of honesty. The main emphasis, however, is not so much on the face as on the tail of the monster throughout the Canto. It is mentioned in the first line and is referred to five times altogether. Fraud's sting is appropriately in the tail and Geryon tries to keep it hidden (9); nevertheless we shall see presently that Dante, not unnaturally, has a wholesome dread of it.

The description is heavily allegorical, as we have already discovered. The meaning of the 'image' is declared almost immediately in line 7 and there is something almost heavy-handed in lines 10 and 11. Dante nevertheless presents the monster in a dramatic and highly effective way. The Canto opens with an unattributed 'Ecco', whereupon there is talk of an invincible weapon of war — a kind of laser-beam that passes through every obstacle, natural or artificial — and the first terzina ends with a verb as violent and offensive in sound as it is in meaning. Then the words are attributed to Virgil (4), and we are shown his gesture, that of beckoning the monster to approach ('che venisse': 5). And approach he does ('sen venne': 8), dramatically pushing forward his head and trunk ('e arrivò la testa e 'l busto'). Description then begins, but the account of the snake-like markings — the knots and encircling devices of fraud — leads us via simile to the exotic carpets of the East and the mythology of the Greek past (16–18). The description of appearance yields again to what Dante does best — the evocation of movement. The beaver's posture when it settles itself to attract its prey

(i.e., to lure fishes: 22) was at that time supposed to be with its tail in
the water.

> Lo duca disse: 'Or convien che si torca
> la nostra via un poco insino a quella
> bestia malvagia che colà si corca'.   30
> Però scendemmo a la destra mammella,
> e diece passi femmo in su lo stremo,
> per ben cessar la rena e la fiammella.   33
> E quando noi a lei venuti semo,
> poco più oltre veggio in su la rena
> gente seder propinqua al loco scemo.   36
> Quivi 'l maestro 'Acciò che tutta piena
> esperïenza d'esto giron porti',
> mi disse, 'va, e vedi la lor mena.   39
> Li tuoi ragionamenti sian là corti;
> mentre che torni, parlerò con questa,
> che ne conceda i suoi omeri forti'.   42
> Così ancor su per la strema testa
> di quel settimo cerchio tutto solo
> andai, dove sedea la gente mesta.   45

(My leader said: 'Now we must bend our way a little, as far as that malignant
beast that couches there.' We descended, therefore, on our right and went ten
paces along the edge, so as to keep well away from the sand and the flames;
and when we had reached him I saw upon the sand a little further onwards people sitting near the empty space. Here the Master said to me: 'So that you may
carry away full experience of this ring, go and see their condition. Let your talk
there be brief. Till you return I will speak with this creature that he may lend
us his strong shoulders.' So I went by myself still farther along the extreme edge
of that seventh Circle to where the woeful people were seated.)

There follows a transitional passage (28–45): Dante and his guide have
to walk on the edge of the third Ring of the seventh Circle in order to
avoid the fire raining down on the Violent against nature (sodomites)
and against art, as detailed in the previous two Cantos. The route taken
by Virgil and his charge is mapped here, as everywhere else, with
painstaking precision — with so much plausible detail, in fact, that one
forgets that the story is fictional and is almost tempted to take the
journey as fact, as some of Dante's less sophisticated early readers seem
to have done; note, for instance, the 'ten paces' of line 32. Details such
as this were to spur many, including Galileo 300 years after the poem
was written, to attempt to gauge with mathematical and architectural
detail the size and shape of Hell. The same purpose of imparting
verisimilitude to the narrative is served by Virgil's advice and exhor-
tations. Dante goes 'tutto solo' (44) to his brief encounter with the
usurers. It is worth dwelling for a moment on these two simple words,

unremarkable in themselves, yet, placed where they are and related as they are to Dante's fictional situation at that time, they convey the poet's feeling of forlornness and even dismay at being on his own, without Virgil's protection in the deeper part of Hell. Virgil has thought fit to go alone in order to approach Geryon.

Before we look at Dante's encounter with the usurers in detail, we must briefly dwell on the meaning of usury in this context. Modern dictionaries define the term as the practice of lending money at exorbitant interest. This was not quite so in Dante's time; it meant then just producing money from money. A digression on medieval morality as applied to economics is indispensable at this point, since it would be wrong to assume that all the usurers met by Dante were pawnbrokers or Scrooge-like characters; and, on the other hand, it may not be easy for us to grasp why what we might call nowadays 'investing' or simply lending at a reasonable rate of interest should have been regarded as a detestable sin. The indispensable clues are in Canto XI. As Virgil has explained (XI, 94–111), usury understood in the way I have just mentioned is a sin against art ('art' meaning human industry, any work or craft of man); for it is laid down in Genesis (2: 15; 3: 17 and 19): 'In the sweat of thy face shalt thou eat bread', that is to say, by means of labour and skill applied to appropriate material — the material supplied, in the first place, by the natural world, which is man's proper habitat. The usurer, on the contrary, as stated in Canto XI (109), 'takes another way' and 'puts his hope elsewhere', that is, in the profit he makes from lending money — a sterile occupation, for money itself is a barren thing. Furthermore, usury is a sin against nature, for 'art imitates nature'; another authority invoked by Virgil in Canto XI (101–5), Aristotle, had stated this in his *Physics* (II, 2). And nature is the child of God. It follows that art, being the child of nature, is the grandchild of God, and that (I am quoting Canto XI (95–6) once more) the usurer, who sins against art and therefore against nature, 'offends divine goodness'. One of the earliest commentators of the *Comedy*, Jacopo della Lana, writing between 1324 and 1328, spelt it out when he remarked that if money was invested in cattle or land or vineyards it would be natural for it to bear fruit, for it happens to be the will of God; but for money to produce more money is unnatural and a sin against God. This is why usurers are relegated to a deeper place in Hell than any other of those guilty of violence; even deeper than the rest of the sinners against God and nature, such as blasphemers and sodomites.

Per li occhi fora scoppiava lor duolo;

di qua, di là soccorrien con le mani
quando a' vapori, e quando al caldo suolo: 48
   non altrimenti fan di state i cani
or col ceffo or col piè, quando son morsi
o da pulci o da mosche o da tafani.   51
   Poi che nel viso a certi li occhi porsi,
ne' quali 'l doloroso foco casca,
non ne conobbi alcun; ma io m'accorsi   54
   che dal collo a ciascun pendea una tasca
ch'avea certo colore e certo segno,
e quindi par che 'l loro occhio si pasca.   57
   E com' io riguardando tra lor vegno,
in una borsa gialla vidi azzurro
che d'un leone avea faccia e contegno.   60
   Poi, procedendo di mio sguardo il curro,
vidine un'altra come sangue rossa,
mostrando un'oca bianca più che burro.   63

(Through the eyes their pain was bursting forth; now here, now there they
defended themselves with their hands, sometimes from the flames, sometimes
from the burning soil, like dogs in summer that ply now muzzle, now paw,
when they are bitten by fleas or gnats or gad-flies. When I set my eyes on the
faces of some on whom the grievous fire was falling, I did not recognise any
of them; but I observed that from the neck of each hung a pouch of a certain
colour and device, and on these they seemed to feast their eyes. And when I
came among them, looking about, I saw, azure on a yellow purse, the face and
bearing of a lion; then, as my gaze went further, I saw another, blood-red,
which showed a goose whiter than butter.)

The punishment meted out to these wretched souls is minutely described in lines 46–8, and the description is made more vivid by a simile
(49–51) drawn from animal life and notable for its deliberate use of
coarse language and for its mention of lowly objects. Indeed, the lower-
ing of stylistic register in the terzina did not pass unobserved in the
seventeenth century, when critics took Dante to task for his undignified
poetic language: Paolo Beni remarked that dogs, snouts, paws, fleas,
gnats, gad flies are 'vili e laide cose' ('plebeian and unclean things').
Dante, no doubt, realized this as clearly as Beni, and made sure in this
way that the whole brief episode of the usurers should reflect his profound disdain for these sinners. Animals are prominent throughout,
from the simile we dwelt on a moment ago to the picture gallery of coats
of arms (58–72), where animals are conspicuously present, and, finally,
to lines 74–5, where one of the usurers contorting his mouth into a
vulgar grimace is compared to an ox licking its nose. It is worth noting
that these coats of arms are not engraved on a shield in a heraldic man-

ner, but on a money-bag (55–7), resembling the purse usurers used to wear when sitting at their counters. Notice too that the usurers' gaze is turned towards the object of their obsession — money. Their eyes feed on it.

Dante, the character in the *Comedy*, affects to scorn identifying any of them (he actually says that he recognized none: 54), but then he offers plenty of clues; the coats of arms of their families engraved on their pouches in colourful detail clearly give them away. The early commentators have, indeed, named each one of them and it is very likely that they were right in every case. But there is little to be gained by knowing who they were. The virtual obscurity in which they are left by Dante is in itself an added condemnation. It is enough to say that, apart from a couple of Paduans, they were citizens of Florence (70). The fact of Florentine usurers being singled out amounts to a further indictment of the corruption allegedly brought about in Dante's native city by the economic expansion that had taken place there in the second half of the thirteenth century — an industrial and financial 'explosion' that had made Florence the main centre of manufacturing and banking in the Western world. Dante deplored this as a pollution of that pristine purity — largely mythical, of course — to which he passionately wanted Florence to return. His lack of sympathy with this new-fangled prosperity stemmed partly from a scholar's contempt for mercantile pursuits and partly from an attitude of mind which made him discontented with his own age and which must have been exacerbated by his vicissitudes following his banishment from his native city. In fact, the theme of the corruption of Florence emerges in earnest as early as Canto VI of *Inferno* with Ciacco's prophecy, and comes to the fore once again in Canto XV (67–9; 73–8), as well as in Canto XVI (73–5) where, as I have already mentioned while discussing Canto VI, Dante identifies the main evils of this city as 'the new people and the sudden gains': the 'new people' being, of course, the labourers who had flocked into Florence from the surrounding countryside to satisfy the hunger for manpower of the swiftly-growing industries and who, as Dante thought, had brought in the seeds of corruption and changed the character of the original population. This theme becomes a *leit-motiv* throughout the *Comedy*, reaching its peak in the central Cantos of *Paradiso*.

It should be noted that the usurers and bankers singled out by Dante (for some of them, at least, would nowadays be described as bankers) were all noblemen. Was there a 'class' (or 'anti-class') bias in his holding up members of the aristocracy to scorn? There may well have been.

Dante's 'Comedy'

However it is fair to say that the upper classes of Florence had indeed been increasingly taking advantage of favourable economic conditions and the greater need for credit resulting from the industrial boom; they had engaged in the pursuit of gain and had made a display of luxury; they had also allowed strangers and *parvenus* to infiltrate their ranks. It is debatable whether all this had led to a collapse in their moral standards, but Dante strongly believed it had. What is more, he himself, the scion of a noble family, believed that their conduct ran counter to the chivalrous ideals of courtesy and valour held out in Canto XVI (67) as well as in the *Convivio* (II, x, 8 and elsewhere) as an essential attribute of nobility. Wealth cannot impart 'gentilezza' ('nobility'), as stated in the fourth book of the *Convivio*, since it is base by nature. Its pursuit is an obstacle to spiritual life, and in any case is unworthy of a nobleman, for nobility, as Dante remarks in the *Convivio* (IV, xiii, 14), demands liberality. Seen in this light, the encounter with the usurers has an even greater impact on the reader.

> E un che d'una scrofa azzurra e grossa
> segnato avea lo suo sacchetto bianco,
> mi disse: 'Che fai tu in questa fossa?   66
> Or te ne va; e perché se' vivo anco,
> sappi che 'l mio vicin Vitalïano
> sederà qui dal mio sinistro fianco.   69
> Con questi Fiorentin son padoano:
> spesse fïate mi 'ntronan li orecchi
> gridando: "Vegna 'l cavalier sovrano,   72
> che recherà la tasca con tre becchi!" '.
> Qui distorse la bocca e di fuor trasse
> la lingua, come bue che 'l naso lecchi.   75

(And one that had a sow azure and gravid stamped on his white wallet said to me: 'What are you doing in this pit? Take yourself off and, since you are still alive, know that my townsman Vitaliano will sit here on my left side. Among these Florentines I am a Paduan; many a time they din in my ears, shouting: "Let the sovereign knight come, who will bring the pouch with the three goats!" ' Then he twisted his mouth and thrust out his tongue, like an ox that licks its nose.)

The episode ends with one of the sinners breaking the silence that has been its feature so far. Almost certainly he is to be identified as Reginaldo Scrovegni, the father of Arrico who built the famous chapel bearing the name of the Scrovegni in Padua and frescoed by Giotto. His vindictive, malevolent, brief harangue (66–73) fulfils several functions. In his opening words he is characteristically rude to Dante; he anticipates the future eternal damnation of another Paduan who was still alive in 1300 (68–9); he castigates Florence and Padua jointly as two cities where usury is rampant (70); and he solemnly announces the arrival, in due course, of a Florentine still living in 1300, easily recognizable to his contemporaries as Giovanni Buiamonte dei Becchi, sarcastically laying stress on the title of knight bestowed on him (72). His outburst ends with the vulgar grimace on which I have already dwelt (74–5).

> E io, temendo no 'l più star crucciasse
> lui che di poco star m'avea 'mmonito,
> torna'mi in dietro da l'anime lasse.   78
>   Trova' il duca mio ch'era salito
> già su la groppa del fiero animale,
> e disse a me: 'Or sie forte e ardito.   81
>   Omai si scende per sì fatte scale;
> monta dinanzi, ch'i' voglio esser mezzo,
> sì che la coda non possa far male'.   84
>   Qual è colui che sì presso ha 'l riprezzo
> de la quartana, c'ha già l'unghie smorte,
> e triema tutto pur guardando 'l rezzo,   87
>   tal divenn' io a le parole porte;
> ma vergogna mi fé le sue minacce,
> che innanzi a buon segnor fa servo forte.   90
>   I' m'assettai in su quelle spallacce;
> sì volli dir, ma la voce non venne
> com' io credetti: 'Fa che tu m'abbracce'.   93
>   Ma esso, ch'altra volta mi sovvenne
> ad altro forse, tosto ch'i' montai
> con le braccia m'avvinse e mi sostenne;   96
>   e disse: 'Gerïon, moviti omai:
> le rote larghe, e lo scender sia poco;
> pensa la nova soma che tu hai'.   99

(And I, fearing lest a longer stay should anger him who had warned me to stay but little, turned back from the weary souls. I found my leader already mounted on the croup of the savage brute, and he said to me: 'Now be strong and bold. The descent henceforth is by such stairs as this. Mount in front, for I wish to be between so that the tail may not harm you.' As one who has the shivering-fit of the ague so near that his nails are already pale and he trembles all over at the mere sight of shade, such I became at these words of his: but shame threatened me, which makes a servant brave before his good master, and I settled myself on those ugly shoulders. I wanted to say, but the voice did not come as I thought, 'See that you embrace me!' But he who succoured me another time in another ordeal clasped me in his arms as soon as I mounted and supported me, then said: 'Geryon, move on now; let the circles be wide and the descent slow; remember the new burden you have.')

The passage that follows (76–99) prepares the atmosphere for the description of Geryon's flight — perhaps the most astonishing *tour de force* ever attempted by Dante's imagination. What makes it all the more impressive is the fusion of symbolic and literal meaning, so well managed that allegory never becomes an encumbrance and does not impair the realism of the narrative. Virgil's exhortation as soon as Dante has left the usurers and approached the monster Geryon once again (81) is a signal to the reader that an extraordinary event is about to be enacted; and the almost flippant reference to the 'descent henceforth' being 'by such stairs as this' (82) indicates that the journey into the depths of Hell (that is, the acquisition of knowledge of the utmost human depravity) can no longer be achieved by the pilgrim and his guide with their strength alone. The two poets will indeed resort to the assistance of similar infernal monsters from now on every time they have to go further down in the course of their journey. Here, in order to reach the eighth Circle, reason represented by Virgil must summon the very spirit of fraud from the abyss and master it in order to enable Dante to see it clearly in all its reptile deformity, that is, to know fraud in all its ugliness. Between the Circle of the Violent, where we now are, and the Circle of the Fraudulent there lies quite literally an abyss, a precipice of unimaginable depth, as Dante has explained in Canto XVI (94–105) by means of elaborate comparisons with waterfalls in the Appennines. This is symbolic of the vast moral abyss separating mere violence from fraud, for the latter is an underhand sin; it strikes at the bonds of trust that are meant to draw mankind into a unity, while violence is committed, so to speak, in the open. In the next two lines (83–4) the protection afforded to Dante by Virgil interposing himself between him and Geryon's tail might symbolize — for those who find such details illuminating — that reason is a defence against the worst sting of sinful behaviour. But all these allegorical subtleties are perhaps of less importance than the remarkable observation of the approaching malarial fit (the 'quartan fever': 85–7), the psychological insight of how shame can help us to overcome fear (89–90), the expressive suffix of 'spallacce' (91), and the tenderness and intimacy of Dante's unexpressed wish that Virgil should 'hold him tight' (93). I ought to remark in passing that the word 'forse' in line 95 is not to be taken in its usual meaning of 'perhaps' in this instance, but as a noun signifying peril or ordeal.

> Come la navicella esce di loco
> in dietro in dietro, sì quindi si tolse;
> e poi ch'al tutto si sentì a gioco,   102
>   là 'v' era 'l petto, la coda rivolse,

e quella tesa, come anguilla, mosse,
e con le branche l'aere a sé raccolse.   105
   Maggior paura non credo che fosse
quando Fetonte abbandonò li freni,
per che 'l ciel, come pare ancor, si cosse;   108
   né quando Icaro misero le reni
sentì spennar per la scaldata cera,
gridando il padre a lui 'Mala via tieni!',   111
   che fu la mia, quando vidi ch'i' era
ne l'aere d'ogne parte, e vidi spenta
ogne veduta fuor che de la fera.   114

(As the bark backs out from its berth little by little, so [Geryon] withdrew thence and, when he felt himself quite clear, turned his tail where his breast had been and, stretching it out, moved it like an eel and gathered the air to himself with his paws. I do not think there was greater fear when Phaethon let go the reins and the sky was scorched as it still appears, nor when wretched Icarus felt his loins unfeathering by the melting wax and his father cried to him: 'You're taking the wrong way', than was mine when I saw that I was in the air on every side and saw everything lost to sight except the beast.)

Virgil has ordered Geryon (97–9) to descend slowly. He complies. As he begins his flight (100–2) the smoothness of his movements resembles those of a bark backing out little by little from its berth. Dante draws here a comparison with a manoeuvre that he must have seen many times, and conveys its gradual nature by means of a reduplication ('in dietro in dietro': 101), echoed by another one at the end of Geryon's flight ('al pié al pié': 134) and, for good measure, a third one ('lenta lenta': 115), almost exactly half-way between the other two. Line 104 ('E quella tesa, come anguilla, mosse') is swift, in striking contrast with the four preceding ones, as well as with the passage that follows. It is the first hint that the creature is capable of rapid movement. The very word 'anguilla' is suggestive of slipperiness and apt to convey Geryon's self-propelling motion when he stretches out his previously coiled tail. At a deeper level, it adds a touch of abhorrence, of reptilian sliminess to the description, indicating the insidiousness of deceit and treachery. In the next two terzine (106–11) the two similes recalling the fate of two famous mythological fliers, Icarus and Phaethon, are not predictable clichés, the obvious quotations that come to mind in the context of the beginning of a flight, as some commentators have suggested. They remind us of journeys made in defiance of man's limitations and punished by the gods, and point forward to the 'folle volo' of Ulysses (XXVI, 125) — all three flights being in deliberate counterpart to Dante's 'fatale andare' (*Inferno*, V, 22). The two similes have also the purpose of prepar-

Dante's 'Comedy'

ing us for the transition of Geryon from a bark ('navicella': 100) to what
has been described as a 'macchina volante', a creature without wings
that can miraculously move through the air like a swimmer through
water.

> Ella sen va notando lenta lenta;
> rota e discende, ma non me n'accorgo
> se non che al viso e di sotto mi venta.   117
> Io sentia già da la man destra il gorgo
> far sotto noi un orribile scroscio,
> per che con li occhi 'n giù la testa sporgo.   120
> Allor fu' io più timido a lo stoscio,
> però ch'i' vidi fuochi e senti' pianti;
> ond' io tremando tutto mi raccoscio.   123
> E vidi poi, ché nol vedea davanti,
> lo scendere e 'l girar per li gran mali
> che s'appressavan da diversi canti.   126

(He goes swimming slowly on, wheeling and descending, but I am not conscious
of it except for the wind blowing in my face and from below. I heard now on
our right the torrent making a hideous roar below us, at which I stretched forth
my head and looked down; then I became more afraid at the descent, for I saw
fires and heard wailings, so that, trembling, I cling the closer. And I saw then
— for I had not seen it before — our descent and circling by the great torments
that were drawing near on every side.)

Then comes the *pièce de résistance*, the detailed, realistic description
of this extraordinary event. What would it feel like flying on the back
of a monster into the depth of the abyss of Hell? Dante's answer is a feat
of penetrating psychological insight. For us flying has become commonplace, so that we are all the better able to appreciate the poetic and
imaginative quality of an account that reads so true in every detail. At
first the slow, circular descent made 'audible' by the successive trochees
of 'notando lenta lenta' (115) cannot be perceived by the poet, except
by the wind blowing in his face and from below (117) — an utterly
realistic touch. He is far too afraid to lean out and look. This theme has
already been introduced (85–7) to express his shudder at the prospect
of physical contact with the huge snake's skin (the image of fraud); now
in lines 106–12 as well as in lines 121–3 it is stressed again, this time to
put the novelty and perilousness of his experience of flying in its proper perspective — flying when carried by such a vehicle and amidst
those awe-inspiring surroundings. In spite of these feelings, Dante,
'with everything lost to sight except the beast' (114), is intent on listen-
ing (118–19); the air is filled with the alarming roar of the waterfall

formed by the river Phlegethon tumbling down from the seventh to the eighth Circle; and a little later he can make out the wailings of the next category of damned souls. But above all he keeps his eyes wide open, notwithstanding the darkness surrounding him; little by little, peering through the gloom, he can make out the fires of the next Circle, Malebolge, the place of punishment of the Fraudulent (122), as Geryon's circling downwards very gradually brings it nearer. Note the repetitions 'vidi' . . . 'vidi' twice (112–13 and 122–4), reinforced by 'veduta' (114), 'occhi' (120), 'vedea' (124). The passage from the sense of touch to that of hearing and then the sense of sight is absolutely typical of the almost clinical accuracy Dante uses to obtain his effects of suspense and realism.

> Come 'l falcon ch'è stato assai su l'ali,
> che sanza veder logoro o uccello
> fa dire al falconiere 'Omè, tu cali!',   129
>   discende lasso onde si move isnello,
> per cento rote, e da lunge si pone
> dal suo maestro, disdegnoso e fello;   132
>   così ne puose al fondo Gerïone
> al piè al piè de la stagliata rocca,
> e, discarcate le nostre persone,
>   si dileguò come da corda cocca.   136

(As the falcon that has been long on the wing, and without sight of lure or bird makes the falconer cry: 'Ah, you're coming down!', descends weary, with a hundred wheelings, to where it sets out swiftly, and alights, angry and sullen, at a distance from its master, so Geryon set us down at the bottom, close to the foot of the jagged rock, and, disburdened of our persons, vanished like an arrow from the string.)

The closing lines of the Canto (127–36) are worth dwelling upon. The comparison of Geryon's flight with that of a falcon may seem at first a little inappropriate. We can imagine Geryon as a massive monster, a very different creature from a swift bird of prey, if he can accommodate Dante and Virgil with ease on his 'ugly shoulders' (91). Yet, further consideration of the simile shows its appositeness. It adds another touch of realism to Geryon's flight. It is worth remembering that Dante and his contemporary readers must have been well acquainted with the way a falcon flies, and that this provided a familiar point of reference for the description of the monster descending in rotating circles, like those of a falcon as it returns to earth. Further, the simile indirectly throws light on his behaviour. Up till now he has obeyed Virgil's commands with surprising docility. It is true that he has been described in

derogatory terms throughout the Canto, as a 'foul' being in the opening lines, a 'vile brute' (23), a 'malignant beast' (30) and a 'savage' one
for good measure (80), yet he has in fact shown remarkable sub-
missiveness. He has been a passive instrument of Virgil's will, comply-
ing with every order or request from him. Clearly this is because he cannot do otherwise; there can be no question of his rebelling against the
decrees of Providence, and Dante's journey, which he is assisting, is
part of these decrees. But there is more than a hint in lines 131 and 132
— the final ones of the comparison with a falcon — that he has submit-
ted to his task unwillingly, under duress, and that he too, like the
falcon, is angry and sullen; so much so that, once relieved of his burden,
he vanishes in a flash. Now, this last prodigy of the bulky and hither-
to slow monster hurtling away with unexpected swiftness comes in the
final line of the Canto. Its breathtaking speed is enhanced by contrast
with the previous one; the sound of 'discarcate' is ponderous and drawn
out, and so is that of 'persone', on account of the position of the vowels
and stresses. Heaviness and cumbersomeness and toil are suggested.
Line 135 is like the stretching of a bow before its sudden release while
in line 136 the arrow is actually released. Dante needs no more than four
words for his simile. But what well-chosen words! Rhythm and sound
blend together in these two final lines to produce the desired effect.
After the slow line 135, three words of two syllables, all of them beginning with a hard 'c', follow each other in quick succession to suggest
the speed of the departing arrow and, by implication, the extra-
ordinarily sudden disappearance of Geryon. And the final touch is the
isolation of 'cocca', with its almost bizarre sound, at the end of the line
and the Canto. The three words are heralded by 'dileguò', with its
strong stress on the vowel; and this is where the string of the bow is
released or, leaving the metaphor on one side, where the tension of the
previous line breaks.

A metaphor to describe an allegory: difficult material for the creation of great poetry, one would have thought. Yet, Dante — miracle
of miracles — manages to infuse so much life into it as to make it
memorable.

Purgatorio I

Canto XXVI of *Inferno* (133–5) offers just a glimpse of the Mountain of Purgatory, which Ulysses, in his heroic quest, could not attain, because his thirst for knowledge — human knowledge — was unassisted by Grace. *Purgatorio* is the story of Dante (or of every man who seeks God and, in the full awareness of his sins, willingly undergoes penance) succeeding where Ulysses failed. The contrast is striking, and the memory of the hero who set out and did not return must have accompanied the poet throughout his ideal journey, if even in *Paradiso* (XXVII, 82–3) the mere mention of the columns of Hercules brings forth a reference to 'il varco folle' ('the reckless enterprise') of Ulysses. And in the very Canto to be considered here, in which Dante and Virgil emerge on the island denied to the fearless Ithacan, that memory seems to haunt him; lines 130–2 have the unmistakable ring of an echo of the stirring episode of *Inferno*, XXVI, with their mention of the waters that surround the desert shore never having been sailed by man 'who after had experience of return'; the very word 'esperto' (132) recalls 'a divenir del mondo esperto' ('to gain experience of the world': *Inferno*, XXVI, 98) and in the next line 'com'altrui piacque' is a repetition of an identical formula that occurs at the climax of the Ulysses episode (141).

In the second Cantica of the *Comedy*, *Purgatorio*, then, Dante's story brings us to the very shores of that island that has been barely mentioned in the previous episode, surrounded by the vast expanse of the ocean that covers the southern hemisphere, and situated at the antipodes of Jerusalem. The last Canto of *Inferno* tells how the two poets pass through the centre of the Earth, having left Hell, and emerge through a natural passage, to see the stars again; and we know already that a mountain, higher than any previously seen by Ulysses, rises on this island. It was a happy and original invention to place Purgatory on this mountain and it was a departure from the notions then current, that represented the abode of the purging souls as a sort of annexe of Hell; a subterranean region of ice, fire and torture. Artistic motives certainly played a part in determining this choice; it was indispensable, in a sustained poetic story of this kind, to bring an element of variety to the description of a realm where the inmates, although undergoing a process of purification, still suffer punishments, similar to those of

63

the damned; the sun-bathed mountain, soaring above the waves of the
sea into the purest air, could hardly be more different from the gloom
of Hell! It is above ground, in a region immensely distant from ours,
but more akin to ours than the nether realm. One might more accurately describe this variety as antithesis: antithesis not only in the physical
ambience — the beauty of nature perceived in its most appealing colours as opposed to the horror of the infernal abyss — but also (and it
is here that the other and, possibly, more important motives lie) antithesis between the moral and spiritual conception of Purgatory and
that of Hell.

In a sense time and space are more important, and more vividly
presented, in the *Purgatorio* than in the *Inferno*. Dante's Hell is not 'outside time' altogether. Nevertheless it will go on for ever; the state of
damnation is endless; the damned cannot look forward to an end of
their suffering. But it is precisely this which the souls in Purgatory do
look forward to; being already pardoned, they know that they will suffer only for a definite, limited period. This is why they are so eager to
complete the expiation of their sins, and meanwhile not waste even a
single precious moment of their 'time'. And this desire of theirs finds
symbolic expression in their ascent from Cornice to Cornice of the
'mountain that cleanses as one climbs it' (XIII, 3); which in turn gives
rise to a fresh and wonderfully enhanced feeling for both time and
space; the feeling conveyed on the one hand by the marvellous descrip-
tions of the moving moon and the stars, of sunrise and sunset that accompany the narrative, and on the other by all the landscape poetry,
as it has been called, of Dante's *Purgatorio*. And all these elements, indeed the whole tone and atmosphere of the Cantica, more meditative
and recollected than the *Inferno*, and even tinged by a subtle vein of
melancholy, are fully caught right from this beginning, where the
freshness of awakening nature is mingled with a sense of solemn
mystery. Canto I is thus a fitting prelude; it sets the scene.

I have mentioned the poetry of landscape as being already well in
evidence. It must be understood that the beauty of nature is not vividly
and delicately portrayed just for its own sake; this would hardly have
occurred to the medieval mind. It is so subtly and intimately interwoven with the symbolic meaning of the story as to be inseparable from
it. Dante's artistry had attained by now such a point of refinement, his
mastery over his medium had become so full, that he could make the
concrete, outward scene and the inner meaning coexist, and could convey both the beauty of the one and the profundity of the other

Purgatorio I

simultaneously. The prelude is free from any intrusion of undigested allegory, such as the appearance of the three beasts encountered in the prelude to *Inferno*.

Canto I falls into three main divisions; the first, occupying 39 lines, states the subject of the Cantica and introduces us into the new environment.

> Per correr miglior acque alza le vele
> omai la navicella del mio ingegno,
> che lascia dietro a sé mar sì crudele;   3
>   e canterò di quel secondo regno
> dove l'umano spirito si purga
> e di salire al ciel diventa degno.   6
>   Ma qui la morta poesì resurga,
> o sante Muse, poi che vostro sono;
> e qui Calïopè alquanto surga,   9
>   seguitando il mio canto con quel suono
> di cui le Piche misere sentiro
> lo colpo tal, che disperar perdono.   12

(To course over better waters the little bark of my wit now lifts her sails, leaving behind her so cruel a sea; and I will sing of that second kingdom where the human spirit is purged and becomes fit to ascend to Heaven. But here let poetry rise again from the dead, O holy Muses, since I am yours; and here let Calliope rise up for a while and accompany my song with that strain which smote the ears of the wretched pies so that they despaired of pardon.)

A thrill of liberation runs through the first line, carried by the verb 'correr', and underlined by the strong accent on 'alza le vele', as though, after the anguish and oppression of the 'cruel sea' (3) — the sea of the harsh poetry of *Inferno* and also the sea of unredeemed sin — a favourable wind fills the sails of the little bark of Dante's genius. But soon the poetry of the Canto settles down to a gentler flow, to indicate expectation, wonder, humility and submission; still, however, retaining the joyous undertone imparted by the freer, open place where he now finds himself.

After the second terzina, in which the subject of the *Purgatorio* is formally defined, there follows an invocation to the Muses, a device that Dante has taken over from classical epic, and in particular from Virgil. This is far from being the only place in the *Comedy* where pagan deities are mentioned in a Christian context, a feature of Dante's poetry on which much might be said; here it may suffice to call attention to the adjective 'sante' ('holy': 8) applied to the Muses, and to infer from it that Dante accepted to some extent the myth representing them as the inspirers of poetry, in the sense that they personified in this myth one of the attributes of God. This inference is supported by other passages of *Purgatorio*. For instance, at the end of Canto XXVIII (139–44) Dante takes the myth of the Golden Age as imperfect dream-like recollections of Eden. Calliope is singled out as the Muse whose help, in particular, he wishes to enlist (9), not only because she is regarded as the leader of her band of sisters and because of the etymological meaning of her name (the fine-voiced one), but mainly on account of Ovid's suggestion. It was in Ovid's poem that Dante had read the story of the challenge issued by the nine daughters of King Pierus to the Muses, of their subsequent defeat by Calliope, and of their metamorphosis into magpies; even the verb 'surga' (9) is an echo of Ovid's 'surgit', and signifies that the inspiration now required will have to be even higher than on that victorious occasion.

> Dolce color d'orïental zaffiro,
> che s'accoglieva nel sereno aspetto
> del mezzo, puro infino al primo giro,   15
>   a li occhi miei ricominciò diletto,
> tosto ch'io usci' fuor de l'aura morta
> che m'avea contristati li occhi e 'l petto.   18
>   Lo bel pianeto che d'amar conforta
> faceva tutto rider l'orïente,
> velando i Pesci ch'erano in sua scorta.   21

(The sweet hue of the oriental sapphire which was gathering in the serene face of the sky, clear as far as the first Circle, gladdened my eyes again as soon as I passed out of the dead air which had afflicted my eyes and breast. The fair planet that prompts to love made all the east laugh, veiling the Fishes which were in her train.)

At this point the story proper of *Purgatorio* begins. The poet gazes round him, and takes in the gladness (16) of the world that greets him as soon as he issues from the 'dead air' (17). It is still night, so that he can see the heavenly bodies, but dawn is breaking and colour — what colour! — already strikes his eyes; not just the rich, suffused colour of sapphire, but a more precious, delicate and 'dolce' colour of oriental sapphire (the so-called oriental variety of this stone having a softer and more even hue). The wonderful line 13, slowed down by three pauses and by the skilfully chosen word 'oriental', sets the pace of a solemn, precise, meditative description; note the use of emotive adjectives like 'sereno', 'puro' (14–15), that add a light, heartening quality of clarity and transparency to the sky. The 'primo giro' (15) is variously understood to indicate the first Circle of Heaven (that is to say, the

Sphere of the Moon) or the horizon. Neither of these interpretations is particularly cogent, but the general meaning is not in doubt: the purity of the air ('il mezzo', a scientific term denoting the medium through which images come to us) was perfect as far as the eye could see. The next terzina (19–21) may seem at first a bit dry, with its astronomically precise indication of the position of the planet Venus within the constellation of the Pisces, and with its initial circumlocution ('The fair planet that prompts to love'), which might sound like a piece of superfluous adornment. Yet, a note of joy runs through line 20, a truly exhilarating line, and the mention of 'amar', indeed the very mention of Venus in these terms, is far from being a chance expression that is pressed into service for reasons of metre; for love in its fullest and widest sense is a key word in this Cantica.

> I' mi volsi a man destra, e puosi mente
> a l'altro polo, e vidi quattro stelle
> non viste mai fuor ch'a la prima gente.   24
>   Goder pareva 'l ciel di lor fiammelle:
> oh settentrïonal vedovo sito,
> poi che privato se' di mirar quelle!   27

(I turned to the right and set my mind on the other pole, and I saw four stars never seen before but by the first people. The sky seemed to rejoice in their flames. O widowed region of the north, since thou art denied that sight!)

And now another entrancing sight appears: the four splendid stars of the southern hemisphere, so bright that the sky seems to rejoice in their flames (25). Is Dante referring to the Southern Cross, as some interpreters have believed? It could be that he had heard accounts of it from navigators and astronomers, but this can be neither proved nor disproved. He could not have seen it himself, and it was not recognized as a constellation until a couple of centuries after his death. But does it matter? Whatever the case, it is abundantly clear that these 'quattro stelle' are symbolic; they are described as 'holy' (37) and stand for the four cardinal virtues, as is confirmed by two other passages in *Purgatorio*. If he had in mind some identifiable, real stars, as well as the symbolic ones, it would be difficult to understand what he means by their never (note the definiteness of 'never') having been seen before but by the first people, that is, by Adam and Eve (24). On the other hand a purely symbolic explanation is possible: only our first forebears (if they were, as I believe, 'la prima gente') saw them in their full splendour before the original sin, while they were in the Garden of Eden, which Dante situates on the summit of Purgatory; only they, at that time, had complete possession of the cardinal virtues. Should we infer from this that no one after them was so adorned? Such a conclusion should be accepted with qualifications; there certainly were virtuous people in classical antiquity and after the advent of Christianity, but even they, being involved, as all men are, in Adam's fall, saw the four stars less perfectly. Above all, lines 26–7, with their intense feeling of sadness and regret, emphasized by the adjective 'widowed' (or deprived of something that should be cherished), describing our region of the north, suggest that Dante was fixing his attention mainly on his contemporary world, bereft of virtue and plunged into corruption and strife by the struggle between popes and emperors; a struggle that, in Dante's view, was caused by the confusion of the spiritual and temporal Powers.

> Com' io da loro sguardo fui partito,
> un poco me volgendo a l'altro polo,
> là onde 'l Carro già era sparito,   30
>   vidi presso di me un veglio solo,
> degno di tanta reverenza in vista,
> che più non dee a padre alcun figliuolo.   33
>   Lunga la barba e di pel bianco mista
> portava, a' suoi capelli simigliante,
> de' quai cadeva al petto doppia lista.   36
>   Li raggi de le quattro luci sante
> fregiavan sì la sua faccia di lume,
> ch'i' 'l vedea come 'l sol fosse davante.   39

(When I had withdrawn my gaze from them, turning a little towards the other pole where the Wain had already disappeared, I saw beside me an old man alone, worthy by looks of so great reverence that no son owes more to a father; his beard was long and streaked with white, and his hair the same, a double tress falling on his breast; the rays of the four holy stars so adorned his face with light that I saw him as if the sun were before him.)

When the poet next turns his gaze from the stars, he sees near him an old man standing alone. He has appeared suddenly, unnoticed, miraculously — the first of the miracles of Purgatory, so different from the terrifying supernatural events in Hell in that they are gentle, often instructive, a source of consolation rather than of fear. The apparition could hardly be more impressive in its austere, awe-inspiring, yet paternal features; we learn later on that he is Cato the Younger, the Stoic whose reputation for rectitude was a by-word in Rome, and the staunch opponent of Julius Caesar who, after struggling in vain, inflicted death upon himself, rather than fall into the tyrant's hands.

Purgatorio I

Dante spares no effort to enhance the reverence (32) the sight of him arouses: the adjective 'solo', stressed by being placed at the end of line 31, adds solemnity to this figure standing in isolation against the vast background; and the noun 'veglio' (a somewhat rarer and more poetic alternative to 'vecchio') applied to a man who died before he was fifty years old (and Dante may have known this) is another detail meant to heighten the respect of which he is worthy; his looks (34–6) betoken a venerable integrity. Of course, the description of Cato's personal appearance finds its authority in Lucan's *Pharsalia* (II, 372–6), but with significant modifications. Lucan tells how Cato had allowed his 'horrificam . . . caesariem' and his 'maestam . . . barbam' ('shaggy hair'; 'grim beard') to grow as a sign of mourning at the inception of the civil war. There is nothing grim or horrific, nothing sad in Dante's portrait; rather, an ennobling sable-silvered halo surrounding those patriarchal features. But what creates a resplendent brightness are the rays of the four holy stars that shine on his face 'as if the sun were before him' (37–9). Cato is so infused with the cardinal virtues, that God himself, of whom the sun may be taken as the symbol, illumines him. Clearly the dazzling, supernatural light in which this character is presented, as well as his function and meaning, require some explanation.

A veritable chorus of admiration for Cato had descended from classical antiquity down to Dante, and his judgement of the qualities of this historical figure keeps close to his main sources, even though the powerful imprint of his originality re-creates, so to speak, the historical Cato as a complex and impressive character in the *Comedy*. Lucan has already been quoted, as one of the strongest inspirations; in his pages Dante found a glorification of the Stoic virtues of this man, a giant in the midst of civil strife, while in Cicero's works he read the highest praise of his moral fortitude. Likewise, Horace, Sallust, Valerius Maximus, Seneca had spoken of him in laudatory terms, and Dante may well have known the writings of some of them. But it was Virgil himself who, next to Lucan and Cicero, supplied the most effective suggestion; Virgil, who moved in Augustan circles and could hardly, therefore, be suspected of unduly favouring one who had opposed the great-uncle of his patron, made Cato lord and law-giver to Elysium. This occurs in the *Aeneid* (VIII, 670), in the course of the description of Aeneas's shield: 'Secretosque pios: his dantem iura Catonem' ('far apart from the good, and Cato giving them laws'). What greater tribute than this testimony from a spokesman of the victorious party to a vanquished hero?

It would, however, be an oversimplification to say that Dante places

Cato where he is chiefly on the authority of Virgil. There are many problems raised by his presence in Purgatory. Although Dante offers few clues for their solution in the *Comedy*, he must have weighed these matters carefully, and indeed there are several clues in his other works — the *Convivio* and the *Monarchia*. As a starting-point, we ought to bear in mind that, while Cato is chosen as the guardian of Ante-Purgatory (that is, of the lowest region of the mountain, where those who were late in repenting of their sins have to wait before starting to expiate them), and is therefore the holder, so to speak, of a temporary office, until the Last Judgement, there is a clear indication in line 75 that he will eventually be saved; for on the great day his 'vesture' (body) will rise in splendour with his soul to celestial happiness. Yet, how could a suicide be admitted to *Purgatory*, let alone achieve salvation? Ought he not to be in Hell, in the Ring of the suicides? It is often surmised that Dante treated pagan suicides differently from Christian suicides, on the ground that suicide was viewed in a different light by the ancients, and they were to be judged in the *Comedy* according to pagan morality. This might be acceptable, if Cato were relegated to Limbo, but Dante clearly condones his action altogether, indeed, sees it as admirable; he calls it 'inenarrabile sacrificium' in the *Monarchia* (II, 5, 15: 'a wonderful sacrifice'). Could he have found support for his judgement in Christian writers? Augustine and Thomas Aquinas are often quoted in this connection. Both, of course, condemn suicide as always inexcusable, and the former explicitly includes Cato in his condemnation. However, both imply some very few exceptions: Augustine (*De Civ. Dei*, I, 17–26) describes Samson as being prompted by the Holy Ghost, and the Holy Virgins, who encountered martyrdom by drowning themselves at the time of the persecutions against the Christians rather than be defiled, as obeying a divine command. Thomas specifically comdemns Cato's deed as not prompted by fortitude, but rather by fear (*Summa Theol.*, 2a 2ae, 125, 2 ad 2; cf. 64, 5; and his commentary on Aristotle, *Nicom. Ethics* III, 7, lectio 15). But in the *Supplement* to the *Summa* (95, 6 ad 6), while again roundly condemning suicide, Thomas adds: 'unless it be done under divine inspiration, as an example of fortitude'. Clearly, in spite of Augustine's and Thomas's statements to the contrary, Dante must have held Cato's suicide to come within this category. The motive of divine inspiration is expressly stated in a passage of the *Convivio* (IV, v, 16) where, after listing the glorious deeds performed under 'divina inspirazione' by many heroes of republican Rome, he breaks into the highest possible eulogy of Cato:

Purgatorio I

'O sacratissimo petto di Catone, chi presummerà di te parlare?' ('Who would dare to speak freely of the god-like figure of Cato?'). This impossibility of adequately praising him is explained later in the same book (IV, xxviii, 15): 'what mortal man was worthier to signify God than Cato? Certainly none.' If Dante attributed to him an almost God-like quality (and what more could he have said to indicate his admiration of him?), it was mainly on account of his sublime final gesture, for, as he wrote in the *Monarchia* following fairly closely the text of Cicero's *De Officiis*, Cato 'had shown how much freedom should be prized by preferring to depart from life a free man, rather than remain alive without freedom'. Freedom, let us remember, is the central theme of *Purgatorio*, and Cato, by opting for liberty at the cost of his life, is seen as the greatest upholder of this cause; he has also gone through his existence as a paragon of virtue, indeed, as stated in a passage of the *Convivio* (IV, xxvii, 3), inspired by Lucan, 'he deemed that he had been born, not for himself, but for his country and for the whole world'. Would it be too much to say that the sacrifice of this pre-Christian martyr, of the worthiest man to signify God, may have seemed, in its motivation and in its value, not unlike later sacrifices within the Christian tradition? One can, at any rate, conclude that normal standards do not apply to Cato's suicide, according to the idealized image of him that Dante had formed through his readings of classical poets and prose writers. Be that as it may, this issue remains the knottiest problem concerning the Roman character in *Purgatorio*.

But there are others too. How could a pagan be given access to Paradise? Here the difficulties are less arduous, as there are instances of pagans being saved in the *Comedy*: the Emperor Trajan, the Trojan Ripheus, as well, of course, as the poet Statius. It is true that Dante takes pains to explain their salvation in every case. For Trajan, he accepts a medieval legend; for Ripheus, following Virgil's assertion that this man had been most pious and just, he states that the three theological virtues were to him a form of baptism; and for Statius he invents a secret conversion to Christianity. No similar justification is put forward for Cato; yet, this most righteous of men, this mirror of virtue must have appeared to Dante in a position analogous to that of the other pagans whom he represents as saved. Once again Lucan may have been partly instrumental, for one could find indications in his poem that Cato's attitude to religion, if it did not actually foreshadow Christianity, might have pointed in that direction. 'Jupiter est quodcumque vides, quocumque moveris' ('Jupiter is whatever you can see, wherever you move'), Lucan makes Cato say (*Pharsalia*, IX, 580); it is Jupiter alone rather than the gods, and the Stoic pantheism of this statement could well look like monotheism to a sympathetic reader.

A further cause of perplexity is Cato's having died to frustrate the triumph of Caesar, the founder of the Empire, considered by Dante as an instrument of Providence. But here it is not even necessary to resort to Lucan's resounding, immortalizing line: 'victrix causa deis placuit, sed victa Catoni' (*Pharsalia*, I, 128: 'the victorious cause was dearest to the gods; the cause of the vanquished to Cato'). It is enough to reflect on Dante's view of early and republican Roman history, as unfolding in accordance with the designs of God to prepare in Rome the establishment of those twin conditions for human happiness — the Church and the Empire, the spiritual and the temporal Powers. We learn from the *Monarchia* that the great Roman heroes, endowed by the divine will with nobility, piety, righteousness, the spirit of justice and military valour were all admirable, whether they belonged to the winning or the losing side, for they were all furthering the mission destined for Rome. Caesar was the instrument of God, but Cato was even nearer God than Caesar, for even the universal Empire should not trespass on what is God's greatest gift to man — freedom. The contrast between Caesar and Cato, far from escaping him, must have been uppermost in Dante's mind, if he places in the last Canto of *Inferno* Brutus and Cassius, together with Judas, as the most despicable traitors mangled by Lucifer in the lowest pit of Hell, whilst he puts Cato in the very next Canto, the first of *Purgatorio*, as if to underline the point that the need for liberty is at least equal to the need for a universal Empire.

It is clear now that the presence of Cato at the threshold of *Purgatorio* is dictated by the coherent image Dante had formed of this man as the highest symbol of freedom. Of course, the freedom for which the historical Cato had died was political freedom, whereas the 'libertà' of the celebrated lines 71–2, which Dante is seeking and Cato certainly represents in the *Comedy*, is that far wider and comprehensive concept which forms the main theme of *Purgatorio*: freedom from sin and evil passions and, even more, freedom of the will (or of reason), which implies freedom of the immortal soul to strive for the vision of God. Dante does not draw a sharp line of distinction between civil and moral liberty; all liberties were seen as interdependent, indeed spiritual freedom could be fully ensured only if the universal emperor was properly exercising his temporal power and guaranteeing political freedom.

'Chi siete voi che contro al cieco fiume

fuggita avete la pregione etterna?',
diss' el, movendo quelle oneste piume.   42
    'Chi v'ha guidati, o che vi fu lucerna,
uscendo fuor de la profonda notte
che sempre nera fa la valle inferna?   45
    Son le leggi d'abisso così rotte?
o è mutato in ciel novo consiglio,
che, dannati, venite a le mie grotte?'.   48

('Who are ye that have fled the eternal prison against the blind stream?' he said,
shaking those venerable locks. 'Who has guided you or who was your lantern
in coming forth from the profound night that holds in perpetual blackness the
valley of Hell? Are the laws of the abyss thus broken, or has a new decree been
made in Heaven, that, being damned, you come to my cliffs?')

After this long digression, back to the text of Canto I. The second section occupies exactly half of the Canto (40–108) and consists of the
dialogue between Virgil and Cato, the central part of which (52–84) is
Virgil's longest speech in the *Comedy*, apart from his doctrinal
discourses. There is a sharp change at this point in the tempo of the
poetry; after the solemn, slow description of the first section, a note of
tension intervenes; which goes to show that the more meditative, or
even elegiac, atmosphere to which I referred earlier, as dominating
many parts of *Purgatorio*, admits of a wide range of emotions, and
even of drama. There is, indeed, a dramatic element in the encounter
we are witnessing of two ancient Romans, so different both in their personalities and in the fate Dante assigns them. From the beginning (43–8)
Cato's words are in keeping with that character of austerity, of severity
that had been attested by ancient writers; 'durus', 'rigidus' are the
epithets Lucan had reserved for him. At the sight of the two pilgrims,
he suddenly breaks the silence of the starlit night with a series of sharp
questions meant to ascertain the identity of the unusual travellers. The
'blind stream' (40) is the rivulet the poets have followed upward in their
journey from the centre of the Earth.

    Lo duca mio allor mi diè di piglio,
e con parole e con mani e con cenni
reverenti mi fé le gambe e 'l ciglio.   51
    Poscia rispuose lui: 'Da me non venni:
donna scese del ciel, per li cui prieghi
de la mia compagnia costui sovvenni.   54
    Ma da ch'è tuo voler che più si spieghi
di nostra condizion com' ell' è vera,
esser non puote il mio che a te si nieghi.   57
    Questi non vide mai l'ultima sera;
ma per la sua follia le fu sì presso,

73

Dante's 'Comedy'

che molto poco tempo a volger era.   60
    Sì com' io dissi, fui mandato ad esso
per lui campare; e non lì era altra via
che questa per la quale i' mi son messo.   63
    Mostrata ho lui tutta la gente ria;
e ora intendo mostrar quelli spirti
che purgan sé sotto la tua balìa.   66
    Com' io l'ho tratto, saria lungo a dirti;
de l'alto scende virtù che m'aiuta
conducerlo a vederti e a udirti.   69

(My Leader then laid hold of me and with speech and hand and sign made me reverent in knees and brow, then answered him: 'Of myself I came not. A lady descended from Heaven for whose prayers I succoured this man with my companionship; but since it is thy will to have it made more plain how in truth it stands with us, it cannot be mine to deny thee. This man never saw his last hour, but by his folly was so near to it that very little time was left to run. I was sent to him, as I said, for his deliverance and there was no other way but this on which I have set out; I have shown him all the guilty race and now purpose to show him those spirits that cleanse themselves under thy charge. How I have led him would be long to tell thee; there descends from above virtue which aids me in bringing him to see thee and to hear thee.)

Virgil's behaviour and reaction are no less typical and worthy of note: he is perturbed, and hastily makes Dante kneel and take up an attitude of reverence. His reply to Cato is indicative of the gentleness that is usually associated with him, of his dignity and courteousness, of his gift for ornate and persuasive eloquence, and the exquisite word and the 'bello stile'. At the same time it is a slightly disjointed reply, with repetitions, one of which does not go unnoticed ('Sì com'io dissi': 61), with a desperate desire to please or even to flatter (66, 69), and with an anxiety to invoke higher authority for their journey, as if to excuse himself (this again is done twice, 52–4; and 68–9; the words 'da me' (52) mean 'on my own initiative'). After his first assurance that they are not trespassing in Purgatory, he tries to soothe Cato's feelings by stating (57) that it cannot be his will to deny a fuller explanation. Lines 59–60 are in need of some comment, as it is difficult to see how Dante's folly could have literally brought him near his last hour. Surely they admit only of an allegorical meaning: by his folly, that is, because of his sins, Dante has come so near spiritual death that little time is left to run, if, of course, divine Grace did not come to his succour.

    Or ti piaccia gradir la sua venuta:
libertà va cercando, ch'è sì cara,
come sa chi per lei vita rifiuta.   72
    Tu 'l sai, ché non ti fu per lei amara

Purgatorio I

in Utica la morte, ove lasciasti
la vesta ch'al gran dì sarà sì chiara.   75
    Non son li editti etterni per noi guasti,
ché questi vive e Minòs me non lega;
ma son del cerchio ove son li occhi casti   78
    di Marzia tua, che 'n vista ancor ti priega,
o santo petto, che per tua la tegni:
per lo suo amore adunque a noi ti piega.   81
    Lasciane andar per li tuoi sette regni;
grazie riporterò di te a lei,
se d'esser mentovato là giù degni'.   84

(May it please thee to be gracious to his coming. He goes seeking liberty, which
is so dear, as he knows who gives his life for it; thou knowest it, since death
for it was not bitter to thee in Utica, where thou didst leave the vesture which
in the great day will be so bright. The eternal edicts are not broken by us, for
this man lives and Minos does not bind me; but I am of the Circle where are the
chaste eyes of thy Marcia, who in her looks still prays thee, O holy breast,
that thou hold her for thine own. For her love, then, do thou incline to us. Allow
us to go through thy seven kingdoms. I will report to her thy kindness, if thou
deign to be spoken of there below.')

I have already drawn attention to the splendid and often quoted lines
71–2; I would like to stress the skill with which Dante interweaves into a statement of the purpose of his journey a reference to Cato's own
suicide, which links up with the next terzina introduced by the ringing
'Tu 'l sai', which is meant to show the Roman hero the respect accord-
ed him by the two travellers. Virgil's *captatio benevolentiae* culminates
in lines 78–84, where he enlists to his aid the memory of Marcia, Cato's
wife, who is another inhabitant of Limbo and offers to tell her on his
return of his gratitude to her husband. Dante learned the story of Marcia from Lucan, and made much of it in the *Convivio*. She had been the
wife first of Cato, then of another, and after the death of her second
husband, she had wished to return to her former husband (*Convivio*,
IV, xxviii, 13–19).

The involutions of Virgil's speech, his humility and respect at his first
introduction into Purgatory are meant to show awareness of his condition: he is a soul who, not being saved, finds himself in the presence
of more privileged souls; gone are the confidence and authority he
displayed in *Inferno*. However another and deeper meaning is to be
seen in his attitude of perturbation: he represents human reason, facing the symbol of a higher condition of spiritual freedom, which cannot be attained by the unaided human will.

    'Marzïa piacque tanto a li occhi miei

75

mentre ch'i' fu' di là', diss' elli allora,
'che quante grazie volse da me, fei.   87
　　Or che di là dal mal fiume dimora,
più muover non mi può, per quella legge
che fatta fu quando me n'usci' fora.   90
　　Ma se donna del ciel ti move e regge,
come tu di', non c'è mestier lusinghe:
bastisi ben che per lei mi richegge.   93

('Marcia so pleased my eyes while I was yonder', he said then, 'that whatever kindness she sought of me I did; now that she dwells beyond the evil stream she cannot move me more, by the law which was made when I came forth from thence. But if a lady from Heaven moves and directs thee, as thou sayest, there is no need for fair words; let it suffice thee to ask me for her sake.)

This is made plain by the first part of Cato's rejoinder (85–93) where Virgil's delicate but misjudged flattery is firmly but not brusquely rejected. The poet appeals to Cato's tenderest emotions; but earthly affections, based on human considerations, are no longer of any avail for one who is bound by the law mentioned in line 89, the law that separates those that dwell beyond the evil stream (88), that is, beyond Acheron, from those who have been admitted to Grace. This law, Cato says, came into force when he 'came forth from thence', usually taken to mean when he was brought out of Limbo by Christ, together with the other souls worthy of salvation. If there is still a shade of impatience in the 'non c'è mestier lusinghe' (92) and in the 'bastisi ben' of the next line, the instructions that follow are imparted concisely but calmly. They refer to the ritual of purification and initiation of Dante before he sets out on the second stage of his journey and, with tension slackening, prepare the atmosphere for the final section of the Canto.

　　Va dunque, e fa che tu costui ricinghe
d'un giunco schietto e che li lavi 'l viso,
sì ch'ogne sucidume quindi stinghe;   96
　　ché non si converria, l'occhio sorpriso
d'alcuna nebbia, andar dinanzi al primo
ministro, ch'è di quei di paradiso.   99
　　Questa isoletta intorno ad imo ad imo,
là giù colà dove la batte l'onda,
porta di giunchi sovra 'l molle limo: 102
　　null' altra pianta che facesse fronda
o indurasse, vi puote aver vita,
però ch'a le percosse non seconda.   105
　　Poscia non sia di qua vostra reddita;
lo sol vi mostrerrà, che surge omai,
prendere il monte a più lieve salita'.   108

Purgatorio I

(Go then, and see that thou gird him with a smooth rush and bathe his face so as to remove from it all defilement, for it would not be fitting to go with eye dimmed by any fog before the first minister of those of Paradise. This little island, round about its very base, down there where the wave beats on it, bears rushes on the soft mud; no other plant which would make leaves or harden can live there, not yielding to the buffets. Afterwards let not your return be this way; the sun, which is now rising, will show you where to take the mountain at an easier ascent.')

The first instruction is to gird Dante (or rather, re-gird, if the 'ri' of 'ricinghe' is meant, as it seems, to recall a previous girding) with a smooth rush (94–5); that is, with a plant that, having neither leaves nor a hard stem (103–4), yields to the shock of the waves (105). The yielding rush is the symbol of humility (the 'umile pianta': 135); and the girding is a necessary pre-condition to the undergoing of penance, in so far as humility disposes the soul to a willing acceptance of punishment and suffering. It is almost certain that this regirding harks back to the ungirding of *Inferno*, XVI, where Dante flung down into the abyss a cord unloosed from his waist, as a signal to the monster Geryon. This cord is probably a Franciscan cord, and therefore a symbol of Franciscan virtues, which, one might imagine, were no longer needed in the lower part of Hell, but now become necessary again as a preliminary to purgation. The second instruction is to bathe Dante's face (95–6), so as to remove from it all defilement left by his journey through sin, and to prepare him for the sight of the first of the angels (the 'first minister': 98–9) that guard the Terraces of Purgatory.

The next terzina (100–2) directs our eyes for the first time to the physical features of the island: to its muddy shores beaten by the sea, and to the rushes, which are the only plants that grow on them. The contours are left deliberately vague in the dim light, and this vagueness accentuates an impression of foreboding of supernatural events, an air of mystery.

> Così sparì; e io sù mi levai
> sanza parlare, e tutto mi ritrassi
> al duca mio, e li occhi a lui drizzai. 111
>   El cominciò: 'Figliuol, segui i miei passi:
> volgianci in dietro, ché di qua dichina
> questa pianura a' suoi termini bassi'. 114
>   L'alba vinceva l'ora mattutina
> che fuggia innanzi, sì che di lontano
> conobbi il tremolar de la marina. 117

(With that he vanished, and I rose up without speaking and drew close to my Leader and set my eyes on him. He began: 'Son, follow my steps; let us turn back, for this plain slopes down from here to its low bounds.' The dawn was overcoming the morning breeze, which fled before it, so that I descried far off the trembling of the sea.)

'Così sparì' (109); the vanishing of Cato is as sudden and unexplained as his appearance has been; and Dante, who never utters a word in this Canto, rises up from the kneeling position he has held throughout the conversation between Cato and Virgil, without speaking, almost awe-struck by the solemn ritual that is about to be enacted. Although Virgil pronounces a few more words, introduced by the affectionate vocative 'Figliuol' (112), the final section of the Canto strikes one as dominated by silence, as befits the slow and deliberate act of purification that is about to be performed in the first light of day, and as befits the mood of expectation and wonder of the pilgrim, just awakened from the sleep of sin into a daylight that presages the beginning of his cleansing and his ascent.

If the first shimmering of daylight, so delicately described in the masterly lines 115–17, has also a symbolic value, its unfailing impact is emotional. The highly poetic image of the victorious breaking of the dawn and of the poet descrying the waves touched by the breeze forms such a texture of suggestive words and of almost musical notations, that one is loath to anatomize for fear of spoiling. It blends a picture of the rippling waters perceived, rather than seen, 'di lontano', through a distance, together with a feeling of restrained and inward joyfulness, expressed by 'vinceva' and, even more, by the subdued trembling vibration of line 117: 'conobbi il tremolar de la marina'.

> Noi andavam per lo solingo piano
> com' om che torna a la perduta strada,
> che 'nfino ad essa li pare ire in vano.   120
>   Quando noi fummo là 've la rugiada
> pugna col sole, per essere in parte
> dove, ad orezza, poco si dirada,   123
>   ambo le mani in su l'erbetta sparte
> soavemente 'l mio maestro pose:
> ond' io, che fui accorto di sua arte,   126
>   porsi ver' lui le guance lagrimose;
> ivi mi fece tutto discoverto
> quel color che l'inferno mi nascose.   129

(We made our way over the lonely plain, like one who returns to the road he has lost and, till he finds it, seems to himself to go in vain. When we were at a part where the dew resists the sun, since, being in shade, it is little dispersed, my Master gently laid both hands outspread on the grass. I, therefore, aware of his purpose, reached towards him my tear-stained cheeks and on them he wholly restored that colour which Hell had hidden in me.)

Purgatorio I

The mood of the pilgrim and of his guide, as they set out over the lonely plain, is captured in the next, somewhat pensive terzina (118–20): an absorption in what they have seen and gone through (Dante's cheeks are tear-stained: 127), and a haste to resume their journey. Then the ritual begins, surrounded by an aura of religious composure. The cleansing of Dante is performed 'soavemente' ('gently': 125) by Virgil, with dew collected from the fresh grass. Lines 122–3 have exercised the ingenuity of interpreters, but they need not detain us long. The meaning is roughly the same, whether we take 'adorezza' to be a verb (which, by the way, would have been coined by Dante for the occasion) or follow the reading of Petrocchi's recent critical edition, as I do here. The word 'orezza', derived from 'aura', occurs elsewhere in *Purgatory*, and the expression 'ad orezza' stands for 'in a cool, shaded place' where the dew would resist the sun.

> Venimmo poi in sul lito diserto,
> che mai non vide navicar sue acque
> omo, che di tornar sia poscia esperto.   132
> Quivi mi cinse sì com' altrui piacque:
> oh maraviglia! ché qual elli scelse
> l'umile pianta, cotal si rinacque
> subitamente là onde l'avelse.   136

(We came then on to the desert shore that never saw man sail its waters who after had experience of return. There he girded me as the other had bidden. O marvel! for, such as was the lowly plant he chose, such did it spring up again immediately in the place where he had plucked it.)

The Canto ends with another miracle, enacted on the mysterious desert shore, 'sì com' altrui piacque' (133), 'as the other [Cato] had bidden'. Or is it 'as God had willed'? Probably both; the sense is deliberately two-fold, in that, underlying the obvious allusion to Cato's command (94–5), there is a deliberate recall of the closely similar phrase ('com'altrui piacque'), placed also emphatically at the end of the line, which was Ulysses' comment on his shipwreck at the end of Canto XXVI of *Inferno* (141) in sight of the mysterious 'dark mountain'. Notice that that shipwreck, and therefore implicitly the identity of that mountain with the Mountain of Purgatory, have been evidently alluded to in the immediately preceding terzina of our Canto (130–2). Such deliberate poetical ambiguity would moreover be perfectly consonant with the whole quasi-magical and supernatural character of the scene, a feature that is immediately reinforced by the fact that, as soon as Virgil has plucked the rush and placed it round Dante's waist, the lowly plant springs up again. 'Oh maraviglia': the gasp of wonderment is still audible down to the last line of the Canto. Of course, the immediate springing-up again of the rush is a reminiscence of the golden bough torn by Aeneas from a tree in Diana's grove, just outside the entrance to Hades, and quickly succeeded by another of the same metal: 'et simili frondescit virga metallo' ('and the spray bears leaf of the selfsame metal': *Aeneid*, VI, 144). And there is also a verbal echo of the Virgilian 'primo avolso' ('when the first is torn away': *Aeneid*, VI, 143) in line 136 ('l'avelse'). Dante loved to follow Virgil's footprints whenever he could. One should not, however, forget that the rush growing in Purgatory is also a symbol, and the message of the miracle must be that, once the penitent has accepted humility, more acts of humility will follow each other inexhaustibly.

'Oh maraviglia!' we can repeat with Dante, as has been done by others before us after reading this Canto, dominated as it is by the towering figure of Cato and bathed, at the beginning and at the end, in a light of mystic serenity, which prepares us for that long ascent towards purification and redemption, towards the Terrestrial Paradise and Beatrice, that is the story of *Purgatorio*.

Purgatorio V

As in the case of Inferno and of Paradise, the moral structure of the second realm is based on ten divisions. Purgatory proper consists of seven Cornices, surmounted by the Terrestrial Paradise, which makes eight. To achieve the perfect number ten Dante added the two Terraces of Ante-Purgatory, with which we are concerned in Canto V.

If Purgatory is the antechamber of Paradise, Ante-Purgatory is the antechamber of the antechamber. Purgatory proper begins on the further side of the gateway at which Dante and Virgil arrive in Canto IX. For it is only beyond this gateway that they find the seven Cornices on which the seven so-called Deadly Sins or Vices are purged away, beginning with pride (Cantos X–XII) and ending with lust (Cantos XXVI–XXVII). And it is only as the souls climb these Cornices that they — each on the Cornice or Cornices appropriate to it — undergo a suffering that is properly speaking purgatorial, that is to say, inwardly purificatory and remedial. This is not the case with the souls encountered before that gate is reached, those of Ante-Purgatory. Here by contrast the suffering imposed on the souls is simply the legal penalty of being made to wait for a given period of time before being allowed to pass on to their inward purification on one or other of those seven Cornices. Since they desire this purification intensely, the delay is painful, but it is not at all inwardly remedial. It has however the character of a punishment corresponding, as a sort of 'contrapasso' (cf. *Inferno*, XXVIII, 142), to the fact that all of these souls have been guilty of postponing until the very end of their lives their conversion to God and repentance for their sins. These then are the negligent or 'late-repentant'. They fall into four groups — respectively, (on the first Terrace) the excommunicated who have died under the ban of the Church (Canto III), and (on the second Terrace) those who repented late merely through indolence (Cantos IV–V), the late-repentants who have suffered a violent death (Canto V), and finally those who have neglected their spiritual duties through excessive preoccupation with worldly cares, a group comprising mostly princes and rulers or statesmen (Cantos VI–VIII). These then are the inhabitants of Ante-Purgatory. All of them, as I have said, suffer a kind of 'contrapasso' corresponding to their negligence. But besides this reason, at least two others can be adduced for Dante's having constructed (as the orthodox teaching on Purgatory left him free to do) his Ante-Purgatory. The first, which applies to all the sinners here, is that the special condition of these sinners lends itself easily and naturally to touching expressions of their reliance on prayers offered for them on earth that their time of mere waiting may be shortened (cf., e.g., Manfred's words, Canto III, 136–45). A second reason, applying only to those who have died excommunicate or by violence, is that it gives Dante the opportunity to stress the important doctrinal point that in the last resort salvation depends on God alone, and that at the moment of death God can always be trusted to give Grace to those who sincerely desire it, irrespective of the Church's absolution.

Ante-Purgatory is, of course, the lowest part of the mountain and it is, therefore, the first to be visited by the two poets. At the beginning of Canto V Dante and Virgil, having already met the excommunicated, are in the second Terrace of Ante-Purgatory; in the latter part of Canto IV they have come across the first group of negligents, those who have their own laziness to blame for their procrastination; they spend their time sitting about, the very image of indolence, and the whole scene is described at a leisurely pace, in which human sympathy and a good deal of broad-minded understanding are subtly interwoven with gentle irony as well as a vein of melancholy. The scene continues in the first few lines of Canto V, which is otherwise wholly concerned with the late-repentants who have died a violent death.

Now, this Canto shows a striking contrast with the previous one. Indolence and slowness of movement are replaced here by action and haste: the souls don't sit about, they move, and don't just walk, but run. This serves a dual purpose, at once artistic and moral: it adds that variety to the narrative which constantly stirs the reader's interest in a hundred ways throughout the *Comedy*, and it suitably reflects the state of mind of souls who are impatient to begin their purgation. Furthermore, the drama and bustle of their deaths is also symbolized by their behaviour. The very choice of vocabulary enhances the dynamic character of the action and aims at conveying the solicitude of the penitents: verbs, as you will notice, abound, above all verbs of action and movement, while adjectives are scanty and used only when they are indispensable — never for a purely descriptive or ornamental purpose.

The text can be broadly divided into two parts: the former (1–63) being concerned in a general way with various groups of inhabitants of

Purgatorio V

this region of the second Terrace; and the latter with three distinct episodes in quick succession.

> Io era già da quell' ombre partito,
> e seguitava l'orme del mio duca,
> quando di retro a me, drizzando 'l dito,   3
>   una gridò: 'Ve' che non par che luca
> lo raggio da sinistra a quel di sotto,
> e come vivo par che si conduca!'.   6
>   Li occhi rivolsi al suon di questo motto,
> e vidile guardar per maraviglia
> pur me, pur me, e 'l lume ch'era rotto.   9

(I had already parted from those shades and was following in the steps of my Leader when one behind me, pointing his finger, cried: 'See, the rays do not seem to shine on the left of him below and he seems to bear himself like one alive.' I turned my eyes at the sound of these words and saw that they kept looking in amazement at me and at the light that was broken.)

The surprise exhibited by the souls of the indolent at the sight of a living being (one through whom the rays of the sun do not seem to shine) who is permitted to visit their realm (4–9) is a motif that recurs again and again in the *Comedy*, and one that I think Dante introduced in order to add verisimilitude to his story, while at the same time reminding his readers of the extraordinary quality of his experience. Moreover the detail of the penitent pointing his finger (3) does not seem to me to be pure padding or just a vivid touch, but to carry on the mild irony of the previous Canto, since it shows us this soul confining himself in his laziness to the least possible effort rather than jumping to his feet, or even raising his arm. The repetition 'pur me, pur me' (9) has been seen by several commentators as an expression of annoyance, or of unease, or of vanity on the part of Dante at the insistent gaze to which he is subjected. I think, on the contrary, that here the poet is putting himself as it were in the shoes of the soul who has spoken, and is trying to convey his or her wonder.

> 'Perché l'animo tuo tanto s'impiglia',
> disse 'l maestro, 'che l'andare allenti?
> che ti fa ciò che quivi si pispiglia?   12
>   Vien dietro a me, e lascia dir le genti:
> sta come torre ferma, che non crolla
> già mai la cima per soffiar di venti;   15
>   ché sempre l'omo in cui pensier rampolla
> sovra pensier, da sé dilunga il segno,
> perché la foga l'un de l'altro insolla'.   18
>   Che potea io ridir, se non 'Io vegno'?
> Dissilo, alquanto del color consperso
> che fa l'uom di perdon talvolta degno.   21

Dante's 'Comedy'

('Why is thy mind so entangled', said the Master, 'that thou slackenest thy pace? What is it to thee what they whisper there? Come after me and let the people talk. Stand like a firm tower that never shakes its top for blast of wind; for always the man in whom thought springs up over thought sets his mark farther off, for the one thought saps the force of the other.' What could I answer but 'I come'? I said it, suffused somewhat with the colour that sometimes makes a man deserving of pardon.)

There follows a sharp rebuke from Virgil for Dante's tarrying; its sternness has seemed to many interpreters somewhat disproportionate to the fault, and has caused perplexity; was Virgil angry because of his charge's vanity? or because of his lack of dignity? Others are nearer the mark: it is necessary that Virgil should come forward to correct Dante's attitude of indulgence towards the indolent, an attitude that was artistically highly effective, but morally unjustifiable: in fact, he means to drive home the lesson that you should not allow yourself to be distracted by any pretext once you have entered the path of expiation and purification; for this would 'set the mark farther off' (17). Furthermore, if one analyses Virgil's reproaches, one sees that they are aimed as much at the inertia and languor of the indolent as at Dante's lingering; notice the contempt with which he refers to them ('le genti': 13) and to what they say ('ciò che quivi si pispiglia' (12) where the unusual form 'pispiglia' has derogatory overtones as compared with the more ordinary 'bisbiglia', and could be freely rendered by 'the senseless babble they indulge in'). Lines 14 and 15 have become part of every Italian's stock of quotations owing to their Dantesque ring and clear-cut conciseness; they echo similar images in the Scriptures and, even more, in the *Aeneid*. Dante certainly has in mind Virgil's 'stat ferrea turris' (VI, 554), or 'rupes immota' (VII, 586), but his 'torre ferma' has a more universal meaning, embodied as it is in a precept valid for all men. This precept is further clarified in the next three lines: distractions from the main purpose abound, and 'thus the native hue of resolution Is sicklied o'er with the pale cast of thought'. Note that wool-gathering and frittering away one's time are particularly abhorrent to the poet; he never tires of reproving it; not long before, in Canto III (78), he has said: 'ché perder tempo a chi più sa più spiace' ('loss of time most grieves him that knows best'). Far from resenting the rebuff, Dante shows due contrition (19–21) and introduces us to the second group of the negligent.

> E 'ntanto per la costa di traverso
> venivan genti innanzi a noi un poco,
> cantando *'Miserere'* a verso a verso.   24
>   Quando s'accorser ch'i' non dava loco

Purgatorio V

per lo mio corpo al trapassar d'i raggi,
mutar lor canto in un 'oh!' lungo e roco;   27
  e due di loro, in forma di messaggi,
corsero incontr' a noi e dimandarne:
'Di vostra condizion fatene saggi'.   30
  E 'l mio maestro: 'Voi potete andarne
e ritrarre a color che vi mandaro
che 'l corpo di costui è vera carne.   33
  Se per veder la sua ombra restaro,
com' io avviso, assai è lor risposto:
fàccianli onore, ed esser può lor caro'.   36
  Vapori accesi non vid' io sì tosto
di prima notte mai fender sereno,
né, sol calando, nuvole d'agosto,   39
  che color non tornasser suso in meno;
e, giunti là, con li altri a noi dier volta,
come schiera che scorre sanza freno.   42

(And meanwhile people were coming across the slope a little in front of us, singing the *Miserere* line by line. When they perceived that I did not give passage to the rays through my body they changed their song to an 'Oh!' long-drawn and hoarse, and two of them as messengers ran to meet us and asked us: 'Let us know of your condition.' And my Master said: 'You may go back and report to those who sent you that this man's body is true flesh; if they stopped for seeing his shadow, as I suppose, they have sufficient answer. Let them do him honour and it may profit them.' Never saw I kindled vapours cleave the clear sky at nightfall or sunset clouds in August so swiftly as these returned above and, when they reached the rest, wheeled back with them to us like a troop running with loose rein.)

Lines 22–4 convey the rhythm of a procession of penitents; this is achieved by all three hendecasyllabic lines of the terzina having verse accents (or rhythmic stresses) in the same position (that is, on the second, sixth and tenth syllables). The singing of the Fiftieth Psalm (one of the seven penitential Psalms) is appropriate to souls who died a violent death, for the *Miserere* has not been sung on their deathbeds. The next passage does not require much detailed comment; it is a skilful alternation of narrative, monologue and dialogue, into which information as to the state of these souls is inserted naturally and in an effortless manner. After their initial surprise, expressed by a long-drawn-out and raucous interjection of wonder and dismay, the penitents' reactions, as already noted, are impetuous and agitated: their messengers run (29) towards the two pilgrims and their question (30) is direct and succinct. Virgil's explanation ends with a hint that is precious for the souls (36), for it implies that Dante is in a position to revive their memory among the living, who will be encouraged to pray

Dante's 'Comedy'

God for them, and thus will shorten the period of their purgation — a hint that is eagerly taken up (50). After this the messengers return to their fellow-penitents even more speedily than they came, their darting back being compared to the flash of shooting stars or of sunset lightning (37, 38: according to the Aristotelian notions of the time, both phenomena were believed to be caused by the kindling in the atmosphere of vapours from the earth); the swift expression 'sol calando' (39), a Latinism, the equivalent of an ablative absolute, is indicative of the rapidity with which the scene unfolds.

> 'Questa gente che preme a noi è molta,
> e vegnonti a pregar', disse 'l poeta:
> 'però pur va, e in andando ascolta'.   45
>   'O anima che vai per esser lieta
> con quelle membra con le quai nascesti',
> venian gridando, 'un poco il passo queta.   48
>   Guarda s'alcun di noi unqua vedesti,
> sì che di lui di là novella porti:
> deh, perché vai? deh, perché non t'arresti?   51
>   Noi fummo tutti già per forza morti,
> e peccatori infino a l'ultima ora;
> quivi lume del ciel ne fece accorti,   54
>   sì che, pentendo e perdonando, fora
> di vita uscimmo a Dio pacificati,
> che del disio di sé veder n'accora'.   57
>   E io: 'Perché ne' vostri visi guati,
> non riconosco alcun; ma s'a voi piace
> cosa ch'io possa, spiriti ben nati,   60
>   voi dite, e io farò per quella pace
> che, dietro a' piedi di sì fatta guida,
> di mondo in mondo cercar mi si face'.   63

('These people that press on us are many and they come to petition thee', said the Poet: 'therefore go right on and listen as thou goest.' 'O soul that goest for thy bliss with those members with which thou wast born', they came crying, 'stay thy steps for a little; look if thou hast ever seen any of us, that thou mayst carry news of him yonder. Ah, why dost thou go on? Why dost thou not stop? We were all slain some time by violence and were sinners up to the last hour. Then light from Heaven gave us understanding, so that, repenting and forgiving, forth we came from life at peace with God, who with desire to see Him pierces our heart.' And I replied: 'However I gaze in your faces I do not recognise any; but if I can please you in anything, spirits born for bliss, tell me, and I will do it by that peace which in the steps of such a guide makes me seek it from world to world'.)

The return of the messengers with their astonishing news is the signal for a new flurry of action; the souls rush back (41–2) and urgently beg, indeed, cry out to the poet (48) to remember them to those who knew them. Their breathless anxiety is expressed by the double question in line 51; but now, when they introduce themselves (52–7), the flow of their words becomes more gentle through a subtle interplay of internal pauses and of slow rhymes such as those in 'ora' and 'ati', and their speech acquires a lyrical and more pensive quality as befits souls who have repented and forgiven, have seen the light of Heaven and are at peace with God. Note, too, the masterly enjambment (55–6), followed by a very peaceful, slow line: 'fora Di vita uscimmo a Dio pacificati'. Dante's reply (58–63) is couched in terms of the utmost courtesy, as usual in Purgatory, and in the name of that salvation in Paradise which both the pilgrim and the souls aspire to ('that peace which . . . makes me seek it': 63; 'cercar mi si face' is equivalent to 'si fa cercare da me', literally 'makes itself sought by me').

Thus ends the prelude that sets the scene for the three memorable episodes that follow: three very different characters come in succession to the foreground and recount their experiences of violent death and repentance.

> E uno incominciò: 'Ciascun si fida
> del beneficio tuo sanza giurarlo,
> pur che 'l voler nonpossa non ricida.   66
>   Ond' io, che solo innanzi a li altri parlo,
> ti priego, se mai vedi quel paese
> che siede tra Romagna e quel di Carlo,   69
>   che tu mi sie di tuoi prieghi cortese
> in Fano, sì che ben per me s'adori
> pur ch'i' possa purgar le gravi offese.   72
>   Quindi fu' io; ma li profondi fóri
> ond' uscì 'l sangue in sul quale io sedea,
> fatti mi fuoro in grembo a li Antenori,   75
>   là dov' io più sicuro esser credea:
> quel da Esti il fé far, che m'avea in ira
> assai più là che dritto non volea.   78
>   Ma s'io fosse fuggito inver' la Mira,
> quando fu' sovragiunto ad Orïaco,
> ancor sarei di là dove si spira.   81
>   Corsi al palude, e le cannucce e 'l braco
> m'impigliar sì ch'i' caddi; e lì vid' io
> de le mie vene farsi in terra laco'.   84

(And one began: 'Each of us trusts in thy good offices without thine oath, provided lack of power do not thwart the will; therefore, speaking alone before the rest, I beg of thee, if ever thou see the land that lies between Romagna and

87

that of Charles, that thou do me the courtesy to beg them in Fano that good prayers be made for me, only that I may purge away my grievous sins. From thence I sprang, but the deep wounds from which poured the blood in which I had my life were given me in the midst of the sons of Antenor, where I thought to be most secure. He of Este had it done, who was incensed against me far more than justice warranted; but had I made my flight towards Mira when I was over-taken at Oriaco I should still be yonder where men breathe. I ran to the marsh, and the reeds and the mire so entangled me that I fell, and there I saw form on the ground a pool from my veins.')

The first of the three characters is not named, but the notoriety of his tragedy was such that the details supplied were enough for his contem-poraries to recognize him. He was Iacopo del Cassero, who came of a fairly prominent family of the Marches, the district lying on the Adriatic side of Central Italy between Romagna and 'that of Charles' (69), the kingdom of Naples, as it was then, ruled by Charles II of An-jou. Iacopo's native town was Fano (71), but he held high political of-fice in several other city-states on the same side of Italy; he was a Guelph and had seen service as an ally of Florence in the campaign against Arezzo in which Dante too had taken part, and one could well speculate as to whether the poet might have met his fellow-soldier on this occasion. It was Iacopo's misfortune to fall foul of Azzo VIII, the Marquis of Este and Lord of Ferrara ('quel da Esti': 77). Iacopo was then *podestà* or administrative head of Bologna, and had to take the in-itiative in thwarting Azzo's ambition to extend his domains to include this town; it is reported, moreover, that he descended to personal in-sults, and Dante certainly implies (77–8) that, although the Marquis's wrath was disproportionate to the wrongs he had suffered, it was not groundless. When in 1298, just two years before the fictitious date of Dante's journey, Iacopo was appointed *podestà* of Milan, he took the precaution of travelling from Fano by a circuitous route in order to avoid crossing his enemy's Ferrarese territory; he went to Venice by sea and continued by land through that marshy and low-lying area, cross-ed by rivers and canals, which was already in Paduan territory, just behind the Venetian lagoon. Here, where he thought he was most secure (76), he was overtaken by the assassins dispatched by Azzo and slain. It was a near thing, for, had he decided to flee towards Mira (79), he would have escaped his pursuers, but on the spur of the moment he chose to go in the opposite direction, towards the marsh, where the reeds and the mire hampered his movements (82–3). There is also a hint of the Paduans contributing by treachery to the success of the ambush, in their being described as 'Antenori' (75), for Antenor, the Trojan

Purgatorio V

prince and mythical founder of Padua, was taken by Dante in the *Inferno* as one of the prototypes of treachery (XXXII, 88).

A strong undercurrent of emotion can be detected in Dante's treatment of Iacopo's tragic story (evidently this event had left a deep and lasting impression), although Iacopo's own words sound dry and detached, in their precision as to topographical detail; one might say that he speaks as a soldier would of a skirmish. There is no direct mention of forgiveness here, but one would be justified in thinking that this is implied both by his oblique admission that he provoked his murderer and by the fact that neither the latter, nor those who struck the fatal blow are named; repentance for his sins can be read into line 72. Above all, a vein of sadness and grief mixed with dread colours this episode, and imparts a moving quality to it, especially where the hounded man refers to the horrible perforations or gashes ('fóri', not just 'ferite') from which his blood pours (73–4), and in the last, tragic lines where the fallen fugitive watches a pool form from his veins amidst the reeds and mire, and his life draining away.

Poi disse un altro: 'Deh, se quel disio	
si compia che ti tragge a l'alto monte,	
con buona pïetate aiuta il mio!	87
Io fui di Montefeltro, io son Bonconte;	
Giovanna o altri non ha di me cura;	
per ch'io vo tra costor con bassa fronte'.	90
E io a lui: 'Qual forza o qual ventura	
ti traviò sì fuor di Campaldino,	
che non si seppe mai tua sepultura?'.	93
'Oh!', rispuos' elli, 'a piè del Casentino	
traversa un'acqua c'ha nome l'Archiano,	
che sovra l'Ermo nasce in Apennino.	96
Là 've 'l vocabol suo diventa vano,	
arriva' io forato ne la gola,	
fuggendo a piede e sanguinando il piano.	99
Quivi perdei la vista e la parola;	
nel nome di Maria fini', e quivi	
caddi, e rimase la mia carne sola.	102

(Then another spoke: 'Pray, so may that desire be satisfied which draws thee to the high mountain, do thou with gracious pity help mine. I was of Montefeltro; I am Bonconte. Neither Giovanna nor any other has care for me, so that I go among these with downcast brow.' And I said to him: 'What force or what chance took thee so far from Campaldino that thy burial-place was never known?' 'Ah', he replied, 'at the foot of the Casentino a stream crosses called the Archiano, which rises above the Hermitage in the Apennines. To the place where its name is lost I came, wounded in the throat, flying on foot, and bloodying the plain. There I lost sight and speech. I ended on the name of Mary and there fell and only my flesh remained.)

Dante's 'Comedy'

Another warrior and a man who has been deeply involved in political and military strife now takes the stage. He too is a chastened soul who begins his speech, like Iacopo, with a courteous request for prayer; prayer is all the more necessary, as neither Giovanna (presumably, his wife) nor any of his relatives remember him, as he remarks despondently (89–90). Note the different tenses of the verb 'to be' in line 88: this soul still *is* Bonconte, but *was* of Montefeltro, for such mundane things as titles of nobility belong to the past and have become irrelevant.

Whereas Iacopo was a Guelph and an ally of Florence, Bonconte, the Count of Montefeltro, was a Ghibelline leader and had commanded the army of Arezzo in 1289 in the battle of Campaldino against Florence; he had died in the rout inflicted on his forces by their Florentine foes. Now Dante too fought bravely in this battle in the ranks of the Florentine cavalry. This is reliably and circumstantially attested to by an early fifteenth-century biographer, Leonardo Bruni, who had seen and quotes a now-lost autograph letter of the poet, while it is also in keeping with what Dante himself states in the *Inferno* and is lent further credence by this very episode. It is true that Dante does not recognize Bonconte, but probably he never met him personally. It is noteworthy, however, that as soon as he learns the name of the soul who has spoken he puts the question that must have occurred to those who had fought at Campaldino when, after the battle, Bonconte's body could not be found: what then had happened to it (91–3)?

Bonconte's answer begins with an account of his death: nine lines (94–102), the first four of which graphically outline the landscape of the place of the encounter, well known to those who have visited the upper valley of the Arno (Casentino), where a wide plain is crossed by the Archiano, a tributary of the main river, and is surrounded by the thickly-wooded hills in which the Hermitage of Camaldoli is situated. Only two stark lines (98–9) suffice to describe the desperate flight of the unhorsed knight (he, too, is 'forato' rather than simply 'ferito'), dripping blood over the plain. And then suddenly the end; but not before he had time to utter the name of Mary (101) — thus expressing repentance.

Bonconte's account, like Iacopo's, is factual and, at first sight, unemotional, both here and in the thirty or so lines that follow; now on the slopes of the Mountain of Purgatory he can view the harrowing scene of his death with a steady eye. But, whatever the tone of Bonconte's story, I doubt whether any reader can remain unmoved by line

102: 'caddi, e rimase la mia carne sola', for Dante has managed to pack into it his own emotion and compassion; the heavily accented first word of the line, followed by a pause, sounds like the thud of a heavy and now lifeless man suddenly falling. The rest of the line conveys with the utmost economy the pathos of the scene: a body, that a moment ago was still a human being feeling and hoping, and is now lying prostrate in the solitude of the plain, and round it the silence that has descended after the tumult of the battle and the frantic clatter of fleeing steps.

It may seem a bit surprising, however, that Dante should tell us nothing of that battle, especially if he had had first-hand experience of it; in fact he tells us nothing either of Bonconte's previous life, or of his sins. He focuses his tale entirely on the last few minutes of this character's existence, as he has done in the case of Iacopo, avoiding all other factual or historical or political considerations. Bonconte is portrayed not as the former political opponent, nor as the enemy in battle, but just as a soul pardoned by God and set on its slow way to Heaven. The underlying reason for this treatment is, I think, that at this moment Dante is dealing with something more momentous than history or politics — the importance of repentance at the time of man's supreme experience, when the fate of his soul is sealed; next to this, human passions pale into insignificance. As a result, the impact of these episodes on the reader is far more powerful: Bonconte and Iacopo and other characters we meet in Ante-Purgatory (such as Manfred in Canto III) acquire a relevance that is universal without losing their individuality; they become types or symbols and their stories are invested with the same force and grandeur that myths had in the ancient world.

> Io dirò vero, e tu 'l ridì tra ' vivi:
> l'angel di Dio mi prese, e quel d'inferno
> gridava: "O tu del ciel, perché mi privi?   105
>   Tu te ne porti di costui l'etterno
> per una lagrimetta che 'l mi toglie;
> ma io farò de l'altro altro governo!".   108

(I will tell the truth and do thou tell it again among the living. God's angel took me, and he from Hell cried: 'Oh thou from Heaven, why dost thou rob me? Thou carriest off with thee this man's eternal part for a little tear that takes him from me. But with the other I will deal in other fashion.')

This is further borne out by the rest of Bonconte's tale, which is no less remarkable. For an angel and a devil were ready for his soul at the moment of his death (104), and when the devil finds himself deprived of his prey by the silent angel he turns on the wretched body in his impotent fury, after loudly complaining that a little tear should outweigh a plethora of sins (106-8).

> Ben sai come ne l'aere si raccoglie
> quell' umido vapor che in acqua riede,
> tosto che sale dove 'l freddo il coglie.   11
> Giunse quel mal voler che pur mal chiede
> con lo 'ntelletto, e mosse il fummo e 'l vento
> per la virtù che sua natura diede.   11
> Indi la valle, come 'l dì fu spento,
> da Pratomagno al gran giogo coperse
> di nebbia; e 'l ciel di sopra fece intento,   11
> sì che 'l pregno aere in acqua si converse;
> la pioggia cadde, e a' fossati venne
> di lei ciò che la terra non sofferse;   12
> e come ai rivi grandi si convenne,
> ver' lo fiume real tanto veloce
> si ruinò, che nulla la ritenne.   12
> Lo corpo mio gelato in su la foce
> trovò l'Archian rubesto; e quel sospinse
> ne l'Arno, e sciolse al mio petto la croce   12
> ch'i' fe' di me quando 'l dolor mi vinse;
> voltòmmi per le ripe e per lo fondo,
> poi di sua preda mi coperse e cinse'.   12

(Thou knowest well how there gathers in the air the moist vapour which changes to water again as soon as it rises where the cold condenses it. There came that evil will which seeks only evil with his intellect and stirred the mists and the winds by the power his nature gave. Then when day was spent he covered the valley from Pratomagno to the great range with cloud and so charged the sky overhead that the pregnant air was turned to water. The rain fell and there came to the gullies that which the ground refused and when it gathered into the bigger streams it poured headlong to the royal river with such speed that nothing stayed its course. The raging Archiano found my frozen body near its mouth and swept it into the Arno and loosed on my breast the cross I made of myself when pain overcame me. It rolled me along the banks and over the bottom, then covered and swathed me with its spoils.')

What the devil does is to resort to the supernatural powers that (as theologians recognized) he retained, and to cause a violent storm, the gathering and raging of which are minutely described in scientific as well as poetic terms (109-23). The first terzina (109-11) summarizes the Aristotelian explanation of the formation of rain; the next one (112-14) the working of the devil's evil will; and the three that follow, the livid landscape of the plain and the hills under the thickening clouds and then the pouring rain that makes the gullies overflow, transforming the bigger streams into wild torrents; the royal river (122), that is, one that ows into the sea, is, of course, the Arno. The result of this elaborate tmospheric upheaval engineered by the demon is seen in lines 124–9: 1at poor frozen body is pushed into the Arno by the rushing waters, olled along the banks and over the bottom, and buried under stones nd mud. The disappointed devil has had his meagre revenge, and has oosed the cross that Bonconte has made with his arms on his breast.)nce again, in these lines, dwelling on the ravages wrought by the lements on the miserable remains, one can detect a note of compas- ion felt by the poet for his fellow-creature.

Oddly enough, there is an element in the story that is not wholly fan- iful, namely, the storm. It is probable that a cloudburst such as the one escribed did occur after the battle of Campaldino, and that in giving n account of it Dante was drawing on his experience as an eye-witness. Ve know for certain, at least, that on that 11 June 1289 the sky was overed with clouds during the battle, for Dino Compagni tells us so 1 his *Chronicle*: 'l'aria era coperta di nuvoli, la polvere era grandissima' 'the sky was covered with clouds, and the dust was very great': I, x); nd a thunderstorm in the late afternoon is more than likely after a hot, vercast day at that time of the year.

As for the contest between angel and devil, this is a frequent feature n medieval legends, but this particular instance has an interesting •eculiarity; a parallel contest has been described in Canto XXVII of the *nferno*. Now the soul that has been disputed in the previous contest •etween St Francis and one of the Black Cherubim is that of Guido da Aontefeltro, Bonconte's own father. Guido too is a man of action, a oldier and a statesman. On the approach of old age he had done his •est to secure the salvation of his soul by making his peace with the :hurch and joining the Franciscan Order. No wonder that St Francis imself comes to meet his soul at death; but, as Guido recounts in Canto XVII, after he had begun his expiation he yielded to a request made by ope Boniface VIII, and advised him to make use of fraud. It is true that he Pontiff had absolved him in advance from his sin but, as the devil nockingly remarks when he comes to carry away his soul to Hell, there s one thing Guido had not done — repent. Now we can clearly grasp he full meaning of the Bonconte episode, where the events leading up o the drama and the outcome itself are reversed in every particular; nd the two contests for the two souls can be seen as concrete examples •f divine justice overturning in its infallibility the superficial opinions •f men, who could well believe Guido to have been saved by his saintly ife in old age, and Bonconte to have been damned owing to his sudden death without absolution. They serve to highlight the absolute necessity of repentance irrespective of the presence or absence of the Church's absolution; for Guido's long period of penance has been made useless by one sin without repentance, while for Bonconte one instant of repentance redeems a whole life of sin.

> 'Deh, quando tu sarai tornato al mondo
> e riposato de la lunga via',
> seguitò 'l terzo spirito al secondo,   132
> 'ricorditi di me, che son la Pia;
> Siena mi fé, disfecemi Maremma:
> salsi colui che 'nnanellata pria
> disposando m'avea con la sua gemma'.   136

('Pray, when thou hast returned to the world and art rested from the long way', the third spirit followed on the second, 'do thou remember me, who am Pia. Siena gave me birth, Maremma death. He knows of it who, first plighting troth, wedded me with his gem.')

All we have to consider is the last seven lines of the Canto, but they have a special claim to close attention. After the two warriors, a fragile woman now comes forward, and the contrast could hardly be greater. Suddenly the drama and the tragedy of Iacopo and Bonconte, the fury of a devil and the pelting rain of a thunderstorm are replaced by a subdued voice and by the unmistakable, yet not quite distinct, presence of a lady. She is Pia, that much we know about her, though little else is certain. Most early commentators give her a surname, Pia de' Tolomei, though not all of them agree. It seems that she was the wife of Nello dei Pannocchieschi, a military commander who lived a turbulent life, and it is alleged that he had her put to death because of his jealousy, or so that he could contract another marriage. There is also more than one version of the manner in which she was murdered in his castle in lonely Maremma: a majority of early commentators say that he ordered his servants to catch her unawares, and throw her out of a window. But one has to admit that there is no documentary evidence whatsoever to tell us who she was or how and why she died; we must take it that she met a violent death, but one that gave her time to repent of her sins and to forgive. Her disappearance was probably wrapped in mystery, and Dante, who may have been in the dark as to the circumstances as much as we are, did not choose to embroider. We must be thankful that he obeyed his artistic instinct, for in this particular instance, if we are the losers as regards historical detail, we are immeasurably the gainers as regards poetry.

Purgatorio V

Pia's speech consists of two parts, each of three lines; the first one is interrupted by a most skilfully inserted pause (132), and is a delicately expressed request for remembrance: the main verb, 'ricorditi' (133), is not an imperative, but a subjunctive, an entreaty rather than a demand; and the feminine touch of the first two lines — showing her to be more solicitous for the pilgrim's welfare than for herself — is enough to indicate gentleness and thoughtfulness. Her very reticence implies discretion and a self-effacing nature. But the whole portrait is made of shadow rather than of light, of silence rather than of sound; Pia remains in our minds not as a distinct outline, but as an image drawn with pastels, in a *sfumato* tone. I borrow my metaphors from painting, but music would be more apt, for Dante relies here on soft musical suggestions that defy analysis; note, for example, the effectiveness of the two rhyming words 'via' and 'Pia' at the end of lines 131 and 133, marking two pauses and resounding in the mind.

The last three lines contain all she has to say about herself; again, apart from the places of her birth and of her death, no statement, none of the names, landscapes and detailed circumstances that are found in the other two episodes, not even a word about her murderer; just a hint: he who had wedded her knows it all. She lingers briefly on the ceremonies of plighting troth and giving the wedding ring in the day that must have been the most memorable of her life. What remains unsaid stirs our imagination more than anything she might have said.

I have often referred to contrast and variety while discussing these three episodes; it is time to point out what they have in common. They all evoke the world of the city-states, full of vitality, but also of strife, the turbulent world of Guelphs and Ghibellines, of feuds and enmities — that world which Dante aimed at restoring to harmony and happiness. Blood is a recurring theme in the stories of Iacopo and Bonconte, blood flowing profusely from their veins; but neither Iacopo nor Bonconte, let alone Pia, show resentment while telling their tales of violence and bloodshed, only sadness at the memory of the ravages inflicted on their bodies and at the recollection of the mad cruelty of man's hatred for man. Each one of them, however, is anxious in the first place to ask for prayer and remembrance; for the experience that has brought them to the slopes of Purgatory has convinced them of the power of prayer. When all has seemed to be lost under the weight of their sins, the sudden revelation of God has turned the whole situation upside down — and all is literally saved. Dante so vividly describes for us the outward drama of their deaths mainly in order to convey the drama which mattered most and which took place in their minds at the supreme moment of repentance and forgiveness.

Purgatorio VIII

After leaving the second Terrace of Ante-Purgatory, our pilgrim and his mentor entered a beautiful flowery valley that is the temporary dwelling of those who have neglected their spiritual duties through excessive preoccupation with worldly cares — i.e., princes and rulers, who form the last class of souls in Ante-Purgatory. At this point Dante and Virgil are being guided by another poet, the thirteenth-century Italian troubadour from Mantua, Sordello, who joined them just before they reached the valley of the princes. It is well to bear in mind that Dante probably considered Sordello as particularly well suited to act as a guide during this stage of the ascent, because he was the author of a famous diatribe in Provençal in which he had taken to task the various princes of his time. We can assume that Dante saw a similarity between Sordello's views and his own. At the end of Canto VII it was Sordello who pointed out the most notable among the souls in the valley, in a comprehensive review of the monarchs and rulers of Europe.

Canto VIII concludes the account of the poets' visit to the valley of the princes. This Canto holds a particular attraction for me for several reasons: its shape; its general tone (it is suffused with reminiscence and nostalgia, and with feelings such as gentleness and tenderness and sadness all present at the same time); and the portraits it offers of two remarkable men. Let us begin with its shape. The Canto could be divided into five sections — a prelude, so to speak, describing the evening prayer of the souls (down to line 18), followed by the appearance of two angels coming to protect the valley from a serpent. Between the arrival of the angels and their swift putting the serpent to flight, however, an encounter with one of the souls is inserted, so that the drama of the angels and the serpent is enacted in two separate sections; finally, another encounter brings the Canto to its close. Far from detracting from its compactness, such a treatment, which I am tempted to liken to a piece of inlaid work, adds an element of variety. And, what is more important, this variety is still compatible with an overall unity by virtue of the general tone, peculiar to this Canto. It is, then, one of the most ingeniously constructed Cantos of the *Comedy*. Dante had already been experimenting with the artistic device of splicing one episode into another, for instance in Canto X of the *Inferno* where the encounter with Cavalcante suddenly interrupts his conversation with Farinata. The same technique is adopted no less effectively here.

> Era già l'ora che volge il disio
> ai navicanti e 'ntenerisce il core
> lo dì c'han detto ai dolci amici addio;   3
>   e che lo novo peregrin d'amore
> punge, se ode squilla di lontano
> che paia il giorno pianger che si more;   6
>   quand' io incominciai a render vano
> l'udire e a mirare una de l'alme
> surta, che l'ascoltar chiedea con mano.   9
>   Ella giunse e levò ambo le palme,
> ficcando li occhi verso l'orïente,
> come dicesse a Dio: 'D'altro non calme'.   12
>   '*Te lucis ante*' sì devotamente
> le uscìo di bocca e con sì dolci note,
> che fece me a me uscir di mente;   15
>   e l'altre poi dolcemente e devote
> seguitar lei per tutto l'inno intero,
> avendo li occhi a le superne rote.   18

(It was now the hour that turns back the longing of seafarers and melts their heart the day they have bidden dear friends farewell and pierces the new traveller with love if he hears in the distance a bell that seems to mourn the dying day, when I began to cease hearing his words and to gaze at one of the souls that had risen and was signing with his hand to be heard. He joined his palms and lifted them together, fixing his eyes on the East as if he said to God; 'For naught else I care.' '*Te lucis ante*' came from his lips with such devoutness and with notes so sweet that it drew me out of myself, and then the rest joined him sweetly and devoutly through the whole hymn, keeping their eyes on the celestial wheels.)

The celebrated lines with which the Canto opens establish the atmosphere. Their mood — Dante's mood — is attuned to that of the souls in the valley, who are not entirely detached from those they cherished on earth and have now left behind, and who at the same time are yearning to achieve salvation. It is the sunset hour, but this indication of time, precise like so many others in the *Comedy* (it is the hour of the compline hymn: 13), is conveyed poetically not in direct terms, but by reference to a state of mind that all of us have experienced at the end of a day, when the fading light and the sounds we associate with nightfall combine to induce a feeling of melancholy. It has been said that this is the passage in which Dante comes nearest achieving that 'poetic vagueness' which appealed to romantic taste. There is no need, however, to attribute to him romantic feelings *avant la lettre*; we can take it for granted that, like everything else, or almost everything else in the *Comedy*, the opening of the Canto is consciously and deliberately written, and is intended to add pathos to the scene that is about to unfold. Moreover, the theme of a seafarer's or a pilgrim's departure and of the undefined desires and homesickness that afflict him in the evening hour of the first day of his journey is not unconnected with another theme, most indirectly implied here, but destined to come more and more into focus as the Canto progresses, until it will dominate its final lines. I mean the theme of exile, of departure from one's home town, of separation for ever from one's closest friends and relatives and from all the things one has held dear. Dante knew this only too well from experience. As for the means with which he expressed it, the sheer musicality of the lines defies analysis. I will only hint at their complex rhythms, enhanced by enjambment, at the deliberately 'soft' or 'sweet' sounds of the words in terms of Dante's own theory (*De vulgari eloquentia*, II, vii, 6), with the most significant and evocative ones being given added prominence by being placed in a rhyming position: 'disio', 'core', 'addio', 'amore', 'lontano', 'more'. Even the objects mentioned here are such as to stir emotion; the distant bells — not joyous bells, but those which toll the knell of parting days.

Line 7 marks a characteristic change of sense, as we pass from hearing to seeing; Dante ceases to hear the words of Sordello, who has been pointing out and characterizing the souls of rulers at the end of Canto VII, and also those of the souls who have been chanting the hymn *Salve Regina* while he was speaking. Now one of them rises and, after asking for silence with a gesture (9), takes up a deliberately stylized pose of supplication (10–12). We can visualize him in this attitude if we think of the figures often seen in Tuscan frescoes of the time or in Byzantine mosaics. This unnamed soul strikes a contrast with those of famous kings, emperors and princes who fill the previous Canto, from Rudolph I of Habsburg to Philip III of France, from Charles I of Anjou to Henry III of England and many others, a dazzling array of monarchs who have until recently been so powerful. Now, in the twilight hour, we are shown not one of the great figures of history, but 'una de l'alme' (8), simply a penitent, in whom the poet almost identifies himself to the point of sharing in his ecstasy.

> Aguzza qui, lettor, ben li occhi al vero,
> ché 'l velo è ora ben tanto sottile,
> certo che 'l trapassar dentro è leggero. 21

Dante's 'Comedy'

(Here, reader, sharpen well thine eyes to the truth, for now, surely, the veil is so fine that to pass within is easy.)

The pointed warning in lines 19–21 is easier to translate than to explain. It has exercised the ingenuity of critics throughout the centuries, and several diverse interpretations have been put forward, so we must be careful not to fall into that trap which one of the earliest commentators, Benvenuto da Imola, warned readers to avoid six centuries ago: 'I do state and believe that interpreters of Dante make him say that which never crossed his mind.' Looking then at the text, is it easy to pass through or, literally, within the veil of the literal meaning (21) because the deeper allegorical meaning beyond the veil is almost self-evident (the veil being thin: 20), as most ancient commentators explained? No, thought other critics from the sixteenth century onwards, this interpretation does not hold water. Notice how solemnly Dante warns his readers. Would he go out of his way to make them prick up their ears in order to take something that is easily discernible anyway? Does he not, on the contrary, mean that the allegory behind the literal meaning is so difficult that it is easy to pass through the veil without grasping it? Unsatisfactory too, retort those who favour the first interpretation; the meaning of the allegory will be found to be, in fact, altogether obvious and unmistakable; besides, 'trapassar dentro' ('to pass within') the veil can only mean to grasp the allegorical sense and this, Dante tells us, is easy. There is, however, a way out of this dilemma; a clue can already be found in one of the earliest commentaries, in fact, in one endowed with a special authority, as it was compiled by the poet's second son, Pietro di Dante, who lived for several years with his father during his exile and must have learnt from him what he had meant to convey in the more controversial passages. 'Since now the veil (that is, the literal meaning) is so fine (that is, so manifest and clear), that it is easy to pass through it', wrote Pietro, 'one has to beware lest one misunderstands the truth wrapped in the letter of the text.' The key words, then, are in line 19, 'sharpen well thine eyes to the truth'. Do not miss or misunderstand the lesson that the allegorical scene soon to be described is meant to impart. There have been similar warnings before, e.g., in *Inferno*, IX (61–3), likewise to be followed by the enactment of a kind of drama. These occasions when Dante directly apostrophizes his readers are stylistic devices not unknown to classical authors and adopted in his times by sacred orators and moralistic writers, but unprecedented in a poetic work in the vulgar tongue. Dante puts them to good use to add vividness to the narrative and also to remind us of the spirit in which he is writing. He wants to make you sit up and take notice of the truth lying behind the meaning of the text.

> Io vidi quello essercito gentile
> tacito poscia riguardare in sùe,
> quasi aspettando, palido e umìle;   24
>   e vidi uscir de l'alto e scender giùe
> due angeli con due spade affocate,
> tronche e private de le punte sue.   27
>   Verdi come fogliette pur mo nate
> erano in veste, che da verdi penne
> percosse traean dietro e ventilate.   30
>   L'un poco sovra noi a star si venne,
> e l'altro scese in l'opposita sponda,
> sì che la gente in mezzo si contenne.   33
>   Ben discernëa in lor la testa bionda;
> ma ne la faccia l'occhio si smarria,
> come virtù ch'a troppo si confonda.   36
>   'Ambo vegnon del grembo di Maria',
> disse Sordello, 'a guardia de la valle,
> per lo serpente che verrà vie via'.   39
>   Ond' io, che non sapeva per qual calle,
> mi volsi intorno, e stretto m'accostai,
> tutto gelato, a le fidate spalle.   42

(I saw the noble host silent then, looking up as if in expectancy, pallid and lowly, and I saw come forth from above and descend two angels with flaming swords broken short and without their points. They wore garments green as new-born leaves, which they trailed behind them, beaten and fanned by their green wings. One came and took his stand a little above us and the other alighted on the opposite bank, so that the company was held between. I plainly discerned their flaxen hair, but in their faces my eyes were dazzled, as a faculty is confounded by excess. 'Both come from Mary's bosom', said Sordello, 'to guard the valley, because of the serpent which will come presently.' I, therefore, not knowing by what path, turned round, all chilled, and pressed close to the trusty shoulders.)

The first part of what has been likened to a mystery play follows this warning. As I have already remarked, its allegory is plain enough in its general outline, although its details may not be quite so clear and may lend themselves to more than one interpretation. But these need not detain us for too long. Two angels come down from the Empyrean Heaven ('from Mary's bosom': 37). They are armed with flaming swords broken short and without their points (26–7). There are many explanations for this, but none that completely eliminates perplexity. The likeliest, to my mind, is that the truncated points signify that the protection they offer (that is, God's protection) is a manifestation of God's justice and compassion; the swords are weapons for defence, not for attack. The angels themselves stand as a defence against temptation, symbolized by the serpent mentioned in line 39, whose appearance will take place in the second part of the mystery play. The green colour of their garments and wings (28–9) has been acknowledged since the earliest times to denote hope, in the sense of a confident reliance on God's help in time of need, and especially in time of temptation. Note, however, the immediacy with which Dante indicates the precise shade of green colour (28) and the almost visual impact of the concise comparison used to convey it.

It is clear from the souls' knowledge of what is about to happen that the mystery play, or sacred rite, is repeated at the same time every evening, its stages unfolding one after another — confident prayer (16–18), expectancy of temptation (24), dramatic arrival of the angels (25–7), to be followed after the interlude of Dante's encounter with Nino Visconti by the actual appearance of the serpent. So far, so good. It is when attempts are made to discover for what purpose the mystery play is enacted every night that doubts begin to emerge. In brief, are the souls in the valley subjected to the ordeal of temptation at frequent regular intervals? Is this part of their process of purgation, a kind of punishment or fitting retribution, in the shape of recurring fear of temptation, for their having yielded to it during their lifetime? The answer, I think, must be no. The souls in Ante-Purgatory are on their way to certain salvation and must be proof against temptation; nor are they undergoing the sort of punishment that will be undergone, in various forms, by the souls of the seven Cornices of Purgatory proper, from Canto X to Canto XXVII (cf. Virgil's remark: 'you are now arrived at Purgatory': IX, 49).

In order to acquire a proper understanding of the import of the dramatized parable, it is well, I think, not to lose sight, as most commentators have done, of the prayer the souls have been chanting just before. This is the compline hymn *Te lucis ante*, attributed to St Ambrose. While its first stanza implores the Creator of the world for protection, the second stanza prays him to remove dreams and phantoms of the night, and 'to drive back our adversary, that we be not contaminated': a prayer for protection from temptation in general, then, and in particular against temptation from dreams and visions of the night. Now, it is in direct response to this prayer by the souls 'looking up as if in expectancy' (23–4) that the angels appear and descend. If we

Purgatorio VIII

sharpen well our eyes to the truth, as we have been invited to do by
Dante (19), we can see that what follows is an externalization, or
visualization, of God's answer, in his mercy, to the prayer. For the
souls in Ante-Purgatory, temptation and all its fears (the souls are
described as 'pallid': 24) are but a recollection, an edifying *exemplum*;
whereas for Dante, who is still alive and subject to temptation, and for
all of us mortals, whom the Dante-character represents, it is a lesson
to be heeded. It is, indeed, Dante who does not know by what path the
serpent will come (40), as temptation can assail us from many different
directions and unexpected quarters.

This, I take it, is the main burden of the allegory. Dante's allegories,
however, are often complex and may have more than one meaning. It
is, therefore, worth noting that the mystery play is watched every night
by monarchs and rulers, and only by them; this suggests that it may
also have some specific connection with the temptations to which
princes are exposed by the luxuries of Court life. Following this line of
thought a little further, for what it is worth, we might bear in mind that
the place where the drama is performed, the flowery valley, could well
be taken to represent the splendour with which princes are surrounded on earth.

> E Sordello anco: 'Or avvalliamo omai
> tra le grandi ombre, e parleremo ad esse;
> grazïoso fia lor vedervi assai'. 45
>   Solo tre passi credo ch'i' scendesse,
> e fui di sotto, e vidi un che mirava
> pur me, come conoscer mi volesse. 48
>   Temp' era già che l'aere s'annerava,
> ma non sì che tra li occhi suoi e ' miei
> non dichiarisse ciò che pria serrava. 51
>   Ver' me si fece, e io ver' lui mi fei:
> giudice Nin gentil, quanto mi piacque
> quando ti vidi non esser tra ' rei! 54

(And Sordello continued: 'Let us go down now into the valley among the great
shades and we shall speak to them; it will give them much pleasure to see you.'
Only three paces, I suppose, I descended, and was below, and I saw one who
kept looking at me as if he would recognise me. It was now the time when the
air was already darkening, yet not so that it did not make plain between his
eyes and mine what it had shut off before. He made towards me and I made
towards him. Noble Judge Nino, what joy it was to me when I saw thee not to
be among the guilty!)

And now, as the three poets move down into the valley nearer the
'shades of the great' (43–4), one of these makes towards Dante. Line 53

introduces this soul, so to speak, to the reader. Its impact is enhanced by Dante resorting to the device of direct address, in order to convey the joy with which he is filled when he catches sight of his friend and also, perhaps, his surprise at finding him among those who will be saved; for contemporary readers might have inferred from Nino's tempestuous political life and ruthless participation in factions and strife that he had been doomed to eternal punishment in Hell, like his maternal grandfather, Count Ugolino della Gherardesca, the protagonist of one of the most memorable episodes of the *Inferno*. He had, indeed, been politically associated for a time with Ugolino when they had shared the government of Pisa, until they fell out with each other. There followed, through the machinations of their enemies, the murder by starvation of his grandfather. Nino Visconti himself, as a scion of a Guelph family of the aristocracy in prevalently Ghibelline Pisa, was exiled from his native city. He became one of the leaders of the Guelph League, and it was as such that he must have come across Dante in Florence between 1288 and 1293, at a time when both were in their midtwenties. He then went to Sardinia as Judge (or 'Lord', as we might properly translate the epithet in line 53) of lands he had inherited. He died still young in 1296. But of all the political passions and upheavals that were the very fabric of his life there is not even a trace here. In these thirty-three compact lines we are presented with a righteous man, a loving father, a husband full of regret for being forgotten by the woman he had cherished, eager to confide his innermost feelings to a close and trusted friend. The episode is about the private man and not his public life. It is an occasion for Dante to express his abiding affection and regard for one of the friends of his youth; indeed, the portrait of Nino bears every sign of being drawn from life. He is described as 'gentil' in line 53, an adjective that had a wide range of connotations in the thirteenth century. It occurs very frequently in Dante's works (we have, indeed, already met it in line 22), and its significance is discussed at length in the fourth book of the *Convivio*. Here it is rightly translated as meaning, in the first place, 'noble'.

> Nullo bel salutar tra noi si tacque;
> poi dimandò: 'Quant' è che tu venisti
> a piè del monte per le lontane acque?'.   57
> 'Oh!', diss' io lui, 'per entro i luoghi tristi
> venni stamane, e sono in prima vita,
> ancor che l'altra, sì andando, acquisti'.   60
> E come fu la mia risposta udita,
> Sordello ed elli in dietro si raccolse

Purgatorio VIII

come gente di sùbito smarrita.   63
    L'uno a Virgilio e l'altro a un si volse
che sedea lì, gridando: 'Sù, Currado!
vieni a veder che Dio per grazia volse'.   66

(No fair greeting was unspoken between us; then he asked: 'How long is it since thou camest to the foot of the mountain over the distant waters?' 'Oh', I said to him, 'by way of the woeful regions I came this morning, and I am in the first life, though by going thus I gain the other.' And when they heard my answer Sordello and he drew back, like men suddenly bewildered. The one turned to Virgil, and the other to one who was seated there, calling: 'Rise, Currado! come and see what God by His grace has willed.')

In lines 61–3 we note the astonishment shown by Nino and Sordello when they hear Dante stating to Nino that he is 'in the first life'. I ought, perhaps, to mention that Sordello has not yet had his attention drawn to the fact that Dante is still living. The marvel experienced by the shades is a recurring theme and is intended to remind the reader of the exceptional character of Dante's journey. But it should be stressed that there is no pride, no presumption in his statements, here or elsewhere. He is, of course, aware of the privilege granted him, but he acknowledges (66) that he owes it to the grace of God.

    Poi, vòlto a me: 'Per quel singular grado
che tu dei a colui che sì nasconde
lo suo primo perché, che non lì è guado,   69
    quando sarai di là da le larghe onde,
dì a Giovanna mia che per me chiami
là dove a li 'nnocenti si risponde.   72
    Non credo che la sua madre più m'ami,
poscia che trasmutò le bianche bende,
le quai convien che, misera!, ancor brami.   75
    Per lei assai di lieve si comprende
quanto in femmina foco d'amor dura,
se l'occhio o 'l tatto spesso non l'accende.   78
    Non le farà sì bella sepultura
la vipera che Melanesi accampa,
com' avria fatto il gallo di Gallura'.   81
    Così dicea, segnato de la stampa,
nel suo aspetto, di quel dritto zelo
che misuratamente in core avvampa.   84

(Then, turning to me: 'By that especial gratitude thou owest to Him who hides so deep His primal purpose that there is no ford to it, when thou art beyond the breadth of waters tell my Giovanna to plea for me there where the answer is given to the innocent. I do not think her mother loves me longer since she changed the white veil which, in her wretchedness, she must yet long for. By her it is easy indeed to know how long love's fire endures in woman if sight and touch do not often kindle it. The viper which leads afield the Milanese will not make her so fair a tomb as the cock of Gallura would have done.' He spoke thus, his face bearing the stamp of that righteous zeal which burns in due measure in the heart.)

Nino recommends himself to the prayers of his daughter, *his* Giovanna (71), rather than to those of his wife, here referred to as Giovanna's mother (73) — a tacit, delicately expressed reproof, in all likelihood addressed to Beatrice d'Este, who in the same year, 1300, in which Dante set the story of the *Comedy* had contracted a second marriage with the son of the Lord of Milan, Galeazzo Visconti, as stated in line 74 (she had changed the white veil, or widow's weeds). This, Nino goes on to say, will be a matter of regret for her (75), for a couple of years after her marriage, as Dante well knew when he wrote these lines, Galeazzo and his family were driven out of Milan by a rival faction, and Beatrice had to share for several years her new husband's exile and impoverished state. One should not, however, read too much harshness or vindictiveness in lines 76–8, or even see them as an outburst of 'male chauvinism'; this would not be in keeping with the detachment shown by souls in Purgatory. It is pointed out by commentators that the theme of feminine fickleness was a medieval commonplace and had the support of classical writers. It is true that 'femmina' in line 77 has a slightly pejorative force, and that there is more than a hint of bitterness in those three lines; nevertheless, they remain within the boundaries of the moderation that is a main attribute of Nino. One may even detect lingering affection for his wife and sympathy for her misfortunes in the interjection 'misera!' (75). Above all, in assessing the severity of Nino's judgement of the behaviour of Beatrice d'Este, we have to remember that the whole tone of the episode is set by the adjective 'gentil' at the very beginning. His wife's hasty second marriage does not accord with the aristocratic tenets to which much value was attached by that old-fashioned gentleman, Judge Nino, cast in the same mould as Dante.

Looking now at the next terzina, the viper in line 80 was the emblem in the coat of arms of the Lords of Milan, the other, more famous, Visconti family into which Beatrice d'Este had remarried after Nino's death; it is still part of the emblem of the city of Milan, and can be seen on many monuments. The cockerel in the next line was the emblem of the north-eastern portion of Sardinia, Gallura, over which Nino held sway. The episode closes with three memorable lines, which have fixed for ever the image of Nino in the minds of readers of Dante. They convey at the same time undeviating righteousness and moderation as the outstanding features of the man. But the 'zeal' of line 83 requires some elucidation: one could describe it in rather old-fashioned terms as righteous indignation or, in a pedestrian paraphrase, as a 'justified strong feeling'. However difficult it may be to define with precision the shade of meaning conveyed by this word, the terzina rounds off the pen-portrait of Nino and its impact on the reader is unfailing.

> Li occhi miei ghiotti andavan pur al cielo,
> pur là dove le stelle son più tarde,
> sì come rota più presso a lo stelo.   87
> E 'l duca mio: 'Figliuol, che là sù guarde?'.
> E io a lui: 'A quelle tre facelle
> di che 'l polo di qua tutto quanto arde'.   90
> Ond' elli a me: 'Le quattro chiare stelle
> che vedevi staman, son di là basse,
> e queste son salite ov' eran quelle'.   93

(My greedy eyes kept going to the sky just where the stars are slowest as in a wheel nearest the axle, and my Leader asked me: 'Son, what art thou gazing at up there?' And I answered him: 'At those three torches with which the pole here is all aflame.' And he said to me: 'The four bright stars thou sawest this morning are low down yonder and these are risen where those were.')

Dante is appropriately reticent after Nino's outpouring of his intimate thoughts. Lines 85–93 are devoted to a brief religious–astronomical interlude, pursuing one of the interwoven strands of this Canto — that of the gathering darkness as the sun sets. Night has replaced by now the twilight of the beginning of the Canto and three stars become visible in the sky around the South Pole. They clearly stand for the three theological virtues, and this is universally agreed; while the four stars mentioned in line 91, which were described in the opening of Canto I, in the dawn sky, shedding light on Cato, represent the cardinal virtues. According to most commentators, it is to be inferred that the cardinal virtues (justice, prudence, temperance and fortitude) suffice for the active life, symbolized by morning, while comtemplative life, identified with night, requires the theological virtues (faith, hope and charity) as well. I am inclined to agree, particularly as Virgil's pointed remark (91–3), that three new stars have now taken the place of the four morning stars, seems to establish a connection between the two symbolic constellations and, respectively, morning and evening.

> Com' ei parlava, e Sordello a sé il trasse
> dicendo: 'Vedi là 'l nostro avversaro';
> e drizzò il dito perché 'n là guardasse.   96
> Da quella parte onde non ha riparo

la picciola vallea, era una biscia,
forse qual diede ad Eva il cibo amaro.   99
    Tra l'erba e ' fior venìa la mala striscia,
volgendo ad ora ad or la testa, e 'l dosso
leccando come bestia che si liscia.   102
    Io non vidi, e però dicer non posso,
come mosser li astor celestïali;
ma vidi bene e l'uno e l'altro mosso.   105
    Sentendo fender l'aere a le verdi ali,
fuggì 'l serpente, e li angeli dier volta,
suso a le poste rivolando iguali.   108

(As he spoke, Sordello drew him to himself, saying: 'See there our adversary',
and pointed his finger for him to look that way. At that part where the little
valley has no rampart was a snake, such, perhaps, as gave to Eve the bitter food;
through the grass and flowers came the vile streak, turning its head from time
to time and licking its back like a beast that sleeks itself. I did not see and
therefore cannot tell how the heavenly falcons set out, but I saw plainly both
the one and the other in motion; hearing the green wings cleave the air the serpent fled, and the angels wheeled round, flying back abreast up to their posts.)

Suddenly, after this pensive interval, drama ensues as the main action
of the mystery play unfolds in five swift terzine. Its liturgical allegory
is simple and easy to grasp. When one prays to God for His Grace,
temptation is routed. Some of the details are likewise readily
translatable into allegorical terms. As Dante fails to catch the moment
in which the heavenly falcons set out (103–4), but sees them only when
they are in motion (105), so one cannot be sure whence a given evil may
be approaching, nor whence and how God's Grace may intervene. As
for the grass and flowers through which the serpent advances (100),
they may indicate worldly pleasures and attractions. Nevertheless the
overall impression I receive on reading the passage is one of realism.
Similarly, the serpent licking and sleeking itself (102) could represent
the tempter's devices and deceptions; but here too the vivid image of
a writhing snake seems to overwhelm symbolic interpretations. The
sinuous phrasing of lines 100–2 is well fitted for the description of the
movement of a serpent; and the sudden quickness in the next two terzine with the swooping of the angels, the powerful, masterful motion
of their green wings cleaving the air and securing an effortless victory
with lightning speed, are the last act of the mystery play.

    L'ombra che s'era al giudice raccolta
    quando chiamò, per tutto quello assalto
    punto non fu da me guardare sciolta.   111
        'Se la lucerna che ti mena in alto
    truovi nel tuo arbitrio tanta cera

quant' è mestiere infino al sommo smalto',   114
   cominciò ella, 'se novella vera
di Val di Magra o di parte vicina
sai, dillo a me, che già grande là era.   117
   Fui chiamato Currado Malaspina;
non son l'antico, ma di lui discesi;
a' miei portai l'amor che qui raffina'.   120

(The shade that had drawn close to the Judge when he called had not for an instant, all through that assault, removed his gaze from me. 'So may the lantern that leads thee on high', he began, 'find in thy will so much wax as is needful up to the enamelled summit; if thou hast true tidings of Valdimagra or of the parts near it, tell it to me; for there I once was great. I was called Currado Malaspina, not the old Currado but descended from him. To my own I bore the love which here is purified.')

The final section of the Canto is occupied by Dante's encounter with Currado Malaspina, whose presence at the side of Nino Visconti has already been conveyed to the reader in line 65, but so discreetly that it might have passed unnoticed. This is another striking episode. One of its salient features is Dante's own personal involvement, for here, at the very end of his conversation with Currado, is an announcement of the main turning-point of his life — exile, the bitter reality of which had confronted him every day for the last nineteen years of his life and had caused him, as he will put it in Canto XVII of *Paradiso*, to experience how salt is the taste of another man's bread and how hard is the way up and down another man's stairs. I hardly need to remark that this prophecy, like many other such predictions in the *Comedy*, was written after the event, the fictional date of Dante's journey being 1300. In addition, there is in this episode an overt reference to one of the princely families that gave the poet hospitality during his wanderings, the Malaspina. It will become apparent from the reading of *Paradiso*, XVII, that there is a remarkable parallelism between this and the episode relating to Cangrande della Scala; in each of them the generosity of one of Dante's host families is extolled but on this occasion, Foscolo wrote in his *Discourse upon the text of the 'Comedy'*, Dante's praise is warmer with the memory of benefits received.

The Malaspina were Lords of Lunigiana, that part of north-western Tuscany which borders with Liguria on the Tyrrhenian seaboard. The river Magra (116) flows through it. Dante spent a few months at their Court in the latter part of 1306 and, perhaps, in part of the following year. On 6 October 1306 he was appointed by Franceschino Malaspina to act on behalf of himself and of his relatives in negotiations with the

Dante's 'Comedy'

Bishop of Luni, intended to settle controversies about certain castles. Dante did, in fact, come to an agreement with the bishop. Now Franceschino was a first cousin of Currado Malaspina, the protagonist of this episode, both being sons of two sons of Currado I the elder, mentioned in line 119. Currado the younger died in 1294 and Dante had never met him. The character he portrays may have been based to some extent on what he heard about him in the Lunigiana; largely, it is a poetic invention or idealization prompted by aesthetic needs. Currado belonged to the generation that preceded Dante's own (the exact year of his birth is not known); the poet could, therefore, take him as the ideal repository of all those virtues which he fancied to have belonged to previous times and to have disappeared from the world in which he lived; for he had conceived a notion that there had been a Golden Age that had come to an end with the generation before his own — an era of greater honesty, purity and righteousness in public as well as in private life. This was, of course, a somewhat fanciful, idealistic view and a highly personal interpretation of an age gone by. He was thinking of Florence in particular, but also of the behaviour of princes in general. Certain virtues specifically cultivated in Courts, such as chivalry and courtesy, which he also thought had been held in esteem in former times, seemed to him to have largely faded away in his days; he laments their disappearance in a crucial passage of Canto XVI of *Purgatorio* (115–41) and, more briefly, in Canto XIV (88–90).

Now, the encounter with Currado supplies Dante with an occasion to repay his debt of gratitude to his generous and congenial hosts, the Malaspina family, and to hold them up as paragons in a corrupt world, indeed, as representing the survival of a feudal way of life which prized courtesy, liberality and valour. In other words, they are the champions of tradition in an age when everything was rapidly changing and righteousness in all its forms was signally absent. At the same time, he can offer the reader, alongside Nino Visconti's, another portrait of a man after his own heart. Apart from this, the two portraits have little in common with each other; they could even be seen as set in contrast with one another, thus adding to the variety of an essentially varied Canto. Nino Visconti, the fiercely Guelph leader, inexorable in his attitude to his political foes, does not say a word about politics and is entirely absorbed by his private cares, his concern for his daughter, his regrets for his wife's conduct. Currado, on the contrary, does not ask for prayer or indulge in sentimentality, gives away nothing of his feelings and affections;

Purgatorio VIII

his preoccupations are for the reputation of his family in so far as it keeps the tradition of chivalry alive.

The opening lines of the episode characterize Currado at once: he does not for an instant remove his gaze from Dante (111), and seems to take no notice of the mystery play; his singleness of mind, his imperturbability, his inflexibility, his haughtiness, one might almost call it, set the tone for what he tells Dante. He is depicted as another of those high-souled characters, the prototype of whom is Farinata degli Uberti in Canto X of the *Inferno*. The style of his first speech (112–20) bears this out. While the first terzina — attempting to win Dante over — is elaborately worded and full of allusions and metaphors, the second one, in which Currado comes to the point that mattered to him, and the third clipped, almost abrupt, terzina, in which Currado introduces himself, bring to the fore the theme of his former exalted state ('già grande là era': 117) and thus of his family's rank and attributes, which Dante will pursue in his reply. The lantern that leads on high (112) symbolizes, of course, divine Grace; and the wax that is needed for divine Grace to operate is good will. The plain meaning is, therefore: 'So may divine Grace find in thy free will so much fuel as is needful up to the enamelled summit', i.e. to the summit of the Mountain of Purgatory, and thence to the Terrestrial Paradise, or, as some interpreters will have it, to Paradise. The word 'smalto' ('enamel': 114), which is naturally related to 'coloured', and so to flowers, or anyhow to greensward, and hence to gardens, suggests to me, however, that the first of these two interpretations is more likely to be right.

> 'Oh!', diss'io lui, 'per li vostri paesi
> già mai non fui; ma dove si dimora
> per tutta Europa ch'ei non sien palesi?   123
>   La fama che la vostra casa onora,
> grida i segnori e grida la contrada,
> sì che ne sa chi non vi fu ancora;   126
>   e io vi giuro, s'io di sopra vada,
> che vostra gente onrata non si sfregia
> del pregio de la borsa e de la spada.   129
>   Uso e natura sì la privilegia,
> che, perché il capo reo il mondo torca,
> sola va dritta e 'l mal cammin dispregia'.   132
>   Ed elli: 'Or va; che 'l sol non si ricorca
> sette volte nel letto che 'l Montone
> con tutti e quattro i piè cuopre e inforca,   135
>   che cotesta cortese oppinïone
> ti fia chiavata in mezzo de la testa
> con maggior chiovi che d'altrui sermone,
>   se corso di giudicio non s'arresta'.   139

111

('Oh', I said to him, 'I never passed through your lands; but where in all Europe do men dwell that they are not renowned? The fame which honours your house proclaims alike the lords and the country, so that he knows of them who never was there, and I swear to you, as I hope to go above, that your honoured race does not despoil itself of the glory of the purse and of the sword. It is so privileged by nature and by custom that, however the guilty head turn the world awry, it alone goes straight and scorns the evil path.' And he said: 'It is true; for the sun shall not return seven times to rest in the bed which the Ram covers and bestrides with all four feet before this courteous opinion shall be nailed within thy brain by stronger nails than men's talk, if the course of judgement be not stayed.')

Dante's reply takes its cue from Currado's speech and is couched in solemn tones enhanced by rhetorical devices; note the exclamation at the beginning and the interrogation at the end of the first sentence. It is not enough for him to proclaim the Malaspinas' universal fame, he swears for greater emphasis (127) that they in no way belie their reputation for largesse and valour, the chivalric virtues *par excellence* that will likewise be chosen as the attributes of Cangrande della Scala, when Dante will lavish his highest praise on him in *Paradiso*, XVII; while their absence from the modern world will be deplored by Marco Lombardo in Canto XVI of *Purgatorio*. There is some uncertainty as to the meaning of line 131: does the world 'turn away its guilty head', or does 'the guilty head turn the world awry'? I believe the latter makes better sense and I feel inclined to follow the majority of commentators in taking 'the guilty head' to refer to the Pope, who is seen as bearing the main responsibility for the disordered state of the world in several passages of the *Comedy*, and in particular in one I have just mentioned, in Canto XVI (98–114) of this same Cantica.

In the last seven lines of the Canto, Currado's second speech spells out in a few hammering sentences and in prophetic language what the future has in store for Dante; a complex astronomical periphrasis is brought into service to add gravity to the announcement of an event that will take place before the sun returns for the seventh time into the constellation of the Ram, where it was at the fictional date of Dante's journey, that is, before seven years have elapsed. The fact that Dante is destined to experience the courtesy of the Malaspina if the course of divine judgement is not stayed (139) — and it is, of course, impossible for divine judgement to be stayed — means that Dante's fate will be exile. Thus the note on which the Canto closes brings us back full circle to the nostalgic tone of its beginning and

Purgatorio VIII

shows us how Dante could manage to infuse a wide range of emotions and themes into a single Canto, and achieve balance and cohesion of its various elements at the same time.

Paradiso I

The final Canto of *Purgatorio* shows Dante standing with Beatrice on the summit of the Mountain of Purgatory, in the Earthly Paradise, or Garden of Eden, purged of all sins, 'Puro e disposto a salire alle stelle' ('pure and ready to mount to the stars': XXXIII, 145). It is with the ascent to the stars, or to Heaven, referred to here, that the *Paradiso* is concerned. The task that faced Dante at that point in his poem was the most formidable that ever confronted a poet, in view of the subject he had to deal with and the standards he had already set himself. Moreover, the spectacle of human failings, which has been the main subject of *Inferno* and *Purgatorio*, is, generally speaking, more exciting and lends itself to dramatic treatment more readily than eternal bliss and pure contemplation. Dante was now approaching the age of fifty or had just reached it, and had achieved the peak of his technical and intellectual power; in the ensuing years — the last few years of his life — he succeeded in triumphantly overcoming the difficulties inherent in his undertaking, and made his third Cantica worthy of its subject.

Of course, both artistic and theological reasons demanded that his Paradise should be different from his Hell and his Purgatory. Indeed, it is fundamentally different, although the first thing that strikes one is that the symmetry of the two previous Canticas, based on the perfect number ten, is not broken. There are ten divisions both in the *Inferno* and *Purgatorio*; here again, in accordance with accepted doctrine and Ptolemaic cosmology, there are ten concentric Heavens surrounding the central point occupied by the Earth: nine of them revolve, each more swiftly than the one within it. The seven spheres nearest the Earth contain, and take their names from, the seven planets that were known at the time, while the eighth carries the fixed stars in its crystalline substance. Next comes the ninth Heaven, or *Primum Mobile*, which imparts motion to the eight inner Heavens. Finally, round them all, is the infinite space of the Empyrean Heaven, itself unmoved, but communicating motion to the *Primum Mobile* as a final cause and, through the *Primum Mobile*, to all the lower spheres. It is the location of the Supreme Deity.

The similarity between the *Paradiso* and the other two Canticas ends with the tenfold division; for, unlike *Inferno* and *Purgatorio*, where the

114

various circles are peopled with souls, the theologians taught that here all the blessed spirits have their home in the same Heaven, the tenth, or Empyrean. Artistic requirements, however, suggested that an element of variety should be added to the long narrative, together with the possibility of introducing in the lower Heavens at least some encounters with spirits dealing with less sublime, or more worldly, matters than would be seemly in the rarefied atmosphere of the Empyrean, where the souls are absorbed in contemplation. Thus, Dante resorted to the device of imagining that a group of the blessed descends into each of the physical Heavens to meet him and Beatrice, although these souls are not in fact allotted really and locally to these particular Heavens; they are there only for the purpose of manifesting to Dante perceptibly and almost concretely the sphere that influenced them and, consequently, their different degrees of beatitude. Thus, theological orthodoxy is satisfied by all the blessed spirits having their abode in the Empyrean, while, fictionally, the other Heavens too are peopled, so adding to the richness of the story with a succession of different visions and scenarios, and adding to its dramatic range by the variety of the encounters in each Heaven.

Yet, comparatively few of these meetings lead to conversations such as those we have become accustomed to in the earlier Canticas, where our attention was drawn, in turn, to worldly passions, to historical interests, to individual problems; for the discussion of doctrinal matters and the clarification of theological points often dominates the narrative of the *Paradiso*. This does not mean, however, that Dante's poetic inspiration had run dry, as critics used to hold until not so long ago. On the contrary, the nature of his subject-matter makes for an intensification of his poetic effort. His first purpose is to relate an experience that he does not have the knowledge or the power to recall fully (6), for his memory fails him (9); but he proposes to convey what he has retained so as to make it intelligible to his readers and to hold their attention — in other words, poetically. At the same time, he is going to account for the divine order that is inherent in the cosmos, as suggested to him by his assiduous studies in the previous years and by the religious ideals and currents of thought which enjoyed a high degree of popularity and a wide diffusion in his time and in which he was steeped. The task on which he was embarking enabled him, moreover, to express some dominant traits in his own character: a longing for stability and for certainty, and a passionate love of ratiocination, which led him to grapple with the doctrinal issues that he considered fundamental. A solid,

Dante's 'Comedy'

logical basis is thus provided for his account of his mystical experience. Hence, the doctrinal poetry of the *Paradiso*, vibrant with the sustained lyrical effort with which Dante seeks to express both his ineffable vision and its logical justification.

Canto I, intended to be an introduction to the whole Cantica, is an admirable example of this new kind of poetry. It aims to summarize one of the main themes of the *Paradiso* by describing the universe controlled in its every detail by the almighty hand of its Creator, and to convey the beginning of an experience that is to continue to the end of the Cantica — the ascent of man's soul towards God, as exemplified by the story of Dante's own physical ascent.

One finds that the earliest commentaries are most helpful for our understanding of the *Comedy*. For the first twelve lines of Canto I we have not only the very earliest, but possibly the most valuable and authoritative, of all commentaries — by Dante himself; that is, if we accept as authentic, as most people do nowadays, his Letter of dedication of the *Paradiso* to his friend and patron, the Lord of Verona, Cangrande della Scala (*Epistola* XIII). I will lean upon it in the early part of my commentary. Lines 1–36, we learn from this Letter, form the prologue, which, in turn, divides into two parts: lines 1–12 are the *propositio* or preview of what is to follow; lines 13–36 contain an invocation to Apollo.

> La gloria di colui che tutto move
> per l'universo penetra, e risplende
> in una parte più e meno altrove.   3
>   Nel ciel che più de la sua luce prende
> fu' io, e vidi cose che ridire
> né sa né può chi di là sù discende;   6
>   perché appressando sé al suo disire,
> nostro intelletto si profonda tanto,
> che dietro la memoria non può ire.   9
>   Veramente quant' io del regno santo
> ne la mia mente potei far tesoro,
> sarà ora materia del mio canto.   12

(The glory of Him who moves all things penetrates the universe and shines in one part more and in another less. I was in the Heaven that most receives His light and I saw things which he that descends from it has not the knowledge or the power to tell again; for, drawing near to its desire, our intellect sinks so deep that memory cannot follow it. Nevertheless, so much of the holy kingdom as I was able to treasure in my mind shall now be the matter of my song.)

The first terzina gives in a nutshell the gist of Beatrice's discourse in the second part of Canto I; and, at the same time, resounding as it does with Biblical echoes, it solemnly sets the tone for the whole *Paradiso* and states its central themes. Fittingly, its first line proclaims the glory of God. 'Glory', we learn from the Letter to Cangrande, signifies here *divinus radius*, the divine ray, light being the symbol of God *par excellence*; it is an all-pervading splendour (2–3) that penetrates, or identifies itself with, the essence of things, and shines, or manifests itself, in all the complex qualities of things, in different degrees and in various ways throughout the universe according to the greater or lesser disposition of each thing to receive the divine ray. Line 4 proudly affirms Dante's most daring claim: that he *did* go to the Heaven that most receives God's light, that is the Empyrean Heaven (note the stress achieved by the pronoun 'io' being placed after the verb 'fui' in line 5). However the sustained tone of these lines, reflecting both his sense of pride and the sublimity of his subject, is immediately tempered by the becoming humility of what follows; lines 5–9 state his compound inability to tell again what he saw. The Letter I mentioned explains that he did not have the knowledge ('né sa': 6), because he had forgotten, and did not have the power ('né può'), because, even if he remembered and retained it thereafter, nevertheless speech failed him. As illustrated in the next terzina, this is the condition of the human mind, which, drawing near its desire (that is, God), plunges to such depth that memory cannot follow; or, in the words of the Letter to Cangrande, of 'intellect reaching such a height of exaltation that after its return to itself memory fails, since it has transcended the limits of human power'. As all commentators remark, we have here an accurate description of the rapture that mystic writers affirm that they have felt; indeed, the Letter lists a number of these authorities, both from the Old and New Testament and from medieval texts, as proof of the genuineness or, rather, of the credibility of Dante's own fictional experience.

> O buono Appollo, a l'ultimo lavoro
> fammi del tuo valor sì fatto vaso,
> come dimandi a dar l'amato alloro.   15
>   Infino a qui l'un giogo di Parnaso
> assai mi fu; ma or con amendue
> m'è uopo intrar ne l'aringo rimaso.   18
>   Entra nel petto mio, e spira tue
> sì come quando Marsïa traesti
> de la vagina de le membra sue.   21
>   O divina virtù, se mi ti presti
> tanto che l'ombra del beato regno
> segnata nel mio capo io manifesti,   24
>   vedra'mi al piè del tuo diletto legno
> venire, e coronarmi de le foglie

che la materia e tu mi farai degno. 27
    Sì rade volte, padre, se ne coglie
per trïunfare o cesare o poeta,
colpa e vergogna de l'umane voglie, 30
    che parturir letizia in su la lieta
delfica deïtà dovria la fronda
peneia, quando alcun di sé asseta. 33
    Poca favilla gran fiamma seconda:
forse di retro a me con miglior voci
si pregherà perché Cirra risponda. 36

(O good Apollo, for the last labour make me such a vessel of thy power as thou requirest for the gift of thy loved laurel. Thus far the one peak of Parnassus has sufficed me, but now I have need of both, entering on the arena that remains. Come into my breast and breathe there as when thou drewest Marsyas from the scabbard of his limbs. O power divine, if thou grant me so much of thyself that I may show forth the shadow of the blessed kingdom imprinted in my brain thou shalt see me come to thy chosen tree and crown myself then with those leaves of which the theme and thou will make me worthy. So seldom, father, are they gathered for triumph of Caesar or of poet — fault and shame of human wills — that the Peneian bough should beget gladness in the glad Delphic god when it makes any long for it. A great flame follows a little spark. Perhaps after me prayer will be made with better words so that Cyrrha may respond.)

After the *propositio* comes the *invocatio*, in accordance with the examples provided by the classical epic, and in particular by Virgil: a longer and more elaborate invocation, though, for this, the last — and hardest — of his labours (13) than for the two previous ones. In Canto II of the *Inferno* and in Canto I of *Purgatorio* he enlists the help of the Muses, as stated in lines 16–17; now he has need of more powerful assistance, and appeals to Apollo himself. This being a Christian poem, if ever there was one, an intrusion of pagan mythology may cause surprise; and the invocation to Apollo is just one example of the very many references to classical myths that abound in the *Comedy*. A lengthy discussion would be required to suggest a general explanation of this matter; it will suffice here to say that Dante accepted, to some extent, the myth representing this ancient god as the personification of poetry and poetic inspiration, in the sense that Apollo figures one of the attributes of God, as a source of prophetic and poetic inspiration. Let us remember that Apollo stood also for the sun, again a symbol of God; and, above all, take notice of an unmistakable clue in line 28, where he is addressed as 'padre', a vocative reminiscent of Christian liturgy.

The same alternation of pride, for what he has been chosen to see, and humility, because of his incapacity to recount or even recollect it, that we noticed in the opening lines, recurs in the invocation. His longing for the highest recognition of his merit — coronation as a poet in

that very Florentine Baptistry of St John where he was christened —
was destined to remain unfulfilled; this longing is expressed more than
once in the *Comedy*. It is hinted at here in line 15 (the laurel, by the way,
is said to be 'loved' by Apollo, since Daphne had been transformed into
a laurel), and again and more clearly still in lines 25–33, mixed with
regret that so seldom emperors or poets aspire to, or are granted, a
crown. Then Dante suggests that, when a poet yearns for the laurel,
this should favourably dispose God, the inspirer of poetry, to assist him
in his aspiration or, to repeat his words (31–3), this should beget
gladness in the glad Delphic deity. On the other hand, he acknowledges
that, endowed as he is with merely human powers, he cannot hope to
show forth more than a pale image or shadow of the blessed kingdom
imprinted in his brain (23–4).

Just a word on the Marsyas simile (20–1). Marsyas was a satyr who,
having challenged Apollo to a contest in music, and having been
defeated, was flayed by him alive. The myth is outlined with vividness
in these two rapidly flowing lines; but was it appropriate to introduce
it at this point and stress the cruelty or, rather, the barbarity of the
punishment inflicted by the god on the satyr? The explanation of
Dante's choice, to my mind, lies in the fact that the emphasis is not on
the punishment of Marsyas, but on the ease and swiftness of the god's
victory and, implicitly, on his great power; power to provide high
inspiration — and on his omnipotence. Line 34 is a rewording of a dic-
tum then current, but is, nevertheless, notable for its typically Dantesque ring and admirable economy of language. The following two
lines have traditionally been held to mean that other poets who will
follow in his wake will probably achieve even higher inspiration and
improve on his performance. Although this interpretation has recently
been challenged (could Dante envisage a better poem than his own?)
it still seems to me to be almost certainly right. First, it harks back to
a passage in Canto XI of *Purgatorio* (91–117), vigorously stating the
principle of constant progress in art and poetry and, consequently, the
ephemeral character of the primacy achieved by any one artist or poet
at any one time. Secondly, its show of due modesty and humility neatly
counterbalances the proud claim implied in the previous lines: we
gather from them that he, Dante, had set out to be the first of the writers
of verse in the vernacular tongue to be worthy of being described as
'poeta' (29), a term he had earlier reserved for ancient poets; this claim
was, of course, fully justified but, even so, was a high claim to make.

Surge ai mortali per diverse foci

Dante's 'Comedy'

la lucerna del mondo; ma da quella
che quattro cerchi giugne con tre croci,   39
    con miglior corso e con migliore stella
esce congiunta, e la mondana cera
più a suo modo tempera e suggella.   42
    Fatto avea di là mane e di qua sera
tal foce, e quasi tutto era là bianco
quello emisperio, e l'altra parte nera,   45
    quando Beatrice in sul sinistro fianco
vidi rivolta e riguardar nel sole:
aguglia sì non li s'affisse unquanco.   48

(The lamp of the world rises on mortals by different entrances; but by that which joins four circles with three crosses it issues on a better course and in conjunction with better stars and tempers and stamps the wax of the world more after its own fashion. Its entrance near that point had made morning there and evening here and that hemisphere was almost white and the other dark, when I saw Beatrice turned round to the left and looking at the sun — never eagle so fastened upon it.)

With line 37, the Letter to Cangrande informs us, the 'executive part' or, we might say, the substance of the Canto begins. There are now some ambiguities here and there, as befits the description of a state approaching rapture. For instance, there is controversy as to where Dante exactly is at any given point (whether still on the summit of the Mountain of Purgatory, or in the spheres of Air and of Fire immediately surrounding the Earth), although it seems clear to me that he is still in the Earthly Paradise at this moment. But the highly technical astronomical detail in the first four terzine has a degree of precision that contrasts with what is to follow: it is as though the description of cosmic phenomena they contain is meant to be a preparation and starting-point for the mind to grasp the truths that are the very foundation of these same physical facts. The scientific periphrasis in the lines 37–42 and 43–8 aims at pinpointing the time of the year and the time of day at the beginning of his ascent: both are especially propitious (40–2). The diagram reproduced here may help to explain how (39) four circles (the equator, the ecliptic, the colure and the horizon) intersect each other, or rather, the first three are intersected by the horizon so as to form three crosses. Suffice to say that this happens when the sun is in the constellation of Aries, as was then the case and as it was when the world was created, and that the significance of the four circles and three crosses is not confined to the realm of science, but has strong allegorical overtones. The four circles may stand for the four cardinal virtues that we have seen at the beginning of *Purgatorio* too (the four stars shining

Paradiso I

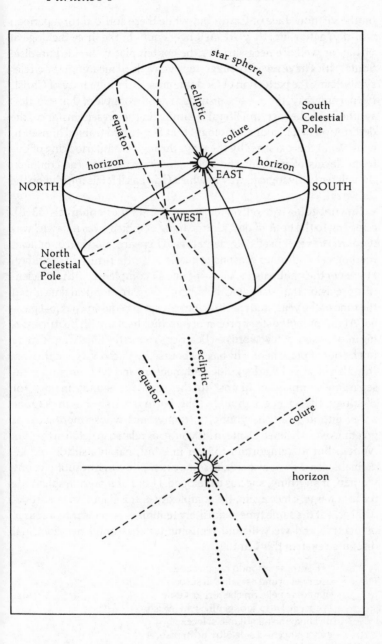

on the virtuous face of Cato); but while these sufficed for a perfect, worldly, active life, they are no longer enough; the three theological virtues as well are necessary for the contemplative life of Paradise. Some critics have recently suggested even a third meaning: the circles symbolizing the perfection of God, the crosses the humanity of Christ. Be that as it may, the passage provides a good example of that effortless synthesis of allegory and literal meaning (in the present instance, the description of a fact of cosmology) that Dante had trained himself to achieve; in this passage, by the way, through the interlocking of different levels of meaning, he also manages to signify the complex, though perfectly logical, way in which God has left His imprint on the universe.

I am not going to dwell on the second part of the periphrasis (43–8), referring to the hour of day, the meaning of which (was it dawn? was it noon?) has exercised commentators. There are good astronomical, theological and other reasons to make us settle firmly for midday. However the unobtrusive 'quasi' of line 44 completes, with the scientific precision that was typical of Dante, the astronomical data about the time of the year, and specifies that the spring equinox has *just* passed. At this point the story proper of *Paradiso* begins with Beatrice gazing into the sun. A few words on Beatrice's role in the third Cantica may not be out of place here. She has, of course, replaced Virgil in the Earthly Paradise as Dante's guide and mentor, and will remain his inseparable companion almost to the end. She stands mainly for theology, the science of divine truths, and as such she has undergone an evolution from the young, attractive girl whose mere gaze or greeting overwhelmed Dante in his youth, as related in detail in the *Vita Nuova*. But it is important to bear in mind that in a subtle and indefinable sense she is also still, to some extent, the same beautiful young woman; if anything, she has developed a kind of maternal solicitude for her charge. Once again, the complexity of this figure, severely doctoral and at the same time exquisitely feminine, is made into a source of poetry; and we will find feminine touches amid her doctrinal discourse even in this Canto I.

> E sì come secondo raggio suole
> uscir del primo e risalire in suso,
> pur come pelegrin che tornar vuole,   51
>   così de l'atto suo, per li occhi infuso
> ne l'imagine mia, il mio si fece,
> e fissi li occhi al sole oltre nostr' uso.   54
>   Molto è licito là, che qui non lece

a le nostre virtù, mercé del loco
fatto per proprio de l'umana spece.   57

   Io nol soffersi molto, né sì poco,
ch'io nol vedessi sfavillar dintorno,
com' ferro che bogliente esce del foco;   60

   e di sùbito parve giorno a giorno
essere aggiunto, come quei che puote
avesse il ciel d'un altro sole addorno.   63

   Beatrice tutta ne l'etterne rote
fissa con li occhi stava; e io in lei
le luci fissi, di là sù rimote.   66

(And as a second ray will issue from the first and mount up again, like a
peregrine falcon that would return home, so from her action, infused by the
eyes into my imagination, mine was made, and beyond our wont I fixed my
eyes on the sun. Much is granted there that is not granted here to our powers,
by virtue of the place made for possession by the race of men. I had not borne
it long, yet not so briefly as not to see it sparkling all over like iron that comes
boiling from the fire; and of a sudden it seemed there was added day to day,
as if He that is able had decked the sky with a second sun. Beatrice stood with
her eyes fixed only on the eternal wheels [the heavenly spheres], and on her
I fixed mine, withdrawn from above.)

Two similes (49–50 and 51) illustrate Dante's urge to imitate Beatrice
and fix his eyes too on the sun; the first simile is taken from the physical
sciences and compares Dante's action to a reflected ray of light
necessarily resulting from a first ray hitting a surface. The meaning of
'pelegrin' in the second one is disputed; some critics think it refers to
a pilgrim, others to a peregrine falcon. The arguments are fairly equally
balanced, and perhaps no choice need be made, though the second
strikes me as more appropriate and poetic, the comparison being, in
this case, with a hawk eager to fly up again with its prey after its
downward swoop. Brought back to a state of virtue by the purification
he has undergone in Purgatory, and having reached, in the course of
this process, the Terrestrial Paradise ('the place [that God] had made
for possession by the race of men': 56–7), Dante is able to withstand
the splendour of the sun for longer than is normally possible for a man,
but not for very long; he turns his gaze to Beatrice, who is still rapt in
the contemplation of the heavenly spheres (64–6). The allegorical
significance is plain: at this point Dante still needs the mediation of
theology to contemplate God; but there is one other aspect of this
passage that is worth noticing — the flood of light in which Dante finds
himself immersed, as though God has added day to day, and decked
the sky with a second sun (61–3); this is the first of the very many

Dante's 'Comedy'

passages in the *Paradiso* (we will find another brief one a little further on) in which the theme of light dominates, a theme to which Dante manages to impart a marvellous, seemingly inexhaustible, variety. Light, of course, is by definition a manifestation of God, who is said in the Bible to be the true light.

> Nel suo aspetto tal dentro mi fei,
> qual si fé Glauco nel gustar de l'erba
> che 'l fé consorto in mar de li altri dèi.   69
>
> Trasumanar significar *per verba*
> non si poria; però l'essemplo basti
> a cui esperïenza grazia serba.   72
>
> S'i' era sol di me quel che creasti
> novellamente, amor che 'l ciel governi,
> tu 'l sai, che col tuo lume mi levasti.   75
>
> Quando la rota che tu sempiterni
> desiderato, a sé mi fece atteso
> con l'armonia che temperi e discerni,   78
>
> parvemi tanto allor del cielo acceso
> de la fiamma del sol, che pioggia o fiume
> lago non fece alcun tanto disteso.   81

(At her aspect I was changed within, as was Glaucus when he tasted of the herb that made him one among the other gods in the sea. The passing beyond humanity cannot be set forth in words; let the example suffice, therefore, for him to whom Grace reserves the experience. If I was only that part of me which Thou createdst last, Thou knowest, Love that rulest the Heavens, who with Thy light didst raise me. When the wheel [the rotating movement of the spheres] which Thou, being desired, makest eternal held me intent on itself by the harmony Thou dost attune and distribute, so much of the sky seemed to me then to be kindled with the sun's flame that rain or river never made a lake so broad.)

The supernatural, the 'passing beyond humanity' (70), of which we have already seen an anticipation in Dante's enhanced ability to gaze at the sun, now becomes the theme. The feeling of 'trasumanar', however, 'cannot be set forth in words' (70–1); to make it intelligible, Dante can only rely on the mythological example of Glaucus (68–9), which he took from Ovid: the story of a fisherman who changed his nature — from human to divine — and became a sea god after tasting a herb endowed with magical properties. Line 70 is, in a way, the pivotal point of the whole Canto, by virtue of its central position and, even more, of its substance. It has always struck me as an awe-filled and awe-inspiring line, on account of its unforgettable, slow, solemn rhythm, achieved by the simple device of having two infinitives of four syllables each one after the other, both ending with the impressive sound of an apocopated 'ar', and of following them for greater em-

124

phasis with an expression in Latin: *'per verba'*. The latter expression gives me a pretext to remark on the abundance of examples of Latin syntax, idioms, vocabulary and sentence-structure in the *Paradiso*, which did not escape the shrewd eye of a far from superficial reader of Dante, whose name may sound unexpected in this context: Niccolò Machiavelli. To take some of the more conspicuous instances, the 'veramente' of line 10 has none of its Italian meaning of 'in truth'; it is an equivalent of the Latin *verumtamen*, nevertheless. And we will soon find another word in pure Latin (*'requïevi'*) in line 97. These examples could, of course, be multiplied; but the point I wish to make is that Canto I is typical in this respect of the doctrinal Cantos of the *Comedy*. Although Dante's genius and intuition led him to write his poem in Italian — an unprecedented and most courageous decision for a work of such erudition — he followed the practice that was normal in his time of using Latin in three of his prose works. At that time bilingualism prevailed in the world of the learned, and it is easy to surmise that an overwhelming proportion of his reading was done in Latin. Now, when touching upon doctrinal matters in his Italian poem, he must have consciously employed latinisms in order to add weight to a serious discussion, but also, to some degree unconsciously, following a habit of mind of long standing that led him to think in Latin when dealing with a scientific subject.

Reverting to the text, Dante's ascent to the Heavens has by now begun, as stated in line 75. Is it only his soul (that part of him that God created last: 73–4) that soars upwards, or also his now weightless body? On this matter he is reticent, echoing the words of St Paul in a similar context ('whether in the body, I cannot tell; or whether out of the body, I cannot tell: God knoweth': II Cor. 12: 2); but it would be unfair for me to do likewise. It is beyond doubt that in the fiction of the poem his body is ascending as much as his soul, as will be shown by a line that occurs a little further on in this Canto and, even more convincingly, by other passages (e.g., *Paradiso*, XXI, 11 and 61; XXVII, 64).

I have already remarked on the importance of the theme of light in the *Paradiso*; almost equally prominent is that of sound — songs and hymns and harmonies that greet the poet as he rises from Heaven to Heaven. This beginning of the ascent, towards the Heaven of the Moon, provides the first example; as he soars through the sphere of Fire, the description relies on the harmony coming from the rotation of the eternal spheres (78) as well as on the sea of light that kindles the sky (79–81).

La novità del suono e 'l grande lume
di lor cagion m'accesero un disio
mai non sentito di cotanto acume.   84

Ond' ella, che vedea me sì com' io,
a quïetarmi l'animo commosso,
pria ch'io a dimandar, la bocca aprio   87

e cominciò: 'Tu stesso ti fai grosso
col falso imaginar, sì che non vedi
ciò che vedresti se l'avessi scosso.   90

Tu non se' in terra, sì come tu credi;
ma folgore, fuggendo il proprio sito,
non corse come tu ch'ad esso riedi'.   93

S'io fui del primo dubbio disvestito
per le sorrise parolette brevi,
dentro ad un nuovo più fu' inretito   96

e dissi: 'Già contento *requïevi*
di grande ammirazion; ma ora ammiro
com' io trascenda questi corpi levi'.   99

Ond' ella, appresso d'un pïo sospiro,
li occhi drizzò ver' me con quel sembiante
che madre fa sovra figlio deliro,   102

e cominciò:

(The newness of the sound and the great light kindled in me such keenness of
desire to know their cause as I had never felt before; and she who saw me as
I saw myself, to quiet the agitation of my mind, opened her lips before I opened mine to ask. And she began: 'Thou makest thyself dull with false fancies so
that thou canst not see as thou wouldst if thou hadst cast them off; thou art not
on earth as thou thinkest, but lightning flying from its own place never ran so
fast as thou returnest to thine.' If I was freed from my perplexity by the brief
words she smiled to me I was more entangled in a new one and I said: 'I was
content already, resting from a great wonder, but now I wonder how I should
be rising above these light substances.' She, therefore, after a sigh of pity, bent
her eyes on me with the look a mother casts on her delirious child, and she
began:)

Dante's bewilderment at what he perceives with his senses, but is unable
to explain to himself, prompts Beatrice to anticipate his question and
to set his mind at rest; here, and again in lines 100–2 (note her 'sigh of
pity'; her attitude similar to that of a mother to a delirious child), she
appears to us as being affectionately solicitous to further Dante's
instruction, and at the same time a trifle impatient of the slowness and
dulness of a pupil who has still some way to go before the full acquisition of knowledge. There is a tone of mild rebuke in her initial 'thou
makest thyself dull', etc. (88), but she soon takes the edge off it with a
smile (95). He is no longer on Earth, she explains to him, but is return-
ing to his own place (93), that is to Heaven, with far greater speed than

that of lightning flying from its own place (92), that is from the sphere
of Fire, whence lightning was then believed to originate. The brief
words Beatrice speaks with a smile to Dante (the grace and elegance of
line 95 hardly need stressing) give rise to a further doubt: how could
it be possible for his body to soar through lighter substances, that is,
through the spheres of Air and Fire (99)? The question offers Beatrice
the opportunity for the first great doctrinal discourse of the *Paradiso*,
on the order of the universe and the natural tendency of the human soul
towards God.

> 'Le cose tutte quante
> hanno ordine tra loro, e questo è forma
> che l'universo a Dio fa simigliante.   105
>   Qui veggion l'alte creature l'orma
> de l'etterno valore, il qual è fine
> al quale è fatta la toccata norma.   108
>   Ne l'ordine ch'io dico sono accline
> tutte nature, per diverse sorti,
> più al principio loro e men vicine;   111
>   onde si muovono a diversi porti
> per lo gran mar de l'essere, e ciascuna
> con istinto a lei dato che la porti.   114
>   Questi ne porta il foco inver' la luna;
> questi ne' cor mortali è permotore;
> questi la terra in sé stringe e aduna;   117
>   né pur le creature che son fore
> d'intelligenza quest' arco saetta,
> ma quelle c'hanno intelletto e amore.   120

('All things whatsoever have order among themselves, and this is the form that
makes the universe resemble God: here the higher creatures see the impress of
the Eternal Excellence, which is the end for which that system itself is made.
In the order I speak of all natures have their bent according to their different
lots, nearer to their source and farther from it; they move, therefore, to different ports over the great sea of being, each with an instinct given it to bear
it on: this bears fire up towards the moon, this is the motive force in mortal
creatures, this binds the earth together and makes it one. And not only the
creatures that are without intelligence does this bow shoot, but those also that
have intellect and love.)

It is noticeable that Beatrice does not answer Dante's question on what
enables him to rise higher than lighter elements or, at least, does not
answer explicitly, for Dante could work out his own answer from the
gist of the whole discourse. As for us who read the story, we ought to
bear in mind, when considering this matter, that physical and spiritual
facts were on the same level of reality for Dante: the tendency of
material bodies to fall and the tendency of man's desire to soar towards

God were two truths to be placed on the same plane, the borderline between the physical and the metaphysical being unmarked, or at least blurred. We ought also to remember that, if the miraculous could be described in the story of the *Paradiso* with verisimilitude, as though it had been a real experience, it was as a result of this intellectual approach.

It would be presumptuous, I feel, to try and throw further light on the meaning of Beatrice's discourse; it speaks lucidly and powerfully for itself, and it will be sufficient to clarify a few points. These last 40 lines are, indeed, the culmination of the whole Canto; they aim at synthesizing the many issues and problems that have been previously touched upon. Thus the opening terzina puts in technical terms what has been more solemnly, but less precisely, stated at the beginning. The word 'forma' (104), being a term endowed with a high degree of technical precision, exemplifies this scientific accuracy of expression; it means something like 'complete realization of being' or, more simply, 'essential formative principle' of all things whatsoever. The 'higher creatures' of line 106 are those possessed of intellect — the angels in the first place; but Dante would have also included men enamoured of wisdom ('the few that reached out early for the angels' bread': Canto II, 10–11) like himself, not to speak of the sages in the Heaven of the Sun. There is order, then, divinely appointed order, for all things throughout the universe, 'per lo gran mar de l'essere' (113): what boundless vastness of infinite spaces is conjured up by these words! I have deliberately stressed them to show what it is that infuses poetry into a doctrinal disquisition that might otherwise be quite dry. All things, then, move to different ports (112), that is, tend towards different goals, according to their bent and their different lots, some being nearer to God and some farther (109–11, echoing the opening of the Canto); the thrice repeated 'questi' (115–17), hammering the point into the reader's mind, refers, of course, to the different instincts of each thing, bearing fire upwards (the 'ne' in line 115 is pleonastic); giving a motive force (or, we might say, regulating the physiology) of mortal, or irrational, creatures; and binding the earth together by what we now know as the law of gravity. The same instinctive love (the 'bow' of line 119) imparts a tendency ('shoots') also to rational creatures, that is human and angelic beings: a tendency towards God.

> La provedenza, che cotanto assetta,
> del suo lume fa 'l ciel sempre quïeto
> nel qual si volge quel c'ha maggior fretta;   123

Paradiso I

> e ora lì, come a sito decreto,
> cen porta la virtù di quella corda
> che ciò che scocca drizza in segno lieto.   126
>   Vero è che, come forma non s'accorda
> molte fiate a l'intenzion de l'arte,
> perch' a risponder la materia è sorda,   129
>   così da questo corso si diparte
> talor la creatura, c'ha podere
> di piegar, così pinta, in altra parte;   132
>   e sì come veder si può cadere
> foco di nube, sì l'impeto primo
> l'atterra torto da falso piacere.   135

(The providence that regulates all this makes forever quiet with its light the Heaven within which turns that of greatest speed, and thither now as to a place appointed the power of that bowstring is bearing us which directs what it shoots at a joyous mark. It is true that, as a shape often does not accord with the art's intention because the material is deaf and unresponsive, so sometimes the creature, having the power, thus impelled, to turn aside another way, deviates from this course and, as fire may be seen to fall from a cloud, so the primal impulse, diverted by false pleasure, is turned to the earth.)

The Heaven that is forever quiet (or satisfied) with the light of God (122), is, of course, the Empyrean, within which turns the fastest revolving Heaven, or *Primum Mobile* (123); it is, indeed, towards the Empyrean that the power of the divine order is bearing them, as to a place preordained for their goal (124–6). The image of the bowstring aiming at a joyous mark is far from inappropriate in the context, and serves also as a link with the related image of the bow we have met a few lines above (119).

In lines 127–35 Beatrice, somewhat unexpectedly perhaps, interposes a parenthesis on the deviations one observes from the natural tendency of the human soul she has been describing. It is as though she suspects Dante of saying to himself: all this is very well, but how is one to explain, then, evil and sin? How does one account for the confusion, disorder and corruption one sees in the world? Or (as an early commentator, Benvenuto da Imola, put it) how is it that so few men attain to blessedness in Heaven? The answer to these unspoken questions touches upon one of the crucial problems of the *Comedy*, that of free will, which has been expounded in Cantos XVI and XVIII of *Purgatorio* and will be further developed in Canto IV of *Paradiso*. Man has the power to follow his natural inclination, but does not always use it (130–2); or, to paraphrase the text more closely: thus sometimes man ('the creature') deviates from this course; man who has the power to turn aside another way, that is, towards evil, although he is naturally disposed to good ('così pinta'). Once again two similes, one before and one after the terzina, serve to add clarity and power of conviction to the point that has been made: the work of a craftsman does not always correspond to his intention, because it may happen that the material is deaf and unresponsive (127–9); the other simile is that of fire, which tends upwards but which may be seen falling from a cloud towards the earth in the shape of lightning (133–4), and so man betrays his primal impulse and turns to earth, diverted by false pleasure (134–5).

> Non dei più ammirar, se bene stimo,
> lo tuo salir, se non come d'un rivo
> se d'alto monte scende giuso ad imo.   138
>   Maraviglia sarebbe in te se, privo
> d'impedimento, giù ti fossi assiso,
> com' a terra quïete in foco vivo'.
>   Quinci rivolse inver' lo cielo il viso.   142

(If I am right, thou shouldst no more wonder at thy ascent than at a stream falling from a mountain-height to the foot; it would be a wonder in thee if, freed from hindrance, thou hadst remained below, as on earth would be stillness in living flame.' Then she turned her eyes again to the sky.)

Now, the logical conclusion of the whole chain of arguments: Dante's ascent is as natural and as little surprising as the fact of the water of a stream flowing downwards, since he, Dante, has been purged from sin in Purgatory and is free of all hindrance (139–40: note the onomatopoeic rhythm of line 138, obtained by a succession of no less than five words of two syllables). If the opposite were to happen, and Dante did not soar above the earth, *that* would be surprising: as surprising as stillness in living flame (139–41).

The Canto concludes with a factual line, seemingly uncharged with emotion. Beatrice's gaze turns again to the contemplation of God; but it is an appropriate and significant conclusion, it seems to me, because it directs our minds to the desire for God; and the desire for God is the ground base for the themes that dominate the Canto.

Paradiso VI

In Cantos II–V Dante and his guide Beatrice ascend to the Heaven of the Moon, which is nearest to the Earth, and then to the second Heaven, where they enter the planet Mercury. Dante is soon surrounded by 'more than a thousand' souls who are almost hidden in the light they themselves radiate. Encouraged by Beatrice, he questions one of them who has offered to enlighten him. In essence, his questions (to be answered in the next Canto) are: who was the soul and why was he there? which implies: what kind of spirits make their appearance in the second Heaven? The final part of Canto V is, in fact, an introduction to Canto VI artistically and stylistically, as well as with regard to the unfolding of the narrative; the scene becomes more and more radiant with light as the Canto draws towards its close, and in the final lines our attention is roused by a display of choice words and rhetorical devices — an indication that something special will happen in the next Canto: the reader's expectations will not be disappointed.

Canto VI ranges through the whole course of Roman history from the origins of Rome to republican and imperial times and then on to Charlemagne. It has been described as 'the celebration of a ritual', and with some justification, for the poet brings a definitely religious outlook to bear on his view of politics. And this Canto is mainly about politics; history is pressed into service in order to explain and justify the order of the world firmly believed by Dante to have been predisposed by God for the happiness of mankind. Since the poet took this standpoint, it would be wrong to expect an objective or dispassionate outline of Roman history; what we find is a highly subjective, indeed idealized, interpretation of events.

A particular feature that distinguishes Canto VI from the other ninety-nine of the *Comedy* is the absence (apart from the concluding lines) of the kind of poetry that appeals to the emotions. Nevertheless it has eloquence, it is a grand overall conception, a poetic *tour de force* of compactness and sustained power, carrying the reader along with breathtaking speed in the sixty or so swift lines that form the central section, from the God-willed beginning, through those miraculous, predestined events, all meant to pave the way to the inevitable climax. Dante had already rehearsed those events and those arguments in the fourth book of the *Convivio* and in the second book of the *Monarchia*, and in both works his prose had taken on an inspired tone; here he gives poetic expression to the same ideas.

It is part of the symmetry governing the vast structure of the *Comedy* that politics should play a dominant role in Canto VI of each Cantica. In the *Inferno*, as we have seen, Dante devotes Canto VI to condemning the factions that rent Florence asunder; in *Purgatorio*, and again here in *Paradiso*, as it will presently become apparent, he rises from party politics in a city-state to a higher vision and points to a remedy for the discords and strife prevailing not just in Florence, but everywhere, both in Italy and in the world — this remedy being the establishment (or re-establishment, as he saw it) of the authority or temporal power of the Emperor over all men. Both in the *Purgatorio* and in the *Paradiso* the rivalry between Guelphs and Ghibellines is the main target of Dante's denunciation. Has number six, one might ask, any special significance in this connection? The question should not be lightly dismissed in view of the great importance Dante attached to numbers. That he attached a symbolic value to number six is clear, I think, from its fairly frequent use in the allegories of the *Comedy*; but the main clue is in the *Convivio* (IV, xxiii, 11 and 15), where the sixth hour of the day, i.e. the one that coincides with noon in the canonical day, is said to be most endowed with nobility and virtue. For this reason, Dante believed (following the gospel of Luke), it was the hour of the death of Christ. One might add the suggestion that etymological links can be seen between number six and Italian words conveying ideas of order and settledness, such as *assestare* or *mettere in sesto* ('to set in order', 'to settle'). Moreover, Dante uses 'sesto' once (*Paradiso*, XIX, 40) in its original meaning of 'compass', an instrument for describing circles ('lo cerchio è perfettissima figura': *Convivio*, II, xiii, 26), which could well be taken to indicate symmetry and carefully measured and controlled activity — in other words, order as opposed to disorder.

A peculiarity that is fairly obvious even at first glance is that, alone among the hundred Cantos of the *Comedy*, this is a monologue from beginning to end, with one and the same spirit speaking without a single line of linking narrative, without the slightest interruption, and with no other character intervening. The speaker is the sixth-century Emperor Justinian, who ruled over the Eastern Empire from Constantinople; in name, as well as in his career, he was an appropriate choice to be the spokesman (if this is the right word) of the spirits in the Heaven of Mercury, and to be made into a symbol of justice in a Canto where the concept of justice (justice in politics, in legislating, in individual behaviour) is constantly in evidence. But, before we come to Justinian, let us look at the opening lines of the Canto.

> 'Poscia che Costantin l'aquila volse
> contr' al corso del ciel, ch'ella seguio
> dietro a l'antico che Lavina tolse,   3
>   cento e cent' anni e più l'uccel di Dio
> ne lo stremo d'Europa si ritenne,
> vicino a' monti de' quai prima uscìo;   6
>   e sotto l'ombra de le sacre penne
> governò 'l mondo lì di mano in mano,
> e, sì cangiando, in su la mia pervenne.   9

('After Constantine turned back the Eagle against the course of Heaven, which it had followed behind him of old that took Lavinia to wife, for two hundred years and more the bird of God remained on the bounds of Europe, near the mountains from which it first came forth; and there it ruled the world under the shadow of the sacred wings, passing from hand to hand, and, so changing, came into mine.)

The first nine lines are a preamble to the Emperor's great speech, and their impressive tone is admirably suited to the purpose of setting the scene for the majestic survey of Roman history that follows; they conjure up vistas of long epochs, of vast spaces, and they introduce the Eagle, 'the bird of God' (4) whose wings are sacred (7), the 'most holy' symbol of the Empire (32). From now on the Roman Eagle will be the subject of Justinian's discourse. These nine lines also serve to fill a gap in the ensuing recital of Roman history, which jumps from the Emperor Titus straight to Charlemagne. They briefly refer to the two hundred years and more (4) that ran from the transfer of the capital to Byzantium, i.e., to the new city of Constantinople ('on the bounds of Europe', not far from the mountains of the region of Troy: 5–6) until the time of the election of Justinian — a slight inaccuracy, for the interval was, in fact, not just over, but just under, two centuries.

The very first line of the Canto is also an occasion for a reference (admittedly, an oblique one) to the fateful donation of Constantine, the alleged grant by this Emperor to Pope Sylvester of the sovereignty of Italy and of the whole West, and therefore the alleged source of the temporal power of the Popes, since Dante's contemporaries saw a link between the so-called donation and the transfer of the capital. Dante, of course, deplored the donation again and again in his works.

Note the undoubtedly deliberate ambiguity of line 2: the capital was moved from west to east, that is in the opposite direction to the course of the sun from east to west; but the seemingly factual expression 'against the course of the sun' could easily be taken to imply: 'against the course willed by Heaven'. This interpretation is corroborated, to my mind, by the reference in the next line to Aeneas ('him of old who took Lavinia to wife'), and to the Eagle having followed him in his journey; for the westward journey of Aeneas from Troy to Italy was regarded by Dante as the first link in the providential chain of events leading to the establishment of the universal Empire of Rome.

> Cesare fui e son Iustinïano,
> che, per voler del primo amor ch'i' sento,
> d'entro le leggi trassi il troppo e 'l vano.   12
> E prima ch'io a l'ovra fossi attento,
> una natura in Cristo esser, non più,
> credea, e di tal fede era contento;   15
> ma 'l benedetto Agapito, che fue
> sommo pastore, a la fede sincera
> mi dirizzò con le parole sue.   18
> Io li credetti, e ciò che 'n sua fede era,
> vegg' io or chiaro sì, come tu vedi
> ogne contradizione e falsa e vera.   21

(I was Caesar and am Justinian who, by the will of the Primal Love which moves me, removed from the laws what was superfluous and vain. And before I had put my mind to the work I believed that there was but one nature, and not a second, in Christ, and with that faith I was satisfied; but the blessed Agapetus, who was Chief Shepherd, directed me by his words to the true faith. I believed him, and what he held by faith I now see as clearly as thou seest that every contradiction is [made up] of false and true [that is, of a pair of contradictory statements, one must be false and one true].)

Though not stated, the contrast between Constantine and Justinian is forcibly conveyed. The former had impaired the unity of the Empire and had moved its capital from the city God had destined for it; Justinian, on the contrary, was clearly regarded by Dante as the great unifier. This emerges from his answer (10–27) to the first question that is put to him. He, formerly an emperor, now plain Justinian (note the different tenses of the verbs in line 10), is in the first place the legislator, the promoter of the *Corpus Juris* — that is, of course, of the great work of co-ordination and rationalization of a mass of laws that had been accumulating for centuries in republican and imperial Rome (10–12). Line 12 is an accurate, succinct description of the nature and purpose of Justinian's compilation; the universal rule of law is the precondition for the political unification of the world, and therefore it is undertaken 'by the will of the Primal Love' (11). Religious and epic tones alternate n the whole of this passage; we will shortly read in line 23 that it is God, of His grace' who inspired him with his high task.

Next, in lines 13–21, Justinian recalls his conversion to the true faith, he word 'fede' being repeated three times (15, 17 and 19) to stress that his was a precondition of his reform and conquests — good works pro-:eed from faith. Justinian's conversion means a repudiation of the Monophysite heresy, in which a misguided desire to affirm that Christ s truly God led to a denial that he was truly man: in short, as the name uggests, the Monophysites asserted that Christ had only one nature, he divine. Now, it is true that Justinian's Empress, Theodora, and the ew Patriarch of Constantinople, Anthimus, had strong leanings owards this heresy; and that Pope Agapetus went to Constantinople n 535 A.D., deposed Anthimus and obtained from Justinian an cknowledgement of the true faith, and of the spiritual power being rested in the Church of Rome; but it seems that the Emperor had never ubscribed to the Monophysite heresy. It is likely that Dante (or his ource, whichever it was) drew the story of Justinian's deviation and onversion from the *Liber Pontificalis*, where it is told in precisely the ame terms.

> Tosto che con la Chiesa mossi i piedi,
> a Dio per grazia piacque di spirarmi
> l'alto lavoro, e tutto 'n lui mi diedi; 24
>   e al mio Belisar commendai l'armi,
> cui la destra del ciel fu sì congiunta,
> che segno fu ch'i' dovessi posarmi. 27

As soon as I took my way beside the Church it pleased God, of His grace, to nspire me with the high task; and I gave myself wholly to it and committed rms to my Belisarius, with whom the right hand of Heaven was so joined that was a sign for me to rest from them.)

he other task of unification undertaken by Justinian (25–7) takes third lace, for the restoration of the Roman Empire to its former territorial oundaries was entrusted to Belisarius. Still, Justinian was successful n this sphere too, even though Spain and Gaul remained unconquered. Iow unlike his behaviour had been from that of later Holy Roman mperors in Dante's own time, who had neglected their duty of exer-ising supreme temporal authority over all men.

There are blemishes in Justinian's record; Dante either did not know f them or chose to ignore them, although some interpreters see in his ffectionate reference to 'my Belisarius' (25) a kind of atonement for he shabby treatment Justinian is alleged to have meted out to him. Be is as it may, the fact remains that Dante aimed at providing a model

for an Emperor striving for peace and justice in harmony with the
spiritual power, rather than at portraying the historical Justinian.

> Or qui a la question prima s'appunta
> la mia risposta; ma sua condizione
> mi stringe a seguitare alcuna giunta,   30
>   perché tu veggi con quanta ragione
> si move contr' al sacrosanto segno
> e chi 'l s'appropria e chi a lui s'oppone.   33

(Here ends, then, my reply to the first question; but its tenor constrains me to
make some addition to it, so that thou mayst see with what reason they act
against the most holy standard, both those that take it for their own and those
that oppose it.)

Having satisfied Dante's curiosity as to his first point, Justinian hints
briefly but very clearly (31–3, and again later on) at the main purpose
of his discourse, which is to prove that both those who support and
those who oppose the holy imperial standard, Ghibellines, that is, and
Guelphs alike, have gone astray, because both sides pursue only their
own selfish motives, instead of obeying the Emperor, and thus they
keep the world in turmoil. Thus, although the central section of Justinian's monologue, setting out the solemn, inexorable unfolding of
Roman history from its inception to its climax, looms largest in the
structure of the Canto, it must be seen as subservient to the issue that
is uppermost in Dante's mind. He means to clinch the point that party
factions and petty squabbles should cease and that all men should
acknowledge the sacredness and dignity of the universal Empire.

There is no doubt, however, that the poet makes this survey of the
flight of the Roman Eagle the centrepiece of the Canto, drawing on all
his mastery of rhetoric and technique. His mind was a storehouse of
reminiscences from several Latin poets, but one can safely say that the
largest number of suggestions were drawn from Virgil's *Aeneid*, many
of them from Book III. I think, though, that Virgil did more than provide a poetic model. Dante recalls in the *Monarchia* (II, i, 2) that when
he was younger he had thought that the Romans had conquered the
world by force of arms alone, without any foundation of right — a view
that he later rejected (*Convivio*, IV, iv, 12). It seems that his study of
Virgil was instrumental in suggesting to him the providential character
of the history of Rome, and it is worth noting that in this Canto Dante
takes up the story where Virgil leaves off. The other general point
worth making about these sixty-three lines (34–96) is the frequent use
of latinisms, exceptionally high even for the *Paradiso*: there is no doubt

that it is deliberate and meant to enhance the effect Dante wishes to produce on his readers.

> Vedi quanta virtù l'ha fatto degno
> di reverenza; e cominciò da l'ora
> che Pallante morì per darli regno.   36
>   Tu sai ch'el fece in Alba sua dimora
> per trecento anni e oltre, infino al fine
> che i tre a' tre pugnar per lui ancora.   39
>   E sai ch'el fé dal mal de le Sabine
> al dolor di Lucrezia in sette regi,
> vincendo intorno le genti vicine.   42

(See what valour has made it worthy of reverence, beginning from the hour when Pallas died to give it sway. Thou knowest that it made its stay in Alba for three hundred years and more, till at the last, still for its sake, the three fought with the three; and thou knowest what it did under seven kings, from the wrongs of the Sabine women to the woe of Lucrece, conquering the neighbour peoples round about.)

The passage begins with a solemn statement (34–5), its rhythm made slower and more impressive by the enjambment 'degno Di reverenza'. The sudden quickening of the pace immediately afterwards is all the more effective. Without any preamble we are rushed into fast-moving narrative of memorable, portentous facts, the 'sacrosanto segno' (i.e. the Roman Eagle) being from now on the grammatical subject of each sentence. The first of these facts is the death of Pallas, son of King Evander, an ally of Aeneas; according to Virgil (Book X), Pallas was slain in battle by Turnus. The significance of this mythical episode (which, like everything else in the *Aeneid*, was treated by Dante as historical truth) lay in the fact that Aeneas inherited the territorial rights of Pallas, and this supplied the legal foundation for the establishment of Roman might and, eventually, of the Empire.

There follows a series of highlights from early Roman history, or even pre-history, for lines 37–8 refer to the three centuries of rule in Alba Longa by the descendants of Aeneas before the foundation of Rome, and line 39 records the duel in which the three Curiatii were defeated by the Horatii. The stanzas move swiftly through the use of anaphora ('Tu sai . . . ' 'E sai' . . . ' 'Sai . . . ') at the beginning of each of them, and the span of time they encompass is invariably a long one: lines 40–2 cover the period of the seven kings of Rome (from the Rape of the Sabine Women in the time of Romulus down to the suicide of Lucretia, which caused the expulsion of the last king, Tarquin).

> Sai quel ch'el fé portato da li egregi

Dante's 'Comedy'

Romani incontro a Brenno, incontro a Pirro,
incontro a li altri principi e collegi;   45
    onde Torquato e Quinzio, che dal cirro
negletto fu nomato, i Deci e ' Fabi
ebber la fama che volontier mirro.   48
    Esso atterrò l'orgoglio de li Aràbi
che di retro ad Anibale passaro
l'alpestre rocce, Po, di che tu labi.   51
    Sott' esso giovanetti trïunfaro
Scipïone e Pompeo; e a quel colle
sotto 'l qual tu nascesti parve amaro.   54

(Thou knowest what it did when borne by the illustrious Romans against Brennus, against Pyrrhus, against the other princes and communes, so that Torquatus and Quinctius, named from his unkempt locks, the Decii and the Fabii, had the fame I rejoice to embalm. It brought low the pride of the Arabs who behind Hannibal passed the Alpine crags from which, Po, thou fallest. Under it, as youths, Scipio and Pompey triumphed, and to that hill beneath which thou wast born it showed itself bitter.)

Four terzine are enough to summarize the whole republican period: the victories in the defensive wars against the Gauls led by Brennus and against the Epirotes led by Pyrrhus (44); the military successes of Titus Manlius Torquatus and of Lucius Quinctius, the famous dictator named Cincinnatus because of his curly hair, rather than his unkempt locks, as Dante mistakenly thought (46–7); a whole cluster of heroes, all belonging to the families of the Decii and the Fabii, are celebrated with figurative myrrh (47–8); while the next terzina (49–51) deals with the wars against the Carthaginians, here anachronistically called Arabs, an appellation applied to the inhabitants of North Africa in Dante's own time, rather than in antiquity. The triumphs of Scipio Africanus and Pompey and the legendary destruction of Fiesole (situated on the hill beneath which Dante was born: 53–4) close the list and lead up to the culminating point.

    Poi, presso al tempo che tutto 'l ciel volle
redur lo mondo a suo modo sereno,
Cesare per voler di Roma il tolle.   57
    E quel che fé da Varo infino a Reno,
Isara vide ed Era e vide Senna
e ogne valle onde Rodano è pieno.   60
    Quel che fé poi ch'elli uscì di Ravenna
e saltò Rubicon, fu di tal volo,
che nol seguiteria lingua né penna.   63
    Inver' la Spagna rivolse lo stuolo,
poi ver' Durazzo, e Farsalia percosse
sì ch'al Nil caldo si sentì del duolo.   66

Paradiso VI

> Antandro e Simeonta, onde si mosse,
> rivide e là dov' Ettore si cuba;
> e mal per Tolomeo poscia si scosse.   69
> Da indi scese folgorando a Iuba;
> onde si volse nel vostro occidente,
> ove sentia la pompeana tuba.   72

(Then, near the time when Heaven willed to bring all the world to its own state of peace, Caesar, by the will of Rome, laid hold of it; and what it did from Var to Rhine, Isère saw and Loire and Seine and every valley from which the Rhône is filled. What it did when it issued from Ravenna and leapt the Rubicon was such a flight as no tongue or pen might follow. Towards Spain it wheeled the host, then towards Durazzo, and smote Pharsalia so that grief was felt on the burning Nile. Antandros and the Simois, whence it set out, it saw again, and the place where Hector lies; then roused itself — the worse for Ptolemy. From there it fell like lightning on Juba, then turned to your west, where it heard Pompey's trumpet.)

If the pace of the narrative was already fast, it now becomes even faster, 'like lightning' (70), in keeping with its subject — the man on whom the spotlight is turned: Julius Caesar, proverbial for the speed of his victories. Even so, no less than six terzine are necessary to run through his exploits, for he has been destined to predispose the world for the *plenitudo temporis*, the time willed by Heaven to bring the world to its own state of peace (55–6), in preparation for the birth of Christ. The figure of Julius Caesar was not seen by Dante as surrounded by a halo. He emerges in a somewhat ambiguous light from the various references made to him in the *Comedy*; sometimes he is presented unsympathetically, with the emphasis on his alleged vices (*Purgatorio*, XXVI, 73) or on his external attributes (his falcon eyes: *Inferno*, IV, 123). Here, however, we find no moral judgement or adverse comment. He appears simply as one of the main links in the series of events that stretched down from Aeneas to Henry VII, as one of the performers of those prodigies which led to the foundation of the Roman Empire, that is, of the universal monarchy, of which he is the true founder, the first Roman Emperor. Even the crossing of the Rubicon (61–2) is not regarded as an act of rebellion, but as an admirable deed, in fact, too great for words. The legal justification for it is found in line 57: Caesar took possession of the Eagle, or, one might say, laid hold of power, by the will of Rome.

The two lines with which the passage begins (55–6) have a fittingly slow, majestic rhythm, in marked contrast to the next one (57), which is so decisive and sharp. Lines 58–60 refer to the conquest of Gaul by listing rivers that bound or cross France; lines 64–6 summarize the first

139

stages of the civil war, with Caesar's Spanish campaign and his victory over Pompey at Pharsalia after landing at Dyrrachium. The reason why 'grief was felt on the burning Nile' (66) is that when Pompey fled to Egypt he was slain by Ptolemy. Ptolemy, in his turn, was shortly afterwards defeated by Caesar (69).

Lines 67 and 68 require close scrutiny. They tell how the sign of the Eagle, following Caesar, returns whence it began its flight when the dictator made a detour in the course of his campaign in order to visit the ruins of Troy; Simois is a river flowing near this city and Antandros is the harbour from which Aeneas sailed on his way to Italy, according to a tradition accepted by Virgil. This interlude in the flight of the Eagle suits Dante's purpose well, because the idea of linking the inception of the Empire with its divine origins has a powerful effect on the reader. His authority was Lucan, but Caesar's Trojan holiday has, in fact, no historical truth in it — it is a poetic invention.

The next terzina (70–2) concludes the story of Caesar's feats with the final stages of the civil war and the defeats of Juba, King of Mauritania, and then of those other supporters of Pompey still remaining in the West.

> Di quel che fé col baiulo seguente,
> Bruto con Cassio ne l'inferno latra,
> e Modena e Perugia fu dolente.　　　　　　　　　　　　75
> Piangene ancor la trista Cleopatra,
> che, fuggendoli innanzi, dal colubro
> la morte prese subitana e atra.　　　　　　　　　　　　78
> Con costui corse infino al lito rubro;
> con costui puose il mondo in tanta pace,
> che fu serrato a Giano il suo delubro.　　　　　　　　81

(Of what it wrought with its next bearer Brutus and Cassius bark in Hell, and Modena and Perugia were in grief. Still weeps because of it the wretched Cleopatra who, flying before it, took from the viper sudden and dreadful death. With him it ran as far as the Red Sea shore. With him it set the world in such peace that Janus's shrine was locked.)

For Dante, Augustus was the second in the series of emperors, and he claims nine lines in the description of the flight of the Eagle. However, if the outlines of Caesar's character have remained somewhat blurred in the previous passage, the figure of Augustus is even less incisively depicted. We learn that he vanquishes Brutus and Cassius (the barking of Brutus (74) should be understood, I think, as a manifestation of grief mixed with rage), and that he routs Mark Anthony at Modena, and Anthony's brother, Lucius Antonius, at Perugia; finally, he causes Cleopatra's suicide and conquers Egypt as far as the shores of the Red

Paradiso VI

Sea (79). But what really mattered to Dante and, indeed, to his contemporaries, is that the rule of Augustus coincided with the birth of Christ, and that at this time universal peace reigned (80–1).

> Ma ciò che 'l segno che parlar mi face
> fatto avea prima e poi era fatturo
> per lo regno mortal ch'a lui soggiace,   84
>   diventa in apparenza poco e scuro,
> se in mano al terzo Cesare si mira
> con occhio chiaro e con affetto puro;   87
>   ché la viva giustizia che mi spira,
> li concedette, in mano a quel ch'i' dico,
> gloria di far vendetta a la sua ira.   90
>   Or qui t'ammira in ciò ch'io ti replìco:
> poscia con Tito a far vendetta corse
> de la vendetta del peccato antico.   93
>   E quando il dente longobardo morse
> la Santa Chiesa, sotto le sue ali
> Carlo Magno, vincendo, la soccorse.   96

(But what the standard that moves my speech had done before and was yet to do throughout the mortal kingdom that is subject to it, comes to seem small and dim if with clear eye and right affection we look at it in the hand of the third Caesar; for the Living Justice that inspires me granted to it, in his hand of whom I speak, the glory of doing vengeance for His wrath. And now marvel at what I unfold to thee: that afterwards it ran with Titus to do vengeance on the vengeance for the ancient sin. Then, under its wings, when the Lombard tooth bit Holy Church, Charlemagne won victory and succoured her.)

And thus we come to the climax of the unfolding of Roman history, the reign of the third emperor, Tiberius, marked by such glory (90) as to dim anything that the sign of the Eagle had done before and was to do later (the Latinism 'era fatturo' (83) adds a portentous quality to the statement, all the more as it is a rhyme word; just like other Latinisms, 'colubro', 'rubro', 'delubro' in the two immediately preceding terzine). The fact that the fame of Tiberius has never overcome the hostile judgement passed on him by Tacitus is entirely overlooked by Dante. It is, in fact, of some interest to note in passing that no Roman emperor, however notorious for his vices, misdeeds or responsibility for the persecution of Christians, is to be found in the *Inferno*. All that matters, in the case of Tiberius, is that his was the glory of doing vengeance for God's just wrath (90). As explained in the second book of the *Monarchia*, Christ's Passion would not have been a punishment, or 'vengeance', for the original sin, and would not have extinguished divine wrath, if it had not been inflicted by a legitimate power; the legitimate character of the Roman Empire and its jurisdiction over all

Dante's 'Comedy'

mankind were therefore necessary conditions for the redemption of the sins of men. Tiberius, the emperor on whose authority Pontius Pilate acted, was then another cog in the mechanism of Providence, and an important one.

However, a later emperor, Titus, wreaks vengeance on the vengeance when he destroys Jerusalem (92–3). Now Dante underlines in line 91 with the intellectual glee of a scholastic theologian the apparent contradiction implicit in an event being at the same time glorious and deserving punishment as a crime (or, to put it different-ly, a just vengeance having to be avenged in its turn). The contradic-tion will be resolved by Beatrice in Canto VII (19–51): if the Passion of Christ is seen in the light of His human nature, it was just, for it punished the original sin; if it is seen in the light of his divine nature, it was a crime, as it was inflicted on the Son of God. Thus, lines 92 and 93, deemed by some commentators to be among the most ingenious and subtle pieces of logic in the whole poem, rest on that dual nature of Christ which had been denied by the Monophysite heresy; they strike me as acquiring an even stronger emphasis on account of their being uttered by Justinian, since earlier in the same Canto we have been told that he repudiated just that heresy and acknowledged the dual nature of Christ. Conversely, it can now be seen that the space devoted to Justinian's attitude towards the Monophysite belief in the first part of the Canto is not excessive, in view of the relevance of the issue to one of the keystones of Dante's religious and political edifice. Justinian's great description of the flight of the Eagle ends with Charlemagne com-ing to the succour of the Church when the Lombards attack it (94–6) — a leap of seven centuries from Titus to an Emperor who was crowned in the year 800; but it serves to establish the continuity between the an-cient Empire of Rome and the modern concept of the Holy Roman Empire.

> Omai puoi giudicar di quei cotali
> ch'io accusai di sopra e di lor falli,
> che son cagion di tutti vostri mali.   99
>   L'uno al pubblico segno i gigli gialli
> oppone, e l'altro appropria quello a parte,
> sì ch'è forte a veder chi più si falli.   102
>   Faccian li Ghibellin, faccian lor arte
> sott' altro segno, ché mal segue quello
> sempre chi la giustizia e lui diparte;   105
>   e non l'abbatta esto Carlo novello
> coi Guelfi suoi, ma tema de li artigli
> ch'a più alto leon trasser lo vello.   108

> Molte fïate già pianser li figli
> per la colpa del padre, e non si creda
> che Dio trasmuti l'armi per suoi gigli!   111

(Now thou canst judge of such men as I accused before, and of their offences, which are the cause of all your ills; the one opposes to the public standard the yellow lilies and the other claims it for a party, so that it is hard to see which offends the more. Let the Ghibellines carry on their arts under another standard, for of this he is always a bad follower who severs it from justice; and let not this new Charles strike at it with his Guelphs, but let him fear its claws, which have torn the hide from a greater lion. Many a time ere now have the children wept for the father's fault, and let him not think God will change arms for his lilies.)

These five terzine draw a lesson from the story that has just been told; the rebuke addressed to both Guelphs and Ghibellines, blamed at the outset by Justinian for the present disorder in the world, is reiterated now in even stronger terms. He reproaches the Guelphs for opposing the yellow lilies of the House of France to the public standard, or universal symbol, of the Empire (100). (The Anjou Kings of Naples enjoyed the support of the Guelphs in their fight against the Emperor. At that time the King of Naples was Charles II, described as 'new' (106) to distinguish him from his father, Charles I.) Likewise, Justinian censures the Ghibellines for claiming the imperial standard as exclusively the emblem of their own party (101–4).

> Questa picciola stella si correda
> d'i buoni spirti che son stati attivi
> perché onore e fama li succeda: 114
>   e quando li disiri poggian quivi,
> sì disvïando, pur convien che i raggi
> del vero amore in sù poggin men vivi.   117
>   Ma nel commensurar d'i nostri gaggi
> col merto è parte di nostra letizia,
> perché non li vedem minor né maggi.   120
>   Quindi addolcisce la viva giustizia
> in noi l'affetto sì, che non si puote
> torcer già mai ad alcuna nequizia.   123
>   Diverse voci fanno dolci note;
> così diversi scanni in nostra vita
> rendon dolce armonia tra queste rote.   126

(This little star is adorned with good spirits whose deeds were done for the honour and glory that should follow them; and when desires mount there thus deviously then the rays of true love must needs mount upwards with less life. But in the measuring of our reward with our desert lies part of our happiness, for we see it to be neither less nor more; thus the Living Justice sweetens our affection so that they can never be warped to any evil. Diverse voices make

Dante's 'Comedy'

sweet music, so diverse ranks in our life render sweet harmony among these
wheels.)

This passage seems to me one of transition. Justinian ceases to be the
stern reprover of petty factions between parties and the solemn nar-
rator of crucial events in human history; his voice takes on the kind of
timbre one might associate with a soul in Paradise, a blessed spirit at
peace with himself and with God. It is difficult to illustrate this timbre
but one might point to the sound of certain rhymes ('raggi', 'gaggi',
'maggi'), to the choice of certain terms ('letizia', 'addolcisce', 'voci',
'dolci', 'dolce'). In Canto V Dante asked Justinian why he was in the
Heaven of Mercury; but the soul of the Emperor also answers here two
associated questions that must have been in Dante's mind: 'Who are
the souls who appear to Dante in the second Heaven?'; and: 'are they
less happy for being in one of the lower spheres?' Justinian explains that
the Heaven of Mercury is adorned with good spirits whose deeds were
performed for the sake of honour and glory, and who therefore pur-
sued the love of God less intensely (112–17). He then goes on to explain
that part of their happiness lies in their awareness of perfect divine
justice, which apportions rewards according to one's deserts (118–20)
— this being a clear development of Piccarda's answer to Dante's question on the same subject in Canto III, 85: 'E 'n la sua volontade è nostra
pace' ('in God's will is our peace'), the main difference being that Piccarda's famous words convey a sense of her femininity; while here the
precision of the explanation befits the *gravitas* of the legislator and
Roman emperor. No evil, Justinian continues (121–3), such as
dissatisfaction with their condition, or envy, can warp the spirits'
affection.

> E dentro a la presente margarita
> luce la luce di Romeo, di cui
> fu l'ovra grande e bella mal gradita.   129
>   Ma i Provenzai che fecer contra lui
> non hanno riso; e però mal cammina
> qual si fa danno del ben fare altrui.   132
>   Quattro figlie ebbe, e ciascuna reina,
> Ramondo Beringhiere, e ciò li fece
> Romeo, persona umìle e peregrina.   135
>   E poi il mosser le parole biece
> a dimandar ragione a questo giusto,
> che li assegnò sette e cinque per diece,   138
>   indi partissi povero e vetusto;
> e se 'l mondo sapesse il cor ch'elli ebbe
> mendicando sua vita a frusto a frusto,
>   assai lo loda, e più lo loderebbe'.   142

144

(Within this same pearl shines too the light of Romeo, whose great and noble work was ill rewarded; but the Provençals who wrought against him do not have the laugh, and indeed he takes an ill road who makes of another's well-doing a wrong to himself. Raymond Berengar had four daughters, each of them a queen, and Romeo, a man of low birth and a stranger, did this for him. And then crafty tongues moved him to call to account this just man, who rendered him seven and five for ten. Romeo left there poor and old; and if the world knew the heart he had, begging his bread by morsels, much as it praises him it would praise him more.')

I have implied that lines 124–6 sound like pure music of the supreme spheres. They could hardly be better calculated to predispose us for the closing part of the Canto, where the speaker introduces somewhat abruptly, but all the more effectively, another spirit in the Heaven of Mercury, Romieu de Villeneuve who was, indeed, a historical character (he was a minister of Raymond Berengar IV, Count of Provence in the first half of the thirteenth century). However I must add that some of the most moving details in Dante's story are clearly made of the stuff that can only be culled from legends. For some reason, Romeo was one of those people round whom legends grew in Dante's time, possibly because his name suggested a pilgrim, a wanderer who had been offered refuge in the Court of Count Raymond and who had given a good account of himself by his 'great and noble work' (129) as a wise and unselfish administrator and able negotiator of brilliant marriages for the four daughters of Raymond. Indeed, all of them actually became queens (133); one was the wife of Edward III of England. The envy of his fellow-courtiers (the Provençals of line 130) induced his lord to demand a reckoning of Romeo's administration (136–7); but he rendered Raymond seven and five for ten (138), i.e., he could prove that under his stewardship the Count's fortune had materially prospered; and then he departed into obscurity as poor as when he had somewhat mysteriously arrived, on his way back from a pilgrimage, if the early commentators are right to read so much in the adjective 'peregrina' (135).

The legendary part of Romeo's story includes his obscure origin, the undeserved disgrace into which he fell and his departure to resume a wandering life as a beggar; but it is also the part that must have had the strongest appeal for Dante. It enabled him to place side by side two spirits whose destinies on earth were in striking contrast with each other: Justinian at the peak of human power, and Romeo 'a man of low birth and a stranger' (135); but both were just men who have been rewarded with the same degree of blessedness in Paradise. Like Justinian, then, Romeo is to some extent a model or type; he symbolizes the dignity of one whose honesty and merits have been rewarded with ingratitude. As a character, he is only sketched in bare outline and on the whole he remains nebulous; but behind the pale image, at least one other, clearer image may be discerned: Romeo's resemblance to Dante is so obvious as to make it superfluous to labour the point. There is no doubt that the unjustly exiled poet ('exul immeritus', to quote his self-description) saw a kindred spirit in the pilgrim; he identified himself with Romeo's behaviour in adversity, with his proud decision to opt for a lonely, precarious but honourable life when faced with the injustice and incomprehension of others. Dante too (he tells us in the *Convivio*, I, iii, 4) had travelled all over Italy 'peregrino, quasi mendicando' ('a pilgrim, almost a beggar'); no wonder he imbued the final lines of the Canto (139–42) with such an intense pathos as to make them one of the lyrical highlights of the whole poem. Their transparent sincerity stems from their being almost an epitome of Dante's own fate in the last nineteen years of his life, and they brilliantly display his ability to convey feelings with the utmost economy of words.

Other parallels have been suggested, the most plausible being that drawn between Romeo and another just man who had served his lord well and had succumbed to calumny and envy, Pier della Vigna, whom Dante had encountered among the suicides, as is told in Canto XIII of the *Inferno*. I would be loath to push the parallel too far, although I recognize that Dante saw some similarity to his own destiny in Piero's fate, just as he did in the fate of Romeo. And perhaps the same note is struck in Canto X of *Paradiso* regarding Boethius (124–9) and Sigier (133–8), though admittedly more faintly in the last case.

A final word about the structure of the Canto. A superficial reading might give the impression that its various sections are somewhat disjointed, but this would be a misguided conclusion. The Canto falls roughly into three parts: the grand review of the course of the Roman Eagle, the introductory section leading up to it, and the final one; and it can be shown that they are mutually integrated and hang together as a coherent whole. The link between the first part and the central section is stated by Dante himself in the words of Justinian (28–32): the tenor of his answer to the first of Dante's questions (Canto V, 127: 'non so chi tu se', 'I don't know who you are') constrains him to make some addition ('alcuna giunta') in order to stress that all men owe reverence and obedience to the imperial authority (whereas the Ghibellines took it as an ally and protector of their own faction, and only of their own faction, and the Guelphs opposed it). The ensuing review of the flight of the Eagle is meant to demonstrate how wrong both parties are.

The link between the central part and the conclusion of the Canto lies in the very motives and impulses that prompted Dante to write the *Comedy* and spurred him on to persevere to the end; for the awareness of being entrusted with the mission of expounding the system devised by Providence for the world in order to secure happiness for mankind was interwoven with a strong feeling of the injustice that he had suffered when exiled from his own native city, Florence. The autobiographical overtones discernible in the Romeo episode are also, in some way, in the background of the rest of the Canto. Dante, a friend of justice rather than of this party or that, willing to pay the price for his choice, is the same Dante who during his exile and because of his exile had taken upon himself the task of persuading his fellow-men to tread the path so manifestly ordained by God.

Paradiso XVII

Having left the second Heaven, Dante and Beatrice rise through those of Venus and of the Sun (Cantos VIII–XIV) and reach the fifth Heaven. In Canto XVII we find them still in this sphere.

It is not by chance, but by design, that the Canto that we are about to examine is placed exactly in the centre of the *Paradiso*: in the symmetrical structure of the *Comedy* there is little room for coincidence. Canto XVII is the culmination of one of the most sustained episodes of the whole poem: Dante's encounter with his ancestor Cacciaguida, which, in its turn, takes place in the Heaven that holds the central position among the nine revolving Heavens, that of Mars, described as a 'stella forte' ('mighty star') in line 77, because it represents *fortitudo*, one of the four virtues that are necessary to the active life. The special place occupied by the fifth Heaven by virtue of its position had already been emphasized in the *Convivio* (II, xiii, 20), and adds to the momentous significance of the episode within the poem. Clearly, this is the place for Dante to bring together the many strands that he has woven into his vast fabric, these are the Cantos in which to embody the quintessence of his conception of man and the universe, and of the purpose of his lifelong work. Yet, on the surface at least, the episode appears to unfold primarily on a personal and historical plane; its bricks and mortar being not so much doctrinal or universal considerations, as the poet's own story and vicissitudes, and a view of the past and present state of Florence, his native city-state. With individual and civic preoccupations coming to the fore, philosophical and theological problems seem to have been discarded or, at least, relegated to the background, and the narrative holds the attention on the literal level. Could it be that an interlude occupying a crucial place in the final Cantica is used purely and simply to bring us down from Heaven to Earth? This would be a rash conclusion indeed. In fact, though many commentators have failed to see it, the narrative proceeds on more than one plane, and there is a deeper meaning and a more exalted purpose behind the story of Dante's meeting with Cacciaguida. In order to pinpoint this meaning and this purpose, a brief summary of the episode is needed.

In Canto XIV the souls of the warrior spirits in the Heaven of Mars form themselves into the pattern of a radiant cross. Soon after the beginning of Canto XV one of them speeds to the foot of the cross like a shooting-star and greets Dante as affectionately as Aeneas's father Anchises had greeted his son in the Infernal Regions, according to the sixth book of the *Aeneid*, which is here explicitly quoted. Then the spirit reveals himself as Cacciaguida, the grandfather of Dante's grandfather, who lived in Florence between the end of the eleventh and the middle of the twelfth century, followed the Emperor Conrad III in the second crusade, was knighted by him, and died in about 1147 fighting against the infidel. At the same time, Cacciaguida draws a vivid picture of the simplicity of life in twelfth-century Florence and goes on to contrast it, particularly in Canto XVI, with Florence in Dante's time, which is described as corrupted and polluted by the immigration of greedy and ambitious newcomers. The encounter reaches its climax in Canto XVII, with which we are now concerned. Here, as we shall see, the poet learns from his ancestor that the future holds in store a life of wandering in exile for him.

For this reason, Canto XVII has been described, with some justification, as Dante's own canto *par excellence*. Yet the theme of his political misfortunes and of the hardships that are the consequence of banishment, which constantly recur both in the *Comedy* and in his other works, ought not to be viewed in isolation but in relation to other themes, all of them present here. First of all, there is the interpretation of Florentine history, which must have been slowly taking shape in Dante's mind during his exile. As we have already seen, this interpretation came to pervade the pages of the *Comedy* more and more and is now spelt out by Cacciaguida: from its pristine, untarnished virtues in the early twelfth century, Florence has sunk to its present depravity and turmoil on account of its rapid growth and the consequent corrupting influx of strangers from the surrounding countryside and townships. It is, of course, an interpretation that no historian would accept as accurate. By 1300 the town had grown beyond recognition, the number of its inhabitants (perhaps about 100,000) was four or five times greater than a century and a half before, and this expansion had brought about problems. However Dante ignores the bright side of the picture: the splendid reality of the city's economic and industrial development, which had made it the most flourishing banking, manufacturing and trading centre in the Western world. This development had caused the increase in the population and, in its turn, was made possible by it. A concomitant to the greater wealth and power of Florence had been the blossoming of painting, sculpture and architecture, not to speak of literature. Dante, however, preferred to focus on the obverse side of the coin. He knew that when he had been exiled he had suffered a great injustice, and he knew that the political upheaval itself that had caused his exile had been brought about by injustice and treachery. In his solitude and isolation, he meditated, naturally enough, upon the causes of the malaise of his town, and formulated this oversimplified and one-sided explanation, which in addition probably owes something to the scorn of an aristocrat and scholar for the mercantile pursuits that were the mainstay of Florentine power and splendour, and to his lack of interest in economic considerations. In fact, he came to feel passionately that the moral decadence he saw was the root of his own, and of his city's, troubles, the two being conceived as indissolubly linked. But, as he evolved that overall design for the welfare of mankind which is so forcefully expounded in the *Monarchia*, he realized that the corruption of Florence was only a facet of the wider corruption that affected the other towns of Italy and indeed the whole world, owing to the fact that the Emperor neglected to perform the duties that had been assigned to him by God, and that the Pope usurped the Emperor's functions. He says explicitly in Canto XVI (58–60) that the original purity of Florence would have remained undefiled by immigration if the people who were most degenerate (i.e. the clergy) had not been a step-mother, but rather as kind as a mother to Caesar (i.e. to the Empire).

The task that Dante sets himself is nothing less than bringing about a solution to this world-wide disorder — in fact, as he sees it, the one possible solution. Indeed, he believes he has been invested by Providence with the mission of making humanity aware of the system ordained by God for its happiness; this, as we shall see, is implied by what Cacciaguida tells Dante in the final lines of Canto XVII. It is clear, then, that the three main themes of the Cacciaguida episode (the poet's exile, the corruption of Florence, which is almost an epitome, or a blueprint, of the corruption of the world, and the mission of salvation, which is the main purpose of the poem) are intimately interwoven; only if all this is borne in mind can we see Canto XVII, as well as the two previous Cantos, in their proper light. It had been his exile that had lifted Dante (and he was deeply aware of this) from the narrow range of local politics to the wide perspective of a universal monarchy set up for the welfare of all men, and had determined and justified the mission he had undertaken. His exile and his mission, his misfortunes and what had come out of them, his banishment and his poem came, therefore, to be seen in one and the same context as something that had been willed by Providence for a higher end. And this went together with a profound belief that the wrongs he had suffered were to be righted; that peace, harmony and virtue were to return to Florence and that the system predisposed by Providence was to be established in the world, for it was unthinkable that God would allow injustice to be perpetuated on earth.

Dante's consciousness of being an instrument of Providence seems to have become firmer with the progress of the *Comedy*, feeding on the growing extent of his poetic achievement. It is first clearly expressed in the last two Cantos of *Purgatorio*. After his confession of personal sin in Canto XXXI, and after being shown, at the end of that Canto, a vision of Beatrice's unveiled glory, Dante is conducted to the centre of the Earthly Paradise where he sees the tree of the knowledge of good and evil, now withered and leafless in consequence of the sin of Adam (*Purgatorio*, XXXII, 13–39; cf. Genesis 2: 9, 16–17). He then sees the tree renewed through the agency of the Gryphon, representing Christ; and then, at the foot of the same tree, sees allegorically enacted the woes and sins of the Christian world, these being represented by a progressive desecration of the Chariot, the symbol of the Church, on which Beatrice first appears (*ibid*. 49–60 and 109–60). To all this Dante is commanded by Beatrice to bear witness, on his return to the world of mortal men, 'in pro del mondo che mal vive' ('for the good of the world that lives ill': 103–5). This command is reiterated in Canto XXXIII, and is coupled with a prophecy of a coming reform of the Church; this reform being associated with some future 'heir of the Eagle', that is, with an Emperor who will be God's minister on earth (*Purgatorio*, XXXIII, 52–4 and 34–45).

It is that reiterated commission to Dante as both poet and prophet which is now solemnly confirmed by Cacciaguida. In this central section of the *Paradiso*, moreover, with five sixths of his task completed, the moment has come — here where the main stress falls precisely on Dante as a citizen of Florence — for placing his exile in its proper setting, for relating it, that is, to the extraordinary vocation first openly revealed to him by Beatrice. Now he can at last portray himself as being another Aeneas, another Paul, whereas the dismayed pilgrim of *Inferno*, II, 32 had said: 'Io non Enea, io non Paolo sono' ('I am not Aeneas, I am not Paul'). Indeed, the first greeting imparted to him by Cacciaguida contains more than a hint that his journey is no less significant than those of the forefather of the Roman Empire and of the great

Dante's 'Comedy'

apostle who describes his *raptus* into the third Heaven (II Corinthians 12: 2–4).

As Aeneas had met his father in Hades, so Dante meets his forebear; it is a happy and poetical stroke of imagination to engineer a kind of family reunion, and to introduce into the poem this figure, almost surrounded by a legendary halo, made glorious by his being a crusader and a martyr who had fought for his faith, and also made venerable by distance in time as well as by ancient nobility. Who could have been more appropriate to play the part that Cacciaguida plays, of the commemorator of a virtuous past, the scathing reprover of the evils of present times, the unflinching but paternally sympathetic prophet of personal misfortunes and announcer of Dante's sublime appointed task, than an ancestor, so near to the poet, and at the same time so far removed? Not even Beatrice would have been appropriate, for she has been instrumental in achieving another goal of Dante's journey, that of purification from sin and attainment of perfection; she has pitilessly rebuked her lover for going astray from the path of virtue and knowledge, and this could hardly have been artistically consistent with a later solemn affirmation of the providential nature of his journey.

Canto XVII can be divided into three sections, the middle one being Cacciaguida's main speech (37–99), and the first one leading up to it.

> Qual venne a Climenè, per accertarsi
> di ciò ch'avëa incontro a sé udito,
> quei ch'ancor fa li padri ai figli scarsi;   3
>   tal era io, e tal era sentito
> e da Beatrice e da la santa lampa
> che pria per me avea mutato sito.   6
>   Per che mia donna 'Manda fuor la vampa
> del tuo disio', mi disse, 'sì ch'ella esca
> segnata bene de la interna stampa: 9
>   non perché nostra conoscenza cresca
> per tuo parlare, ma perché t'ausi
> a dir la sete, sì che l'uom ti mesca'.   12

(As was he who came to Clymene to find out the truth of that which he had heard against himself — he who still makes fathers chary with their sons — so was I, and so I was perceived to be by both Beatrice and by the holy lamp that previously had changed its place for me. Wherefore, my lady said: 'Send out the flame of your desire, so that it may issue well marked with the inward stamp; not in order to add to our knowledge by what you say, but that you may accustom yourself to declaring your thirst, so that drink be poured out for you.')

The simile with which the Canto opens may be felt to be somewhat laboured. Dante has heard so many grave words (23) about his fate, both in Hell and in Purgatory, in the form of prophecies (prophecies after the event: remember that the fictional date of the journey is 1300, whereas the *Comedy* was written several years later), that his mood is one of uncertainty and curiosity, like that of him who still makes fathers wary with their sons (3): that is, of Phaethon, who in Ovid's version of the story had heard doubts expressed as to his being a son of Apollo, and went to his mother Clymene to be reassured (1); whereupon he was allowed by his father to drive the chariot of the sun and so fell to his death. Beatrice encourages Dante to satisfy his thirst for knowledge (7–9), and to ask Cacciaguida, the holy lamp who has previously sped to the foot of the cross for Dante's sake (6). Lines 10–12 explain why Dante has to speak his mind to the blessed spirits, although his words are superfluous, as the souls of Paradise can read his thoughts.

> 'O cara piota mia che sì t'insusi,
> che, come veggion le terrene menti
> non capere in trïangol due ottusi,   15
>   così vedi le cose contingenti
> anzi che sieno in sé, mirando il punto
> a cui tutti li tempi son presenti;   18
>   mentre ch'io era a Virgilio congiunto
> su per lo monte che l'anime cura
> e discendendo nel mondo defunto,   21
>   dette mi fuor di mia vita futura
> parole gravi, avvegna ch'io mi senta
> ben tetragono ai colpi di ventura;   24
>   per che la voglia mia saria contenta
> d'intender qual fortuna mi s'appressa:
> ché saetta previsa vien più lenta'.   27

('Dear stock whence I sprang, and who now soar so high that as it is with minds on earth when they see that no triangle has two obtuse angles, so you, gazing as you do on the point to which all times are present, see contingencies before they exist in themselves — whilst I was with Virgil, climbing the mountain that heals souls and descending into the world of death, things of ill omen were said to me about my future; for which reason, although in myself I feel foursquare against the blows of fortune, I should be glad to hear what chance has in store for me; for an arrow foreseen comes more slowly.')

The question that is asked in lines 13–27 begins with an affectionate form of address; Dante has already called the spirit that has been the seed of his lineage 'padre mio' ('my father'), the root of the tree from which he was descended; his ancestor too has shown the most tender solicitude for him, and described him as his son. Clearly Cacciaguida is a father-figure in the *Comedy*, another giver of that fatherly affection for which Dante was longing and of which he may have been starved in real life, for in the poem there is no lack of father-figures: from the most obvious of them all, Virgil, to Brunetto Latini, Guido Guinizelli and now Cacciaguida. A little later on, in line 35, we will find him designated as 'amor paterno'. Seen in this light, he is even more in keeping with his role.

The question itself that Dante asks has the purpose of eliciting from his forebear the prophecy of his exile. Cacciaguida can see future contingent things (16), that is, earthly events, with the same degree of certainty with which human minds can see obvious geometrical truths (14–17) by gazing on the point in which past, present and future are joined (that is on God: 17–18). He is now asked to enlighten Dante concerning the grave words obscurely hinting bleak developments that he has heard from time to time during his journey. Lines 23–7 give a measure of Dante's moral fibre. Line 27, sinewy and direct, is typical of the poet, although its sentiment is not original, but derived from Latin ancient or medieval sources; the word 'tetragono' (24) is of particular interest; like the simile of lines 14–15, it was, of course, borrowed from geometry, the science that is described in the *Convivio* (II, xiii, 27) as 'sanza macula d'errore e certissima per sé' ('without spot of error and most certain in itself'). It had been used with this meaning before in Aristotle's *Ethics*, but here it is as good as a newly coined adjective, and Dante's authority, as well as its impressive sound, have made it part of the Italian language.

> Così diss' io a quella luce stessa
> che pria m'avea parlato; e come volle
> Beatrice, fu la mia voglia confessa. 30
>   Né per ambage, in che la gente folle
> già s' inviscava pria che fosse anciso
> l'Agnel di Dio che le peccata tolle, 33
>   ma per chiare parole e con preciso
> latin rispuose quello amor paterno,
> chiuso e parvente del suo proprio riso: 36

(Thus did I address the light that first had spoken to me; declaring, as Beatrice wished, all my desire. Nor with dark riddles such as the foolish folk of old were ensnared by, before the Lamb of God who takes sins away was slain, but in clear words and precise speech did that paternal love reply, sheathed and revealed in his own smile.)

Dante's poem is indeed a mosaic of allusions, of well assimilated materials, of concealed and unconcealed quotations; there are two good examples in lines 31 and 33. 'Ambage' is meant to recall the 'ambages' of Virgil's Cumaean Sibyl ('horrendas canit ambages' ('she utters her frightening and intricate prophecy'): *Aeneid*, VI, 99), whereas line 33 is taken straight from liturgical language. Cacciaguida's speech, solemn though it is, has nothing of the dark sayings used by oracles to ensnare 'la gente folle' (the pagans: 31). Its 'preciso latin' (34–5) has aroused some controversy. Did Cacciaguida actually speak in Latin, as he had previously done, or is the term 'latin' used here in the generic sense of 'language', a sense with which Dante often endows it? Sound arguments could be mustered in support of both views, but I doubt if our appreciation or understanding of this passage would be much enhanced thereby. It is more rewarding to linger for a moment on the next line, expressive of the quiet joyfulness of this blessed spirit, the word 'riso', echoed later by 'rideva' in line 121, seeming so apt to the appearance of a spirit in Paradise; it is more than a smile that enveloped and revealed the soul of Cacciaguida as he is about to speak. One might even imagine that it is a glow of pleasure for the heights to which his distant but direct descendant has risen.

> 'La contingenza, che fuor del quaderno
> de la vostra matera non si stende,
> tutta è dipinta nel cospetto etterno;   39
>   necessità però quindi non prende
> se non come dal viso in che si specchia
> nave che per torrente giù discende.   42
>   Da indi, sì come viene ad orecchia
> dolce armonia da organo, mi viene
> a vista il tempo che ti s'apparecchia.   45

('Contingency, which does not extend outside the volume of your material world, is all depicted in the eternal vision; without, however, being thereby necessitated, any more than is a ship that goes downstream by the eye in which it is mirrored. It is from thence that there come to my sight, as to the ear sweet harmony from an organ, the times that are in store for you.)

The first nine lines of Cacciaguida's speech have the purpose of stressing the relationship between free will and predestination. Although, as Dante has already remarked, contingent, or human events are all depicted in God (37–9), it does not follow that free will is impaired (40). However, whereas philosophical and theological arguments are used elsewhere in the poem to define the nature of free will, here a poetic image endowed with singular visual clarity is equally or more effective: the movement of a ship that drops down a stream ('torrente' (42) means a fast-flowing river for Dante) is not determined by the eye in which it is mirrored. The reaffirmation of free will at this point is not only intended to bring into a central Canto a concept that is cruciàl to the poem, but also to emphasize Dante's free and steadfast acceptance both of a mission assigned to him by God and of its corollary, the misfortunes that have involved him in so much suffering. The simile in the next terzina has caused some eyebrows to be lifted. How could the dire events that are about to be recited be described as 'sweet harmony' (44)? Its appropriateness, however, is apparent if one bears in mind that Dante wishes to convey the ease and continuity with which the future reveals itself to Cacciaguida, and that the evils about to be predicted will lead to a glorious outcome; so much so that at the beginning of the next Canto Dante himself savours 'il dolce' ('the sweet') as well as 'l'acerbo' ('the bitter') of what he has been told.

> Qual si partio Ipolito d'Atene
> per la spietata e perfida noverca,
> tal di Fiorenza partir ti convene.   48
>   Questo si vuole e questo già si cerca,
> e tosto verrà fatto a chi ciò pensa
> là dove Cristo tutto dì si merca.   51
>   La colpa seguirà la parte offensa
> in grido, come suol; ma la vendetta
> fia testimonio al ver che la dispensa.   54

(As Hippolytus departed from Athens because of his cruel and treacherous stepmother, so must you leave Florence. This is resolved, it is already being schemed, it will soon be given effect by him who is plotting it there where Christ is up for sale every day. The blame will, as the cry goes, be laid as usual on the injured party; but the retribution will testify to the Truth that deals it out.)

Now the poet, through the vaticination of his ancestor, faces the recital of his banishment and of what it will mean for him (or, rather, what it meant). It is one of the most celebrated passages of the *Comedy*, in its transparently sincere recollection of hardships and adversity, and in its dignified vindication of innocence. Solitude, deprivation and humiliation are to be his lot, he is to be the victim of injustices and false accusations, but is to be proved right in the end, and to rise far above the men and events that have conspired to bring about his misfortunes. Right from the beginning of the prophecy, in lines 49–51, his exile is presented not only as a personal calamity, but as the outcome of a contest in which he is pitted against the chief culprit of the corruption affecting the world, Pope Boniface VIII, who is intent on pursuing his simoniac transactions rather than his functions of shepherd of mankind. Note how scathingly the Pope is branded in these three taut lines. It will be recalled that Boniface was already plotting with the

Paradiso XVII

Black faction of the Florentine Guelphs in 1300 for the overthrow of the White Guelphs in Florence, which took place at the end of 1301, and in which Dante was involved. The prophecy had begun with characteristic directness in the previous terzina where his banishment is announced. The comparison with the banishment of Hippolytus, driven out by the false accusation of his disappointed step-mother Phaedra (Dante had read the story in Ovid) serves to stress from the outset the injustice of the charges laid against him, and casts on Florence too, by implication, the reproach of having been, like Phaedra, a cruel and perfidious step-mother. Although, as usual, public opinion will blame the injured side (52–4), swift retribution will be testimony to the truth, for it is dispensed by God who is Truth — this retribution being a dark hint of the violent deaths of several of those who had been responsible for the upheaval of 1301.

> Tu lascerai ogne cosa diletta
> più caramente; e questo è quello strale
> che l'arco de lo essilio pria saetta.   57
> Tu proverai sì come sa di sale
> lo pane altrui, e come è duro calle
> lo scendere e 'l salir per l'altrui scale.   60

(You will leave everything you love most dearly; and this is the arrow the bow of exile first lets fly. You will know by experience how salty is the taste of another man's bread, how hard is the way up and down another man's stairs.)

These two terzinas demand little comment. Suffice to say that they are couched in a plain style, that their vocabulary is simple: ('ogne cosa', 'lo pane altrui', 'l'altrui scale'). One could, I suppose, weigh every syllable in order to try and extract the secret of their extraordinary intensity, point out the hammering effect of the first two words of each terzina ('Tu lascerai', 'Tu proverai') or the repetition of a key word like 'altrui'; but one would not get much nearer explaining how Dante has succeeded in conveying what it really feels like losing everything loved most dearly and climbing up and down another man's stairs. I, for my part, prefer to consider the subdued and meditative rhythm of a passage that is the distillation of long, cruel experience.

> E quel che più ti graverà le spalle,
> sarà la compagnia malvagia e scempia
> con la qual tu cadrai in questa valle;   63
> che tutta ingrata, tutta matta ed empia
> si farà contr' a te; ma, poco appresso,
> ella, non tu, n'avrà rossa la tempia.   66
> Di sua bestialitate il suo processo

157

Dante's 'Comedy'

farà la prova; sì ch'a te fia bello
averti fatta parte per te stesso. 69

(And what will weigh most heavily on you will be the evil and senseless company with which you must go down into this valley — so ungrateful, so crazy and savage against you will those men prove themselves — but before long it will be their brows, not yours, that will turn red. Their conduct will prove their brutish folly, so that it will be to your honour to have made a party by yourself.)

During the first year or two of his exile, Dante joined forces with the other White Guelphs who had been banished and, inevitably, with the Ghibellines, who had by then a far longer experience of exile; and he played a prominent part in the several attempts that were mounted to re-enter Florence and to oust the new regime. Dante's description of his companions as wicked and senseless (62) may well be coloured by the bitterness of the disagreements that must have supervened; though there is no gainsaying the fact that they were inefficient and irresolute, as well as occasionally unlucky, for their attempts failed one after another; and there are reports of treachery among their ranks. We learn, moreover, that they became ungrateful and insanely hostile towards Dante (64), although we know little about the details of these episodes, apart from unverifiable and vague accounts. As for their brows becoming red (66), this may well refer to shame, but current opinion is that Dante means 'red with blood', following a crushing defeat in the summer of 1304. What really matters is that in lines 68–9 we have his clear-cut and proud statement that he finally parted company with his fellow exiles and made a party for himself. As borne out by the *Convivio*, the *Monarchia*, the *Comedy* and his epistles, the fact is that by then his preoccupations were far higher than party politics, than strife between Guelphs and Ghibellines, or between White and Black Guelphs. These issues paled into insignificance in comparison with the scheme intended to establish ideal conditions for the happiness of humanity, which he saw more and more clearly in his mind. Thus, the moment in which he made a party for himself was a turning-point in his life. From then onwards he could conduct his lone crusade without hindrance from useless and quarrelsome associates and without the distraction of petty local considerations.

Lo primo tuo refugio e 'l primo ostello
sarà la cortesia del gran Lombardo
che 'n su la scala porta il santo uccello; 72
ch'in te avrà sì benigno riguardo,
che del fare e del chieder, tra voi due,
fia primo quel che tra li altri è più tardo. 75

158

Paradiso XVII

(Your first refuge and first shelter will be the courtesy of the great Lombard who bears on the ladder the sacred bird; who will hold you in such kind regard that as between doing and asking, whether on your side or his, that will precede which with others comes later.)

As for the following years of his exile, spent in many different towns and in various Courts, all he tells us here is that he enjoyed the hospitality of the Scala family in Verona. This passage is the only source of information for his early visit to this city, which is likely to have taken place before 1304, if the 'great Lombard' (71) is, as seems probable, Bartolomeo della Scala, who died in that year. The epithet is due to the fact that Verona was largely built on the west bank of the Adige, and therefore in a territory that Dante considered as Lombardy; the imperial eagle was added to the coat of arms of the Scala family (72) when Henry VII invested them with the dignity of vicars of the Empire, although this happened a few years after the death of Bartolomeo. One may wonder at the high praise awarded in the next three lines to Bartolomeo; he is presented as a shining example of liberality, a virtue that is rated among the greatest in the *Convivio* (I, viii), and reaches its perfection when the giver bestows without being asked. One may wonder, for not only has Bartolomeo never been mentioned by Dante before, but whenever another member of the Scala family — his father Alberto, his brother Albuino, his half-brother Giuseppe — have previously appeared in the pages of the *Comedy*, disparaging terms were used. My own view is that Bartolomeo is praised not for his own sake but retrospectively, so to speak, as a compliment to his younger brother Cangrande, who ruled Verona jointly with Albuino from 1308 and then as sole Lord after 1311, for his eulogy follows immediately.

> Con lui vedrai colui che 'mpresso fue,
> nascendo, sì da questa stella forte,
> che notabili fier l'opere sue.   78
>   Non se ne son le genti ancora accorte
> per la novella età, ché pur nove anni
> son queste rote intorno di lui torte;   81
>   ma pria che 'l Guasco l'alto Arrigo inganni,
> parran faville de la sua virtute
> in non curar d'argento né d'affanni.   84
>   Le sue magnificenze conosciute
> saranno ancora, sì che ' suoi nemici
> non ne potran tener le lingue mute.   87
>   A lui t'aspetta e a' suoi benefici;
> per lui fia trasmutata molta gente,
> cambiando condizion ricchi e mendici;   90

159

Dante's 'Comedy'

e portera'ne scritto ne la mente
di lui, e nol dirai'; e disse cose
incredibili a quei che fier presente.   93

(With him you'll see the one who at birth was so stamped with this mighty star
that his deeds will be worthy of note. Not yet, indeed, because of his youth,
have they drawn men's attention, for as yet these wheels have gone round him
only for nine years; but before the Gascon tricks noble Henry, sparks of his
mettle will appear in a disregard for money and fatigue. His large-hearted
liberality will be so famous as to force even his enemies to tell of it. Look to him
and to his munificence; through him shall the condition of many be transformed, the rich changing place with beggars. And concerning him, bear this inscrib-
ed in your memory, but do not reveal it'; and he told me things that shall be
incredible even to those who witness them.)

No other living person is spoken of in the whole poem in terms even
nearly approaching the tribute that is now paid to him: his military
prowess, augured by his birth under the planet Mars (77) and later
abundantly displayed, although not yet apparent in 1300, the fictional
date of Dante's journey, when Cangrande was only nine years old
(79–81); his early promise of magnanimity and valour (83–4), already
evident before the time when the Gascon Pope, Clement V, deceived
the Emperor Henry VII (82) by first supporting him and undertaking
to perform his coronation in Rome, and then backing out and turning
against him in 1312; his sense of justice in helping the deserving poor
at the expense of the undeserving rich (89–90). All this is remarkable
praise indeed, particularly if one bears in mind that line 90 is almost a
paraphrase of the homage to God in the *Magnificat* (Luke 1: 53):
'Esurientes implevit bonis et divites dimisit inanes' ('The hungry he hath
filled with good things; and the rich he hath sent empty away'). But far
more is to come: in lines 91–3 Cacciaguida prophesies that the Lord of
Verona will perform such great things as to be incredible and not to bear
repetition at present. Why is Cangrande so singled out among Dante's
many hosts? Several commentators have been content with referring
to the gratitude felt by the poet for the especial kindness and hospitality
received in Verona during the latter years of his life, and possibly while
he was writing these lines. This may be part of the story; but Dante was
not given to adulation and was not in the habit of stooping to courtly
servility. His real reason for conceiving such admiration for Cangrande
and for entertaining such great hopes (for the 'incredible things' of lines
92–3 are obviously fondly cherished hopes for the future) must rest on
more substantial foundations. And let us also bear in mind that his letter to Cangrande, if indeed it is genuine, is not less explicit in its pro-

fessions of devotion and esteem, and that it even dedicates the *Paradiso* to him.

A clue to what Cangrande stood for in Dante's eyes is probably to be found in line 82, and in the association of his name with that of 'l'alto Arrigo'. Henry VII, elected in 1308, had been the Emperor who had attempted the revival of the medieval idea of the Empire. Right from the time of his election he had made it clear that, unlike his immediate predecessors, he was determined not only to take the imperial crown in Rome, but also to demand from all men the obedience and subjection that was due to the universal Emperor. In other words, he was earnestly attempting to achieve exactly what Dante had longed for; and the poet had written three epistles in order to support his campaign in Italy and probably had begun to write his political treatise *Monarchia* under the impression of what he had seen and heard in these years. After at first apparently succeeding in his undertaking (1310–11), Henry had encountered stronger and stronger resistance, and had died in 1313 with his task far from completed; but Dante, who had placed all his hopes in him, remained faithful to his memory, so much so that in Canto XXX of the *Paradiso* he reserved a seat in the Empyrean Heaven for 'l'alto Arrigo', as he again calls him. Now, Cangrande too had identified himself with the cause of the Emperor who had appointed him vicar, and had vigorously and effectively supported him in his military campaign in Italy. After the death of Henry, his Court had become the rallying-point of the hopes of all Ghibellines. This prince, whose very name had something vaguely mysterious about it, had gained a reputation for political and military skill and resourcefulness, for splendour and generosity, and had inflamed the imaginations of his contemporaries, to whom he seemed the only Italian ruler capable of resistance against papal encroachments. Indeed, he seemed a kind of spiritual heir to Henry VII; all the more so as he coupled his advocacy of the universal Emperor with a devout attitude towards the Church in matters of faith. His position was entirely analogous, then, to that of Dante, who wrote the *Paradiso* after Henry had died and who, in his longing for the realization of his ideal, must have seen in Cangrande another envoy of Providence; with the wisdom of hindsight, we might add against all the odds. This, I believe, is the perspective in which the passage is to be understood.

> Poi giunse: 'Figlio, queste son le chiose
> di quel che ti fu detto; ecco le 'nsidie
> che dietro a pochi giri son nascose.   96

161

Dante's 'Comedy'

Non vo' però ch'a' tuoi vicini invidie,
poscia che s'infutura la tua vita
via più là che 'l punir di lor perfidie'.   99

(Then he added: 'These, my son, are the glosses with which to interpret what
has been said to you; now you know the snares hidden behind a few circlings
[of the sun and the stars]. Yet I would not have you envious of your fellow-
citizens, seeing that your life will far outlast the punishing of their perfidies.')

Cacciaguida's prophecy ends with a glimpse of the timelessness that is
promised to Dante's message; the forecast that his life (98–9), that is,
the effect of his work, will far outlast ('s'infutura' — a typically Dantesque word) the punishment of the Florentines serves as an introduction to the final section of the Canto.

Poi che, tacendo, si mostrò spedita
l'anima santa di metter la trama
in quella tela ch'io le porsi ordita,   102
    io cominciai, come colui che brama,
dubitando, consiglio da persona
che vede e vuol dirittamente e ama: 105
    'Ben veggio, padre mio, sì come sprona
lo tempo verso me, per colpo darmi
tal, ch'è più grave a chi più s'abbandona;   108
    per che di provedenza è buon ch'io m'armi,
sì che, se loco m'è tolto più caro,
io non perdessi li altri per miei carmi.   111
    Giù per lo mondo sanza fine amaro,
e per lo monte del cui bel cacume
li occhi de la mia donna mi levaro,   114
    e poscia per lo ciel, di lume in lume,
ho io appreso quel che s'io ridico,
a molti fia sapor di forte agrume;   117
    e s'io al vero son timido amico,
temo di perder viver tra coloro
che questo tempo chiameranno antico'.   120

(When by his silence the holy soul showed that he had finished putting the woof
into the warp that I had held out to him, I began like one who, being perplex-
ed, longs for advice from a person who sees clearly and wills justly and who
loves: 'My father, I see well how time is spurring towards me to deal me such
a blow as falls the heavier on the more heedless. I shall do well, therefore, to
arm myself with foresight, so that if the place I love most is taken from me, I
shall [at least] not lose others because of my poems. Down through the endless-
ly bitter world and up the mountain from whose lovely crest the eyes of my
lady lifted me, and then passing from light to light through heaven, I have learned things which, repeated, will taste exceedingly bitter to many; while if I'm
a timid friend to truth I fear to lose life among those who will speak of the present age as of times long past.')

Paradiso XVII

Here Dante, in what is almost an inner soliloquy in the form of a dialogue, rehearses the doubts and perplexities that must have assailed him when he started to write the *Comedy*, and, by resolving these doubts in a triumphant solution, he proclaims the purpose of the poem: the fearless propagation of truth for the benefit of mankind. He frames his dilemma as follows: he may be left with nowhere to shelter in after his native city is taken from him, unless he is prudent (109–11), for what he has learnt in Hell, Purgatory and Paradise will be unwelcome to many, if he repeats it (112–17); on the other hand, if he is a timid friend to truth, he will not be remembered by posterity (118–20).

> La luce in che rideva il mio tesoro
> ch'io trovai lì, si fé prima corusca,
> quale a raggio di sole specchio d'oro;   123
>   indi rispuose: 'Coscïenza fusca
> o de la propria o de l'altrui vergogna
> pur sentirà la tua parola brusca.   126
>   Ma nondimen, rimossa ogne menzogna,
> tutta tua visïon fa manifesta;
> e lascia pur grattar dov' è la rogna.   129
>   Ché se la voce tua sarà molesta
> nel primo gusto, vital nodrimento
> lascerà poi, quando sarà digesta.   132
>   Questo tuo grido farà come vento,
> che le più alte cime più percuote;
> e ciò non fa d'onor poco argomento.   135
>   Però ti son mostrate in queste rote,
> nel monte e ne la valle dolorosa
> pur l'anime che son di fama note,   138
>   che l'animo di quel ch'ode, non posa
> né ferma fede per essempro ch'aia
> la sua radice incognita e ascosa,   141
>   né per altro argomento che non paia'.

(The light wherein was smiling the treasure I found in heaven [cf. Matthew 6: 21; 19: 21] first glowed and flashed like a golden mirror in sunlight; and then replied: 'To the conscience grown dark with its own or another's shame, your words will indeed seem harsh; nevertheless, throwing aside all subterfuge, speak out your total vision clearly; and let them scratch where they feel the itch! For if at the first taste your utterance give offence, it will leave vital nourishment once digested. This cry of yours will be like the wind that strikes hardest the highest summits; and that is no small honour! This is why there have been shown you — in these wheels [the heavenly spheres], on the mountain, in the sorrowful valley — only souls known to fame; for the hearer's mind does not dwell on, or put faith in, examples whose origin is unknown and hidden; or any other proof not clearly visible.')

Appropriately, Cacciaguida's light glows brighter as he gives his stern yet stirring reply: 'Tutta tua visïon fa manifesta' ('Make all your vision plain': 128) whatever danger might ensue. These words contain Dante's acceptance of his mission to teach mankind and to further its redemption, with all that this mission implies. It is for him to awaken consciences to their sins and to the evils of the world (124–6); it is for him to nourish mankind with truth, even though his voice will be harsh at first taste (130–3). The outburst of line 129 has disturbed some commentators as being unseemly in the rarefied atmosphere of the fifth Heaven because of the plebeian coarseness of its language. Their squeamishness, however, might be assuaged by the reflection that for Dante this is not a matter to be considered with detachment; all his feelings are involved, and if he puts it in this way, it is because there is no other way that he knows of putting it more vigorously. Besides, this kind of rough language seems to be in keeping with the character of the speaker, who is almost the symbol of a simple, unpolished way of life. Above all, this language fits into a passage the masterly concision of which adds force and elevation to this dignified statement of the purpose of the poem. For here Dante raises us to the lofty region of towering summits and powerful winds in which his poem ranges, and which is evoked by lines 133–4, and declares his awareness of his mission, and his determination to pursue it, even when it may be disagreeable to the powerful of the earth. He has been aiming high, in the full knowledge of his strength and of his task. A memorable, powerful claim is put forward in lines 133–4; the statement that follows them, and closes the Canto, strikes a more prosaic note but is, nonetheless, worthy of attention. Only famous people have been shown to Dante during his journey, because their example strikes the reader's mind more cogently and teaches more effectively than the example of obscure individuals. There are two points to notice: in the first place, the providential nature of his journey is confirmed here by implication, since God himself has pre-arranged every detail; and, secondly, we have in these lines one of the criteria used for the compilation of the poem, set out by the author himself for us to note.

The dialogue with Cacciaguida continues briefly in the next Canto; but what he has to say there is, if such a thing is possible, paradisiac routine. As far as Dante and his mission are concerned, we have reached the climax and the end of the episode. The old crusader has bestowed upon his descendant the insignia of a new crusade.